101 SOFT TOYS

FUN TO MAKE TOYS
FOR CHILDREN
&BABIES

101 SOFT TOYS

FUN TO MAKE TOYS
FOR CHILDREN
&BABIES

ARCO PUBLISHING INC.
New York

Published by
Arco Publishing, Inc.
215 Park Avenue South
New York, NY 10003

© Marshall Cavendish Limited 1984

Library of Congress Cataloging in Publication Data
Main entry under title:
101 soft toys.
1. Soft toy making. I. Arco Publishing. II. Title:
One hundred and one soft toys. III. One hundred and
one soft toys.
TT174.3.A17   1984   745.592′4   84-9394
ISBN 0-668-06248-7

Printed and bound by Grafici Editoriale Padane S.p.A., Cremona, Italy

CONTENTS

Introduction

Hand-made toys have a charm and individuality seldom found in mass-produced toys. This book contains toys to appeal to all ages and tastes – from a simple crocheted ball for a baby to an exquisite puppet straight out of a fairy tale. Some of the toys are simple to make, others fairly complicated; but all will benefit from a careful choice of materials and the willingness to take a few pains in their construction. On these pages and on pages 190-191 you will find useful information on materials and techniques you will need for successful toymaking.

Fabrics and fillings

Many different fabrics can be used for toymaking. Usually a "realistic" fabric is most appropriate – for example, fur fabric for a teddy bear or imitation leather for a doll's shoes; but you can make charming toys using unlikely fabrics, such as the pink flowered print used for the hippo on page 93. Keep a rag bag of bits left over from other sewing projects; these will often eliminate the necessity of buying all new materials for a toy.

When choosing fabrics for toymaking, avoid those that fray easily. Seams on toys are often rather tricky to sew, and a fraying fabric will create unnecessary problems. Felt is a good choice for appliquéd pieces, as its edges require no finishing. For a stuffed animal or a doll, choose a firmly-woven cotton or cotton-synthetic blend, such as poplin or corduroy. Unbleached muslin is the usual choice for a rag doll's body, but stockinet is often preferable for a baby doll, which should be soft and cuddly.

When working with fabrics that have a pile, such as velvet or fur fabric, make sure to place the pattern pieces so that the pile runs as specified. Baste the pieces together before stitching and stitch in the direction that the pile slopes, where possible. In the case of fur fabrics, it may be easier to pin the edges together and work the stitching by hand, using backstitch.

If the toy is to be washable, make sure that any fabrics used for its construction can be washed. It is a good idea to shrink the fabric beforehand unless you are certain that it is pre-shrunk.

Polyester fiberfill is the stuffing generally used for toys. It is washable and non-flammable and should first be teased out to make it light and smooth before being inserted into the toy.

Equipment

You should have on hand certain basic tools and other equipment that are frequently required for toymaking.

Scissors You will need a long-bladed pair for cutting out fabric; small sewing scissors for trimming, cutting yarn and other tasks; and scissors for cutting paper (Note: never use sewing scissors on paper, as it will blunt the blades.) In addition, you may want a pair of embroidery scissors and some pinking shears, for cutting decorative edges.

Needles In addition to general purpose sewing needles, such as sharps or betweens, you may need: crewel needles, which have sharp points and long eyes and are used for embroidery; chenille needles, which have extra-large eyes for embroidering with heavy threads; a tapestry needle, which has a blunt point and is used for joining pieces of knitting, as well as for embroidering on canvas; a curved upholstery needle, which is useful in stitching awkwardly-placed seams; and a long darner, which will take thread through parts of a toy that have been filled with stuffing.

Stiletto This is used for punching holes in fabric.

Knitting needle – medium size This is handy for getting a good point on a small piece, such as an ear, when turning it right side out, and also for inserting stuffing into hard-to-reach places.

Craft knife This is useful for cutting cardboard patterns.

Paper You will need several kinds: dressmaker's graph paper for enlarging designs, tracing paper for trace patterns and, occasionally, ordinary paper for making patterns.

Ruler and yardstick for measuring and marking straight lines.

Right-angled triangle (optional) for drawing square corners; a record album or magazine will serve the purpose.

Tape measure for measuring parts of a toy.

Compass This is often needed for drawing circles.

Fabric glue and tape.

Paintbrushes – fine and medium – for painting features on dolls.

You will also, of course, need thread to match the fabrics; cotton-wrapped polyester is generally suitable, as it is strong and can be used with both natural and synthetic fabrics. Heavy linen thread is needed for some projects.

Transferring pattern markings

Many pattern pieces include markings which must be transferred to the fabric so that the pieces can be joined accurately and decorated. There are several ways of doing this.

Tailor's tacks are ideal for marking points to be joined, as they are visible on both sides of the fabric and are easily removed after stitching. To work a tailor's tack, thread a needle with a double strand of thread, make a small stitch through both pattern and fabric and pull the thread through, leaving a short end, then make another stitch through the same point, leaving a small loop. (If marking two layers simultaneously, leave longer ends and loops.) Cut through the loop and remove the pattern.

Dressmaker's carbon is used on the wrong side of the fabric (except for embroidery designs, as explained below). Place the carbon between the pattern and the fabric with its colored side downward. Using a pencil or a tracing wheel, press firmly on the point or line to be marked. To mark two pieces simultaneously, place them together with wrong sides facing, fold the carbon with colored sides outward and mark as usual.

To transfer an embroidery design, place the fabric right side up and lay the carbon colored side down on top of it. Position the design on top, secure it with pins or weights and go over the lines firmly with a ball-point pen.

A fabric marking pen can also be used for transferring some markings. It has a soft fiber tip, and the mark can easily be removed from most fabrics with a wet cloth (test first), so that you can use it on the right side.

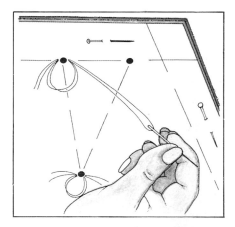

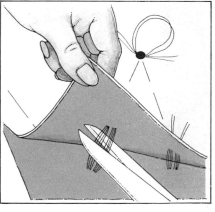

Dolls and puppets

Dolls appeal on many levels: for a little girl a doll may be a companion or someone to mother; for an older child the doll may be an image of herself grown up. And today boys as well as girls are discovering the fun of using dolls to enact their fantasies. Puppets are even better suited to such games, and are excellent for learning coordination, as well as for developing dramatic talents. This section contains dolls of all types, from cuddly baby dolls to elegant costume dolls which would please a collector.

Mary Mary doll rattle

Size
Approximately 11in tall

Materials
Soft plastic doll's head
Small amount of batting
Wooden spoon about 8in long
Piece of stockinet 5in square of ½yd/36in wide panne velvet
1yd of 1¾in wide pleated lace edging
2yd of ⅜in in wide velvet ribbon
8 "silver" bells
About 25 shell-shaped sequins.

Making the pattern — cutting out
For the hat, draw the pattern pieces, following the measurements on the diagram. Cut out the pieces in velvet. For the dress, cut a piece of velvet 24½ × 6¼in . A seam allowance of ⅜in is included.

To make the clothes
Turn under ⅜in hems along both short edges and one long edge (A) of hat brim strip; turn under a ¾in hem along the other long edge. Topstitch hems close to the fold.

☐Gather edge A of the brim to measure 7in. Gather edge B of the main piece to fit edge A. Sew the gathered edges together, RS facing.

☐Fold the main piece along line D and gather the combined edges C and E to measure 5½in .

☐Stitch the two crown pieces together around the curved edge, RS facing. Turn crown RS out. Sew the crown to the main piece.

☐Turn under ⅜in hems along the two side edges and one long edge of the ruffle. Gather the other edge of the ruffle to fit the neck edge of the bonnet, and sew it in place.

☐Sew a length of ribbon over the seam joining the main piece and brim, turning under the raw ends. Matching the center points, stitch

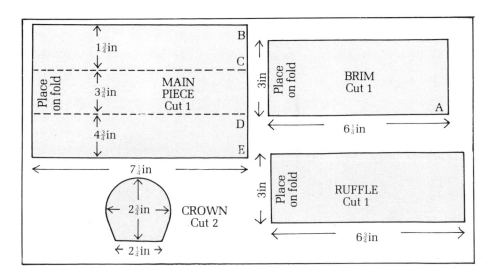

an 18in length of ribbon to the bonnet ruffle, immediately in front of the first ribbon. Sew a piece of pleated edging inside the hat brim.
☐For the dress turn up a ⅜in hem along one long edge, pin a length of pleated edging under the hem and topstitch it in place.

To make the doll
Using a scalpel, cut the doll's face from the back of the head. Wrap a little batting around the bowl of the wooden spoon and cover it with the piece of stockinet. Tie the neck tightly and glue the doll's face to the covered spoon. Re-attach the hair if necessary.
☐Gather the neck edge of the dress and sew it around doll's neck.
☐Cut 8 6m-long pieces of ribbon and stitch them to the top of the dress. Sew a small bell to the end of each ribbon. Stitch a length of pleated edging around the neckline.
☐Sew the sequins around the hem of the dress.
☐Put the bonnet on the doll and tie the ribbons under the chin.

Traditional rag doll

Size
Approximately 24in tall

Materials
⅞yd of 36in-wide unbleached muslin
  for body
1⅛yd of 36in-wide printed fabric for
  dress
⅝yd of 36in-wide red fabric for
  apron
⅝yd of 36in-wide white cotton for
  petticoat and pantalets
2¼yd of eyelet lace edging for
  underclothes
4⅜yd of lace edging for dress and
  apron
Old socks (to be cut down for doll's
  socks)
2 pieces of black felt 8in square
  for shoes and eyes
2oz of brown bulky yarn for hair
½yd of ribbon for hair ties
Scrap of pink felt for cheeks
1lb of washable stuffing
Red and black embroidery thread
  for the features
Narrow flat and cord elastic
5 snaps for dress and shoes

Making the pattern — cutting out
Enlarge the pattern pieces as indicated on the graph, and cut out the pieces for the body and clothes from the appropriate fabrics. Use the ribbed parts of old socks for the doll's socks. Using dressmaker's carbon, transfer the pattern markings to the fabric; a seam allowance of ⅜in is included.

☐Also cut a piece measuring 7½ × 36in from printed fabric for the skirt. Cut and join two pieces of printed fabric to make a strip measuring 70 × 2¾in for the ruffle that goes around the bottom of the skirt.

☐From the white cotton, cut a piece measuring 7½ × 36in for the petticoat. The apron is made from two pieces of red fabric measuring 14 × 7½in and 36 × 2¼in .

To make the doll
Join the two pairs of arms, stitching down one side and up the other, leaving the top edges open. Clip the curves and turn arms RS out. Fill the arms with stuffing, using a knitting needle or a piece of dowel to push the stuffing well down. Make sure that the arms are well rounded and that the hands, by contrast, are not over-stuffed. Turn in the raw edges and overcast them together firmly with a double strand of thread. Work stab stitch on the hands to form the fingers, as shown on page 13.

☐Make the legs in the same way as the arms; but when stuffing them and closing the top edges, make sure that the seams run down the center front and back of the leg. The top edges are closed from one side to the other, perpendicular to the leg seams.

☐For the head and body, first join each of the two pairs from A to B (up the center front/back seam) to form a front and a back section. Clip and press the seam open very carefully, making sure that it will be as unobtrusive as possible. Next join the front and back together in a continuous seam from C to B and down to C. Clip seams and press as before, then turn head and body RS out. Stuff firmly, then turn in the raw edges from C to C and overcast them together. (If desired, a support stick — see page 13 — can be inserted.)

☐Join the arms to the body using double thread, then attach the legs, making sure that both feet point the same way!

☐Make long hair as shown on page 14, using a piece of cardboard 12½in long and winding yarn to a width of 6½in. Sew hair to the head, making a center part, then make two braids and tie them with ribbon.

☐Make felt and embroidered features as shown on page 14. The eyes are made from circles of black felt ⅝in in diameter and the cheeks are 1¼in in diameter.

To make the clothes
First join the ruffle pieces, RS facing, along both short ends. Turn up a short hem on one of the long raw edges and run lines of gathering stitches at the other edge. Join the main skirt piece in the same way, but stitch the seam only part-way up, leaving 1¼in unstitched at the top. Gather the ruffle to fit the skirt, and stitch it to the lower edge, RS facing. Make two gathering lines at the top of the skirt. Join the back bodice pieces to the front at the sides and shoulders, then attach the skirt to the bodice, adjusting the gathers to fit. Finish the raw edges at the back opening of the dress and press them under.

☐Sew the underarm seams of the sleeves and fit them into the bodice; stitch. Turn up a narrow hem at the sleeve edges. Hand-sew cord elastic to the inside of each sleeve, 1½in above the hemmed edge, stretching the elastic as you work, to gather up sleeve.

☐Cut a 1in-wide bias strip from the red fabric, long enough to go around the neck. Press under ¼in on each long edge. Fold the strip in half lengthwise, enclosing the raw edges; press. Use the strip to cover the raw edge of the neck, turning it in neatly at each end.

☐Gather a length of lace to fit the neck and sew it under the binding, as shown in the photograph. Do the same at the sleeve edges. Sew two straight strips of lace in a "V" shape running from the shoulders down to the waistline to meet at the center front.

☐Sew three snaps to the center back opening.

☐On the 14 × 7½in piece of red fabric run two lines of gathering stitches down one long side. Turn up and stitch narrow hems on the other three sides. Using zigzag stitch and easing it around at the corners, attach lace over the hemmed edges. Gather the top edge to measure 7½in. Center the waistband over the gathered edge, RS

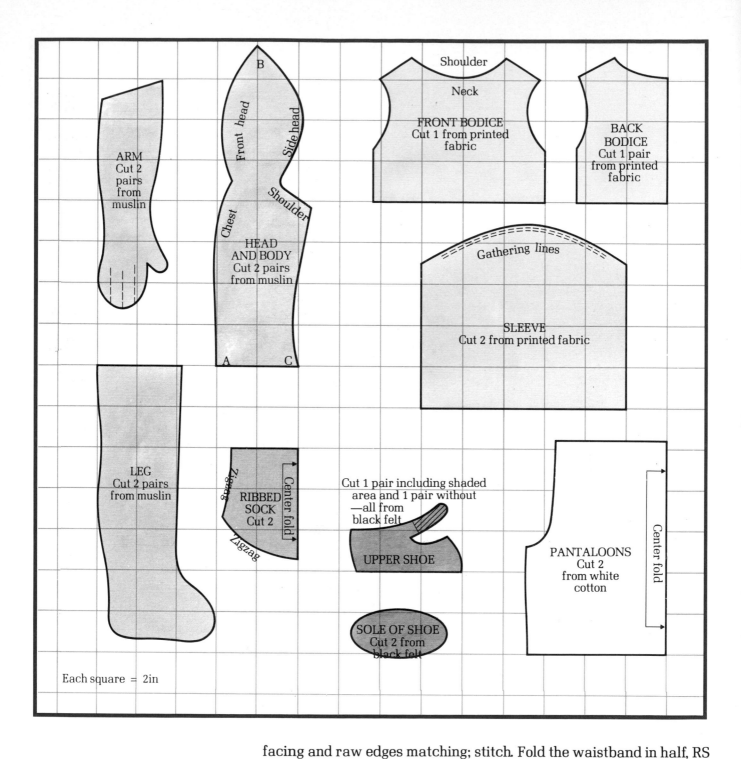

ARM
Cut 2
pairs
from
muslin

B

Front head

Side head

Chest

Shoulder

HEAD
AND BODY
Cut 2 pairs
from muslin

A

C

Shoulder

Neck

FRONT BODICE
Cut 1 from printed
fabric

BACK
BODICE
Cut 1 pair
from printed
fabric

Gathering lines

SLEEVE
Cut 2 from printed fabric

LEG
Cut 2 pairs
from muslin

Zigzag

RIBBED
SOCK
Cut 2

Center fold

Zigzag

Cut 1 pair including shaded
area and 1 pair without
—all from
black felt

UPPER SHOE

SOLE OF SHOE
Cut 2 from
black felt

PANTALOONS
Cut 2
from white
cotton

Center fold

Each square = 2in

facing and raw edges matching; stitch. Fold the waistband in half, RS together, and stitch the tie sections on each side of the apron. Turn them RS out and press, then turn under the remaining raw edge and slipstitch it to the back of the apron along the first stitching line.

☐ Join the petticoat piece along the short edges. Using zigzag stitch, attach eyelet lace to one raw edge. Turn under and stitch the other edge to form a casing, leaving a small gap. Cut flat elastic to fit doll's waist, thread it through the casing and stitch the ends together. Join the inside leg and crotch seams of pantalets. Trim lower edges with eyelet lace and complete waist edge as for the petticoat.

☐ Join each pair of felt shoe tops, then fit them into the soles and stitch them together. Sew snaps to fasten straps. Stitch each sock piece together along the two curved sides, using zigzag stitch.

Stitching

The basic technique for stitching the body is shown here on a one-piece doll, but it applies also to dolls made of separate sections.

When you have cut out the back and front sections, stitch around the outline using a small stitch and leaving an opening in the side of the body. Clip almost to the stitching line on curved edges, then turn the doll RS out and stuff it, using a pointed stick or a knitting needle to push the stuffing firmly into awkward corners. (If the features are to be painted, see page 14.) Slipstitch the opening to close it.

Fingers

The basic mitten-like outline of the hands can be improved by stitching lines to indicate the fingers, using a double strand of thread and sewing right through the hand with stab stitch. Start by dividing the hand in half and making the line between the second and third fingers, then stitch a row on each side to define all four fingers. The same method can be used at the knees and elbows to make the arms and legs bend. This is especially desirable on a one-piece doll, which would otherwise be very stiff.

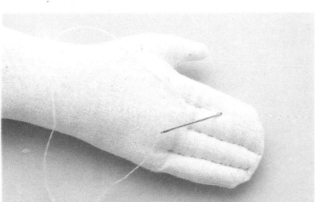

Support stick

To support the head of a large doll and prevent it from flopping around, cut a length of dowel to go through the neck and part-way into the head and body. (Make sure that the ends are blunt.) Wrap stuffing around the stick and tie it in place with strong thread. Insert the stick into the doll, making sure that there is plenty of padding above and below the stick and all around it.

Short hair

To make short hair from ready-cut rug yarn lay pieces of yarn side by side down a strip of paper and hold them in position with tape, as shown. Stitch down the center and then tear away the paper and the tape. Make several strips totaling about 1yd in length, then, working from the outside and spiraling in to the center, pin the strips to the head of the doll. Backstitch the strips in place with a double strand of thread in a matching color.

Long hair

Cut a piece of cardboard as long as the desired finished length of the hair and mark the center point halfway down the strip. Wind enough yarn around the cardboard to make a reasonable head of hair. Tape it in place just above and below the center line on one side of the cardboard. Turn the cardboard over and cut the yarn, cutting across the center. Carefully lift the tape and hair off the cardboard and tape it to paper, then stitch through the center as for short hair.

Hair with bangs

Cut a piece of cardboard 12½in long (or desired length of hair) and about 7in wide. Wind yarn to cover a 5½in width. Cut the yarn along one edge and carefully remove the cardboard. Slip paper under the uncut ends, tape them in place and stitch 2¼in from the ends. Cut the resulting loops. Use the short ends for bangs and the long ends to cover the back of the head. With matching thread, stitch along the bang part and also around the back of the head, from ear to ear, to hold the long hair in place. With the same piece of cardboard, wind a 2in width of hair as shown in "Long hair"; place this on top of the head and tie it in a pony tail.

Stitched and glued features

Using coins as templates, cut small circles from black or blue felt for eyes and slightly larger circles from pale pink felt for cheeks. The eyes should be glued in place about halfway down the face with a gap of about 1¼in between them and the cheeks positioned just below. Use red or pink embroidery thread to backstitch a half circle for the lips and make two French knots above for the nostrils. Work long straight stitches with black thread for eyelashes.

Painted faces

Very attractive painted faces can be made using just black and red, with the red watered down to make pink for cheeks. It is best to practice on spare scraps first, penciling the outline of eyes and lips before filling them in with paint. It is much easier to work on a face that has been stuffed, but remember that it will be necessary to take the stuffing out after the paint has dried so that it can be ironed to fix the dye.

Pierrot the puppet

Size
Approximately 16in tall

Materials
$\frac{3}{8}$yd of 36in-wide white poplin
$\frac{1}{2}$yd of 36in-wide cream crêpe de
   chine
2 strips of cream tulle (pieced if
   necessary), 6in × $1\frac{5}{8}$yd
$2\frac{1}{4}$yd of $\frac{1}{4}$in-wide black satin ribbon
Small amount of black yarn
7oz of stuffing
Pink and black fabric paints
Pink pencil
Fabric glue
2 pieces of $\frac{3}{4} \times \frac{3}{8}$in wood batten,
   8in long
6 screw-in eyelets
$1\frac{1}{8}$in cotter pin
2 washers
Cream buttonhole twist

Making the pattern — cutting out
Enlarge the pattern pieces as indicated on the graph and cut them
out in poplin. Cut the pieces for the clothes from crêpe de chine,
following the measurements given. A seam allowance of $\frac{3}{8}$in is
included.

To make the puppet
Fold the top body piece, RS together, on the fold line; join the side
seams. Turn the top body RS out; stuff. Turn in and slipstitch the
lower edges together.
□Fold each leg in half lengthwise, RS facing, and stitch the shaped
edges together. Stitch the soles to the feet. Turn the legs RS out, stuff
them to the knee and stitch across the marked lines; close the raw
edges with running stitch. Stuff the remainder of each leg, stitching
from one side to the other — not from front to back.

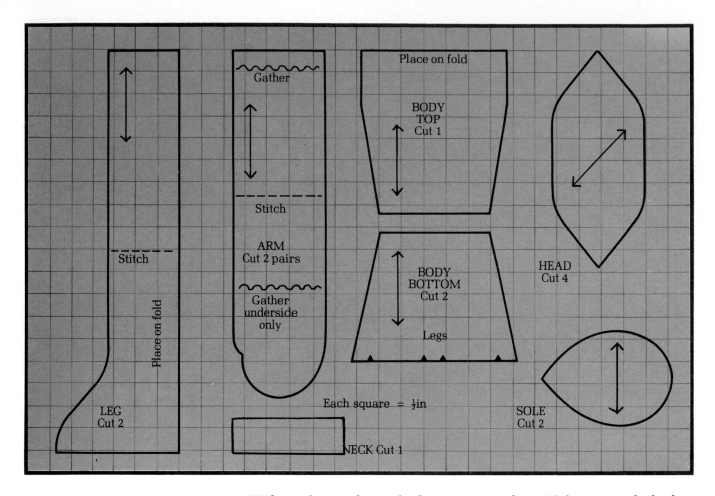

□Place the two lower body pieces together, RS facing, with the legs between them, extending upward through the top edges, with all raw edges even. Baste and stitch the side and lower edges together.
□Turn the lower body RS out and stuff it; turn in and slipstitch the top edges. Faggot stitch the body sections together at the waist.
□Stitch the two pairs of arms together, RS facing; leaving the tops open. Turn the arms RS out and work the hands with a few short rows of stab stitching (see page 13). Gather the underside of each arm slightly to form a wrist. Stuff each arm to the elbow and stitch across it at this point. Stuff the remainder of each arm. Turn in the raw edges and work gathering stitches around them. Pull up gathers and slipstitch the edges together. Faggot stitch the arms to the body.
□Stitch the head pieces together, RS facing, leaving a gap for turning. Turn the head RS out, stuff it and slipstitch opening edges together. Place the two short ends of the neck piece together, RS facing; stitch. Turn in $\frac{1}{4}$in on one edge and slipstitch it to the head. Stuff the neck, turn in $\frac{1}{4}$in on the remaining edge and work gathering stitches around it. Pull up gathers and stitch neck to the body. Using fabric paints, color the shoes, cap and main facial features. Allow paint to dry, then color the cheeks with pink pencil. For the doll's nose, cut a $1\frac{1}{4} \times \frac{5}{8}$in oval from poplin. Place a small amount of stuffing in the center and gather up the edges. Slipstitch the nose to the doll's face.

To make the clothes
Stitch the sleeves to the smock, RS facing, between marked points.
□Fold the smock along the center line with RS facing; stitch the sleeve and side seams. Cut a slit on the fold line about 3in long.

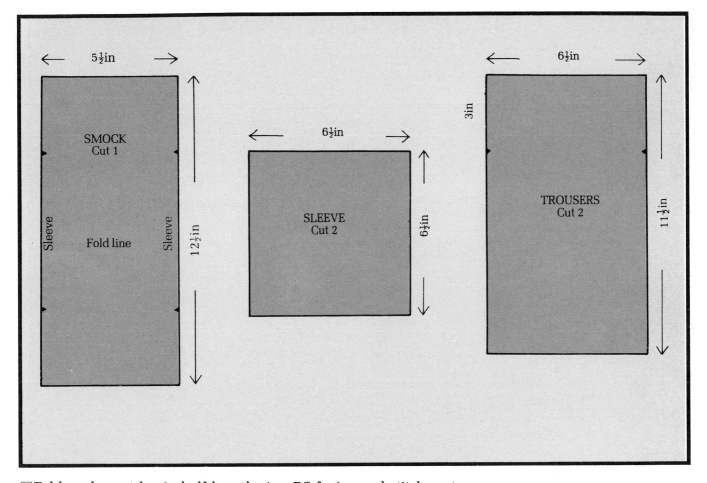

□Fold each pant leg in half lengthwise, RS facing and stitch up to the marked points. Join the two pant legs along the crotch.

□Turn under ⅜in then a further 1¼in around the bottom of each pant leg. Hand-hem it in place. Turn up a ¾in cuff on each one. Repeat for the shirt sleeve cuffs. Turn up a double ¼in hem around the lower edge of the smock.

□Turn under ⅜in on the waist edge of the pants; finger-press. Put the pants on the doll; gather in the waist and slipstitch it to the doll. Put the smock on the doll and catch it in place with a few stitches at the neck.

□Stitch ribbon to one edge of one piece of tulle. Fold both pieces of tulle in half lengthwise; work gathering stitches close to the folds, and draw up tightly. Placing ribboned piece on top, stitch ruffs around the neck of the doll. Glue ribbon around the top of shoes and trim the fronts with bows. Make 6 tiny pompons from black yarn, using the method shown on page 98, and sew them to the puppet as shown in the photograph.

To make the puppet control
Mark the center of each piece of wood and drill a hole through each one at this point.

□Push the cotter pin through the holes in wood, placing a washer at each side. Open out the ends of the cotter pin and hammer them flat. The pieces of wood should be firmly held but able to swivel easily.

□Insert screw eyelets in underside of control as shown. Attach puppet to control with long lengths of buttonhole twist, securing them to backs of knees and hands and sides of head and threading them through the screw eyelets as shown.

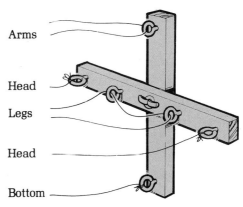

17

Baby Doll

Size
Approximately 11in tall

Materials
⅜yd of 36in-wide unbleached muslin
   for the body
Matte embroidery cotton in four
   colors for the face
Knitting worsted yarn for hair
Strong sewing thread to match the
   unbleached muslin
5½oz of washable stuffing
⅝yd of 36in-wide fabric for the
   dress and pants
2¾yd of narrow lace
2¼yd of ¼in-wide ribbon
1⅝yd of narrow elastic
Scraps of felt or soft leather for the
   shoes

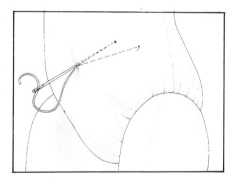

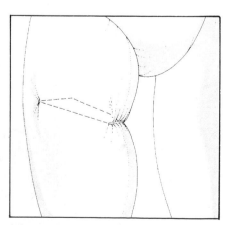

Making the pattern — cutting out
Enlarge the pattern pieces as indicated on the graph, and cut the pieces for the body and clothes from the appropriate fabrics. Using dressmaker's carbon, mark tucks on the WS of the fabric; dimples, creases and the facial features on the RS.

To make the doll
Torso and head Machine stitch two of the gussets together along the single-notched curve between points A and B. Clip the curve and press the seam open.

☐Match the double-notched sides of the joined gussets to the front of the doll at the top of the head, and to the corresponding place on the back. Stitch, clip and press open the seams.

☐Stitch the tucks in the back of body and head. Clip the top tuck only. Join the remaining gusset piece to the bottom of the back, matching the double notches.

☐Machine stitch both side seams. Clip curves where necessary, and turn body RS out.

☐Fill the body with stuffing, making sure the neck firmly supports the head. Using a double thread, work gathering stitches around the neck, following the dotted lines. Pull the thread tightly and fasten it off securely.

☐Turn in the seam allowances on the bottom gusset and body. Slipstitch them together, squeezing the body into shape.

☐Using double thread and a long needle, form the two back dimples and the tummy button. Take a small stitch on one dimple mark, pulling the end of thread through to lodge the knot in the stuffing. Push the needle through to the tummy button and back to the second dimple. Pull tightly to form dimples. Take the needle down to the lower seam and secure the thread where the leg will cover the stitches.

Face and hair Using matte embroidery cotton, work the features following the pattern. Use satin stitch for the cheeks, stem stitch for eyebrows, eyes and mouth. Color the eyes with straight stitches radiating from a central point, using two colors of thread.

☐Thread a tapestry needle with knitting yarn and draw it through the crown of the head. Make loop stitches, working outward from the crown until the face is gently framed. Leave ½in unstitched above the neck line.

Legs and arms Join the leg pieces, leaving the top edges open. Clip the seams where necessary. Turn legs RS out and stuff them. Form the ankles, following the instructions for the neck.

☐To make the knee dimples and crease, make one stitch on a dimple, push the needle through to the back and backstitch along the crease line. Push the needle through again and stitch the other dimple. Fasten off at the top of the leg with a few stitches.

☐With double thread, work gathering stitches around the top of each leg on the seamline. Make sure that the stuffing is tightly packed, then turn under the raw edges and finger-press them in place. Slipstitch the legs to the lower body so that they cover the seams between body pieces and gusset.

☐Stitch and stuff the arms in the same way, leaving the top edges open. Form the fingers by working four large overcasting stitches over the doubled lines, using double thread and taking the needle through the stuffing between stitches.

☐Slipstitch the arms to the body, centering them over side seams.

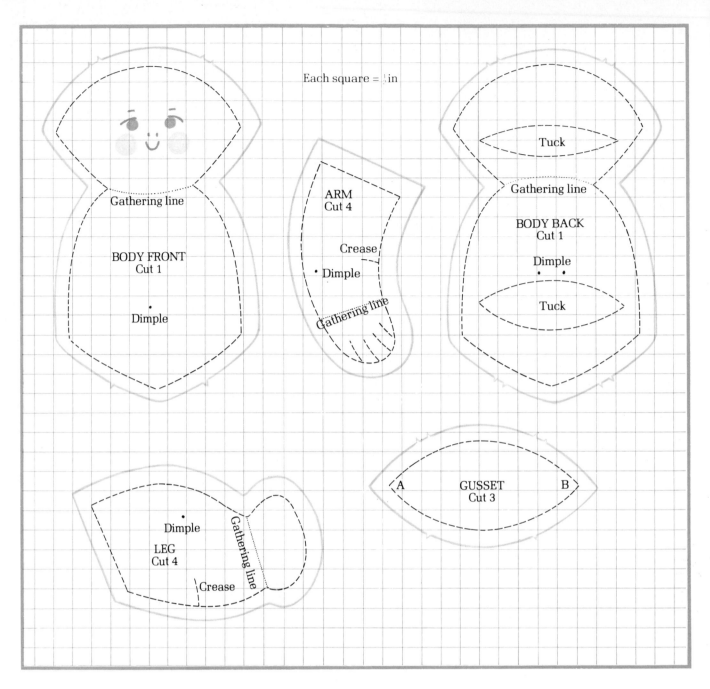

Each square = ½ in

Gathering line

BODY FRONT
Cut 1

• Dimple

ARM
Cut 4

Crease

• Dimple

Gathering line

Tuck

Gathering line

BODY BACK
Cut 1

Dimple
• •

Tuck

• Dimple

LEG
Cut 4

Gathering line

Crease

A   GUSSET
Cut 3   B

To make the clothes
Turn up the lower edge of each sleeve along the fold lines. Machine stitch along the casing lines. Baste a piece of lace under each edge and topstitch it in place. Thread elastic through the casing and pull it up to fit the arm. Sew the elastic ends to the seam allowances to secure them.
☐ Join the center back seam up to the notch. Press the seam open.
☐ Stitch the sleeves to the front and back sections, matching the notches.
☐ Cut a bias strip of fabric, 1½ × 12½ in, to make a casing on the neck. Place RS of casing strip on WS of the neck edge. Baste and machine stitch. Trim seam allowances to ⅛ in.
☐ Turn under the raw edges of the back opening, including the bias strip, and press. Fold the bias strip to the RS of the neckline. Turn under the raw edge and baste and topstitch it in place. Hand sew lace over the seam and thread ribbon through the casing.

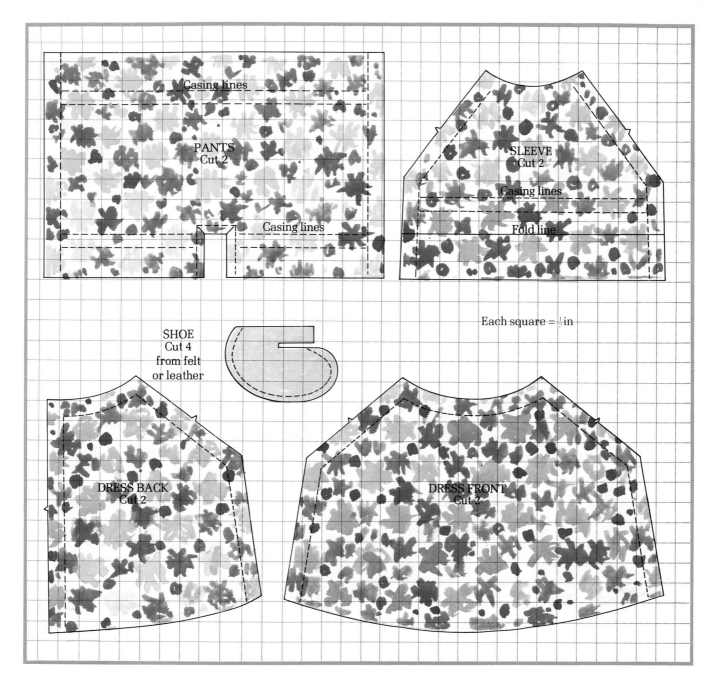

Each square = $\frac{1}{2}$in

☐Turn dress WS out. Stitch side and sleeve seams in one operation.
☐Press under a narrow hem on the lower edge of the dress. Baste a length of lace under the edge and topstitch the hem. Cut two 10in pieces of ribbon. Tie them in bows and sew a bow to each sleeve.
☐Place the two pants pieces together, RS facing. Stitch the inner leg seam and clip the corners. Join the side seams.
☐Turn up $\frac{5}{8}$in on the legs to form casings for elastic; baste and machine stitch along the marked lines, leaving a small gap for inserting elastic. Stitch lace to the bottom of the casing.
☐Make the casing at the waist in the same way, folding under $\frac{3}{4}$in. Thread the elastic through all three casings, drawing it up to fit and sewing the ends together. Stitch up the gaps. Make bows and sew them to each leg casing.
☐Place two shoe pieces together, RS facing. Hand sew along seamlines. Clip curves and turn shoe RS out. Repeat for other shoe. Make and sew a bow to each shoe.

Gretel

Size
Approximately 16in tall

Materials
⅔yd of 36in-wide pale pink
   stockinet
⅔yd of iron-on interfacing
Ball of pale yellow bulky yarn
7oz of stuffing
Stranded embroidery floss in blue,
   pink, cream, brown and black for
   features
⅔yd of 36in-wide pink checked
   fabric for skirt
⅜in of 36in-wide yellow fabric for
   petticoat
⅛in of 36in-wide soft white cotton
   for blouse
½yd each of eyelet lace edging and
   narrow eyelet lace insertion
¾yd of yellow rickrack
½yd each of 1¼in-wide dotted and
   checked ribbon
8in of narrow flat elastic
Scrap of pink felt for shoes
Scrap of white felt for eyes
Small amount of bright yellow yarn
2 buttons for skirt
3 small snaps
Hook and eye

Making the pattern — cutting out
Enlarge the pattern pieces as indicated on the graph. Iron the interfacing to the WS of the stockinet. Cut the pattern pieces from stockinet and felt as indicated. Transfer the features onto the face.
☐For the clothes, cut the following pieces: from checked fabric, one piece 9½ × 12½in , one strip 6¾ × 2¾in and 2 strips 6 × 2¾in: from yellow fabric, a piece 9½ × 12½in; from white fabric, one piece 4 × 8½in and 2 pieces 4 × 4¾in.

To make the doll
Cut ovals of white felt for the eyes and glue them to the face. Using 2 strands of blue and black embroidery floss, work the eyes in satin stitch. Using brown, outline the eyes with short straight stitches and work the eyebrows in stem stitch. Using cream, work the nose in backstitch. Using pink, work the mouth in satin stitch.
☐Join the two back head sections, WS facing, at the center back. Join the back head to the body piece at the neck. Join the face to the front body.
☐Place each pair of arm sections together, RS facing, and stitch all around, leaving the top open. Clip curves and turn arms RS out. Stuff them firmly. Turn in the raw edges and slipstitch them together.
☐Stitch the legs together as for the arms, leaving both top and bottom edges open. Clip curves and turn legs RS out. Hand-sew the soles to the feet. Fill the legs with stuffing and slipstitch the top edges closed, first making sure that the front and back seams are aligned.
☐Place the front and back head and body sections together, RS facing, and stitch around the edges, leaving the lower edge open. Clip curves and turn body RS out. Fill it firmly and slipstitch lower edges.
☐Using strong thread, hand-sew the arms and legs to the body.
☐Cut about 30 pieces of yarn 2in long. Tape them to paper, covering a width of 2½in (see page 13) and stitch ⅜in from one edge. Remove paper and tape. Stitch the bangs to the doll's forehead.
☐Cut about 30 pieces of yarn 24in long. Place them side by side covering a width of 3¼in. Place a strip of paper under the center point, tape yarn in place and stitch as before. Remove paper and tape, and place the yarn on the doll's head, covering the stitching on the bangs. Stitch yarn in place over the center part. Tie it in bunches with a bit of matching yarn at the sides of head and sew bunches in place. Braid the hair and tie it with bows.

To make the clothes
For the skirt, stitch the short sides of the main piece together, RS facing, leaving 3in unstitched at top. Turn under these unstitched edges and topstitch to finish them. Run two lines of gathering stitches along the upper edge. On the lower edge, turn under and press a double ⅝in hem. Topstitch this in place, applying a piece of rickrack at the same time. Topstitch another piece of rickrack ¾in above the first.
☐Pull up the gathering stitches so that the upper edge measures 6in, and distribute gathers evenly. Place the 6¾in waistband strip on the gathered edge, RS facing and raw edges matching, with ⅜in extending on each side. Stitch. Turn in the short ends and fold the waistband to the WS. Turn in the raw edge and slipstitch it to the first line of stitching.

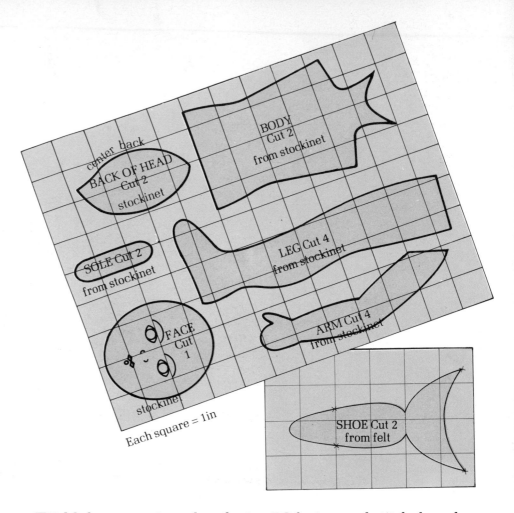

Each square = 1in

□Fold the strap pieces lengthwise, RS facing, and stitch down long edge and one end. Turn straps RS out. Stitch them to front and back of skirt, inside waistband, and sew buttons to the front of waistband as shown in photograph. Sew a hook and eye to the waistband ends.
□For the blouse, fold the largest piece in half widthwise; press. Cut an oval slit in the center of the folded edge, making it 2in wide and $\frac{3}{8}$in deep ($\frac{3}{4}$in when opened) at the center. Round the outer corners of the oval. Slash the fabric through the center, from the oval to one edge, to form the back opening. Turn under $\frac{1}{4}$in on both opening edges and topstitch. Turn under and press $\frac{1}{4}$in on the neck edge, clipping fabric where necessary. Place a length of eyelet lace edging under the edge and topstitch it in place. Stitch eyelet lace insertion on top.
□Place the sleeves on the side edges of the bodice, centering one 4in edge over the crease, RS facing; stitch. Turn under remaining 4in edges and topstitch, applying eyelet lace edging at the same time. Stitch insertion on top.
□Turn the bodice WS out and stitch side and sleeve seams. Turn bodice RS out. Cut 4 pieces of yellow yarn; thread them through insertion at neck and wrists, securing ends at back neck. Sew snaps to back opening.
□Join the center back seam of the petticoat. Turn under and stitch a $\frac{3}{8}$in-wide casing at one edge. Thread narrow elastic through the casing; pull it up to fit doll's waist and stitch ends together. Turn under and stitch a double $\frac{5}{8}$in hem on the lower edge.
□For the shoes, fold the moon-shaped section back to meet the edges and slipstitch it in place. Cut the checked ribbon in half and hand-sew each half to the back of a shoe. Place shoes on feet and tie ribbon into bows.

Sam and Daisy

Making the pattern — cutting out

Enlarge the pattern pieces as indicated on the graphs, and cut out the pieces for the body and clothes from the appropriate fabrics. Also cut, for Daisy's skirt, a rectangle of printed fabric, $33\frac{1}{2}$in × 10in.
□ Using dressmaker's carbon, transfer the pattern markings to the fabric; a seam allowance of $\frac{3}{8}$in is included throughout.

To make the body

Stitch seam A-B on the front body section. Place front and back pieces together, RS facing, and stitch shoulder seams between C and D, and side seams from E to F. Leave the center back seam between A and B open for stuffing. Turn body RS out.
□ Turn in and press $\frac{3}{8}$in on lower edge of the body.
□ Stitch the forehead dart at the top of the face. Embroider the features, using 3 strands of dark brown embroidery floss for the eyes and beige thread for the nose, mouth and freckles. Make sure the stitches are even but do not pull them tightly. It is easiest to work the embroidery if you first baste the face to a piece of lawn, mount it in an embroidery frame and then carefully cut away the lawn from the wrong side.
□ Work the main lines in stem stitch, the center of the eyes with radiating satin stitch worked in a circle, and the freckles with small French knots.
□ Cut 4 circles of pink net, each $1\frac{1}{2}$in in diameter. Sew two to the center of each cheek (making a double layer) using blanket or zigzag stitch.

Sizes

Approximately 24in tall

Materials

For each doll

$\frac{5}{8}$yd of 36in-wide unbleached muslin
1lb of stuffing
Stranded embroidery floss in dark brown and beige
Scraps of pink net
2oz of bulky yarn in light brown

Sam's clothes

$\frac{3}{8}$yd of 36in-wide small plaid fabric
$\frac{3}{8}$yd of 36in-wide large plaid fabric
10in of bias binding to match fabric
2 small buttons
Scrap of striped fabric
8in of narrow elastic
3 snaps

Daisy's clothes

$\frac{5}{8}$yd of 36in-wide brown printed fabric
$\frac{1}{4}$in of 36in-wide white cotton
$1\frac{3}{4}$yd of $\frac{3}{4}$in -wide cream lace edging
$\frac{3}{4}$yd of $\frac{5}{8}$in-wide white gathered lace edging
$\frac{1}{2}$yd of $\frac{3}{8}$in-wide yellow ribbon
8in of narrow elastic
2 snaps

25

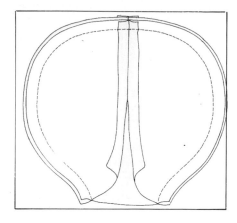

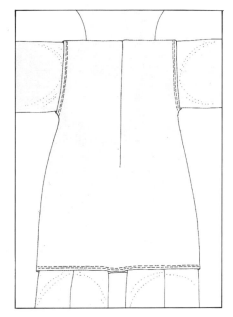

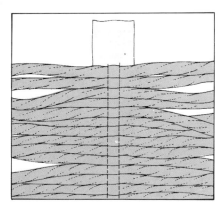

☐ Seam the head back pieces together between X and Z. The remainder of the center back head seam is left open for stuffing. Place front and back of head together, RS facing, and stitch around the edge, leaving the neck edge open.

☐ Turn the head RS out and slip it into the body (still WS out), so that the RS are facing and the neck edges are matching. Make sure that the face is to the front. Baste the neck edges together, then stitch. Press the seam open and turn doll RS out.

☐ Place two leg pieces together with RS facing and stitch all around, leaving the top open. Clip the curve around the feet and turn leg RS out. Fill it firmly, pushing stuffing down into the toes with the help of a blunt stick or knitting needle. Baste the opening edges together so that the front and back seams are aligned. Repeat these steps to make the other leg.

☐ Pin the left leg into the opening on the left side of the body, matching points at F and G, so the leg is hanging down. Repeat for the right leg. Baste and stitch across the lower edges, including the legs, either by machine or with small firm backstitches, so that the legs are floppy.

☐ Place two arm pieces together with RS facing and stitch all around, leaving the top open. Clip the seams and turn arm RS out. Stuff arm firmly, taking care to push the stuffing right into the thumb. Baste the opening edges together to hold the stuffing in place. Repeat for the other arm.

☐ Press under $\frac{3}{8}$in on armhole edges. Pin the arms, thumbs facing upward, into the openings, matching points D and E at each side. Baste and stitch the arms in place as for the legs. Check that all the layers are securely stitched; a double row of stitching is recommended.

☐ Fill the head and body firmly with stuffing, making sure the shoulders and neck are well padded. Turn under the center back edges from point Z on the head to point B on the body. Close the opening by slipstitching the folded edges together. Fasten off securely.

Daisy's hair Cut 35 lengths of yarn 26in long. Place the strands on a sheet of paper so that they cover a width of 8in. Place a strip of tape down the center of the strands, extending tape onto the paper. Machine stitch through tape, yarn and paper, then pull away the paper and tape.

☐ Pin the hair over the crown of the head with the stitching in the center, beginning at the forehead to cover the dart. Backstitch over the part to attach the hair, then catch the hair to the head at each side with small stitches.

☐ Cut the ribbon in half, and tie each half in a bow on each side to form bunches.

Sam's hair Cut 60 strands of yarn, 14in long. Stitch them together as for Daisy's hair, but stitch to one side of center to form a side part. Pin and stitch the hair to the head along the side part. With small stitches, catch the yarn to the head in a random way, so that hair does not appear too neat. Trim the front few strands to form bangs. Cut the ends unevenly to achieve a casual appearance.

To make Sam's clothes
Pin the left front and left back shirt pieces together, RS facing, and stitch the shoulder and sleeve seam A-B and the underarm and sleeve seam C-D. Repeat for the right front and right back pieces. Pin the two sides of the shirt together at one center seamline (E-F), RS facing, and stitch the seam.

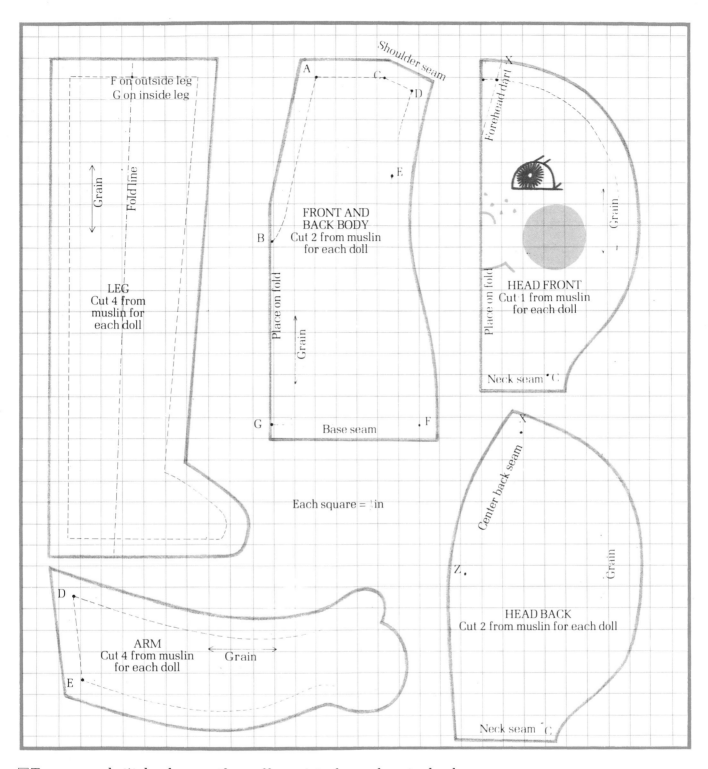

☐ Turn up and stitch a hem on the cuffs, waist edge and center back edges. Stitch bias binding over the raw neck edge. Press the seams and turn shirt RS out. Sew the snaps to the back opening edges; sew two buttons at the top of the center front seam.

☐ Pin the pants pieces together, RS facing, and stitch the crotch seam G-H on center front and back. Stitch the inside leg seams H-I.

☐ Turn under and stitch a casing on the waist edge, leaving a gap. Using a safety pin, thread the elastic through the channel; stitch the ends together securely.

☐ Hem the lower edge of each leg. Cut a square patch of striped fabric and sew it to the left knee with blanket or zigzag stitch.

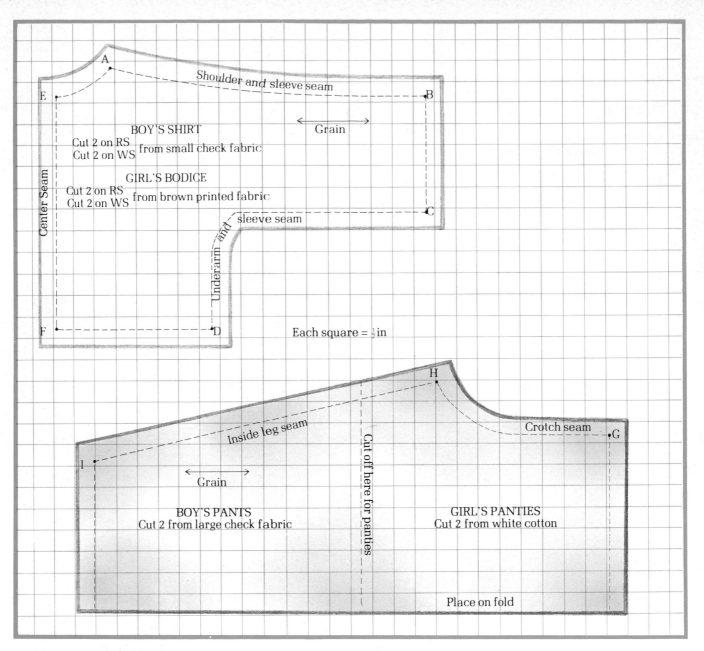

A

Shoulder and sleeve seam

E

B

BOY'S SHIRT
Cut 2 on RS
Cut 2 on WS from small check fabric

GIRL'S BODICE
Cut 2 on RS
Cut 2 on WS from brown printed fabric

Grain

Center Seam

C

Underarm and sleeve seam

F

D

Each square = $\frac{1}{2}$ in

H

Inside leg seam

Crotch seam

G

I

Cut off here for panties

Grain

BOY'S PANTS
Cut 2 from large check fabric

GIRL'S PANTIES
Cut 2 from white cotton

Place on fold

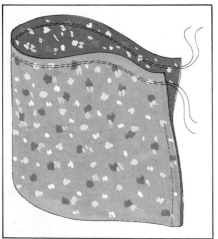

To make Daisy's clothes
Make the bodice section in the same way as Sam's shirt.
☐ Seam the two short ends of the skirt, leaving $3\frac{1}{4}$in at the top unstitched. Make two lines of gathering along the top edge. Pull the gathers up to fit the bodice waist. Stitch the skirt and bodice together, RS facing.
☐ Finish the back opening edges and hem the lower edge of the skirt. Trim the cuffs and skirt hem with lace. Gather the remaining lace to fit around the neckline, and stitch it in place.
☐ Sew the snaps to the back opening at neck and waist.
☐ Make the panties in the same way as Sam's pants. Trim each leg with gathered lace.

Baby doll and basket

Size
Approximately 10in tall

Materials
For the doll
Piece of pale pink stockinet
   12in square for body
Piece of white stretch terry cloth
   10in square for underclothes
½yd of ⅛in-wide turquoise satin
   ribbon for hair bows
1oz ball of brown synthetic fluffy
   yarn for hair
Scraps of brown felt for eyes
Strong thread to match body
Long darning needle
Red and brown embroidery thread
   for features
3½oz of washable stuffing
Cardboard

For the basket
Piece of cardboard 8 × 16½in
1⅛yd of 36in-wide printed quilted
   fabric
⅔yd of 36in-wide white fleece
   fabric for blanket
1½yd of 1½in-wide gathered eyelet
   lace edging
1½yd of ¾in-wide eyelet lace
   insertion
1⅜in of ⅜in-wide turquoise velvet
   ribbon
1¾yd of ¼in-wide turquoise satin
   ribbon

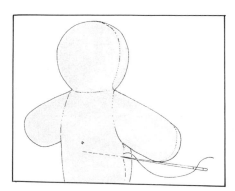

Making the pattern — cutting out

Enlarge the pattern pieces as indicated on the graph, and cut out the pieces from the appropriate fabrics. When cutting out the body, make sure that the vertical ribs of stockinet follow the grain line. When cutting out the basket ends, cut one piece, then use this as a guide when cutting the other seven pieces so that the quilting lines will match. A seam allowance of ¼in is included throughout.

To make the doll

Baste the body pieces together, RS facing. Stitch all around, leaving an opening in the head as indicated. Stitch again along the inside leg. ☐Clip the curved edges and corners. Turn the body RS out. Stuff it firmly and mold it to a good shape.
☐Using strong thread, work a row of gathering stitches around the base of the head in the position marked; pull them up to form the neck and secure the thread firmly.
☐Using strong thread work a line of stab stitch from the shoulder to underarm on each side, pulling the stitches tightly to form a joint.
☐Using the darning needle and strong thread, secure the thread on the seamline below the arm. Take the thread right through the body and out under the other arm. Pull up gently and secure with a backstitch. Repeat several times to form the waist.
☐Cut a piece of cardboard 4¼ × 2in. Wind the yarn thickly over the cardboard widthwise. Backstitch along the loops on one long edge. Cut along the other long edge. This forms the bangs. Place the backstitched edge along the head seam and stitch it in place.
☐Cut a piece of cardboard 6 × 3½in and wind the yarn thickly over it lengthwise. Backstitch along the loops on one short edge. Cut along the other short edge. Position backstitched seam vertically on the center back of the doll's head approximately ¾in above the neck, and stitch it in place. Spread hair over back of doll's head and stitch it to each side, starting at cheeks and working toward neck stitching.
☐Cut two 8in pieces of satin ribbon and tie the hair in bunches.
☐Cut two ⅜in circles from brown felt. Position them on face as indicated on the pattern and stitch them in place, using brown embroidery thread and straight stitches. Using red embroidery thread, work a French knot for mouth. To fasten off, push needle through to back of head, so that stitches are hidden under the hair.

To make the clothes

Stitch the shoulder and side seams of the undershirt, then finish seams. Work a narrow rolled hem around neckline and armholes. Turn up and stitch a narrow double hem at bottom edge.
☐Work a rolled hem around diapers. Position the diapers on the doll and backstitch the ends to secure them. Embroider the safety pins in satin stitch and backstitch, using brown thread.

To make the basket

Mark one base/side and 4 end pieces for lining; set them aside.
☐For the outer section, stitch one pair of end pieces together at center line with RS facing and quilting pattern matching. Trim away the batting; press the seam open. Join the other pair of end pieces.
☐Baste and stitch the end pieces to the rounded ends of the base section. Clip the seams and press them open. Stitch the remaining sides to the base sides. Press the seams open.

□Join the pieces for the lining in the same way. Slip the basket lining into the outer section, WS facing and seams matching. Catch the pieces together at curved seamlines to hold them in place.

□Baste and stitch 47in of gathered eyelet lace around the outside edge of the basket, 1½in from the top edge. Turn ⅜in of the lining edge to the outside and stitch it over the raw edge of the eyelet lace.

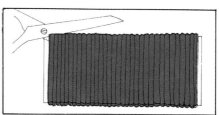

□To make one handle, cut a strip of quilted fabric 14 × 3⅛in. Fold it lengthwise, RS together, and make a ⅜in seam. Turn strip RS out, and press the seam to the center. Stitch handle to the edge of cot with the ends 5in apart. Repeat for the other handle.

□Baste the velvet ribbon around the outside of the basket over the raw edge of lining and slipstitch it in place. Thread 47in of satin ribbon through 47in of insertion. Slipstitch lace around the inner edge.

□Place 8in of gathered eyelet lace RS downward, on the straight edge of one blanket piece, with the shaped edge inwards and the straight edge just overlapping the seamline. Stitch it in place. Finish the side edges of the eyelet lace, so that it fits within the seamlines. Place blanket pieces together, RS facing, and stitch around the curved edge. Clip the curves and turn blanket RS out; press. Turn in straight edge and hem it to WS of eyelet lace.

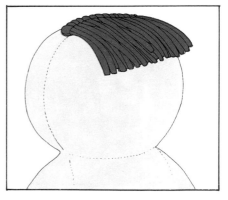

□Topstitch around curved edge. Thread 8in of ribbon through 8in of insertion. Slipstitch trimming to straight edge of blanket.

31

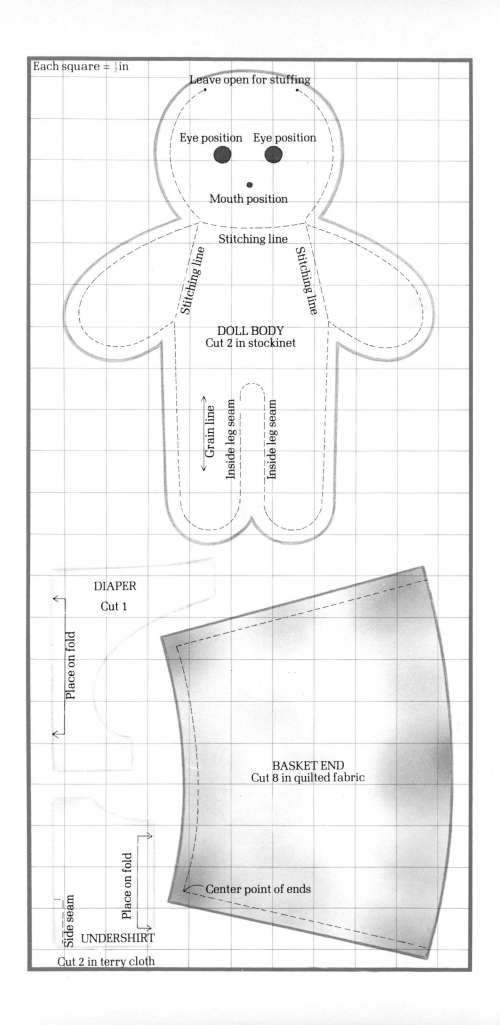

Each square = ½ in

Leave open for stuffing

Eye position   Eye position

Mouth position

Stitching line

Stitching line   Stitching line

DOLL BODY
Cut 2 in stockinet

Grain line

Inside leg seam

Inside leg seam

DIAPER
Cut 1

Place on fold

BASKET END
Cut 8 in quilted fabric

Place on fold

Center point of ends

Side seam   UNDERSHIRT

Cut 2 in terry cloth

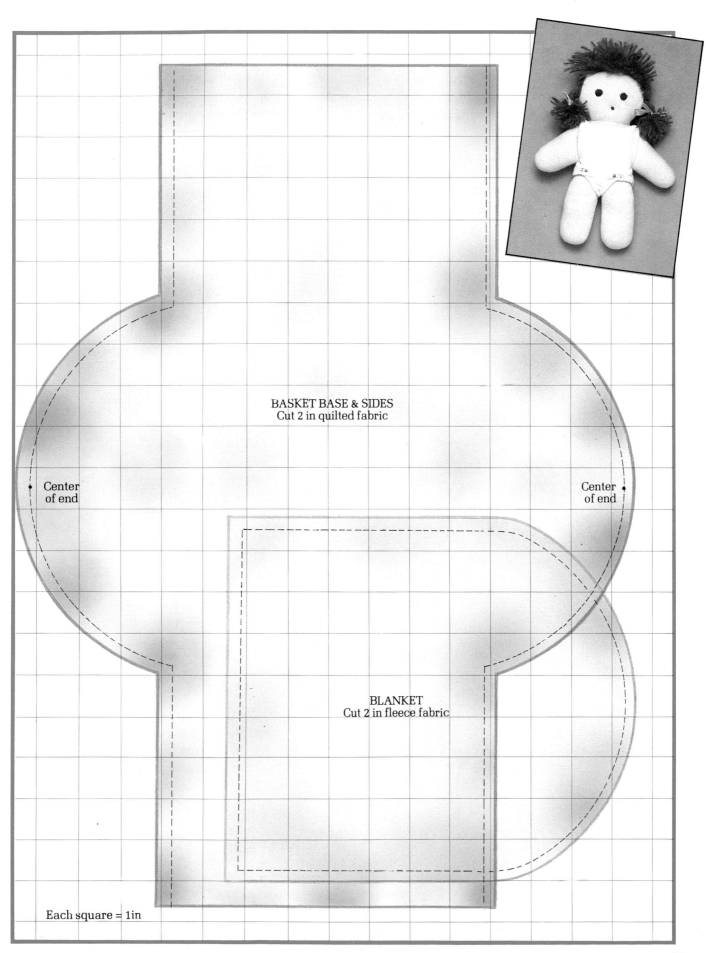

BASKET BASE & SIDES
Cut 2 in quilted fabric

Center
of end

Center
of end

BLANKET
Cut 2 in fleece fabric

Each square = 1in

Victoria

Size
Approximately 19in tall

Materials
⅝yd of 36in-wide unbleached muslin
  for body
¾yd of 36in-wide pink moiré for
  skirt
½yd of 36in-wide fine, soft cotton
  for blouse and pantalets
9oz of stuffing
⅜yd of 2¼in-wide pleated lace for
  cuffs
⅜yd of 1½in-wide eyelet lace for
  pantalets
3in of ⅜in-wide braid for jacket
  trimming
⅜yd of ¾in-wide lace for blouse
  collar
Piece of fine woven straw 7in
  square for hat
1yd of ⅝in-wide blue lacy braid
  for hat trimming
⅜in of 1in-wide cream lace for hat
  trimming
¾yd of ⅝in-wide pink ribbon
Bunch of small fabric flowers
8in of narrow elastic
2 pieces of felt 7in square in gray
  and navy blue for shoes
Small piece of balsa wood for heels
Blue yarn for shoelaces
Small wig strip of doll's hair
Fabric paints for features
1 hook and eye
2 snaps

Make the pattern — cutting out
Enlarge the pattern pieces as indicated and cut the pieces for the body and clothes from the appropriate fabrics. Also cut rectangular pieces for clothes as instructed. A seam allowance of ¼in is included throughout.

To make the doll
First make the arms. Place each pair together, RS facing, and stitch around the edges, leaving the top edges open. Fill them with stuffing, taking care not to overstuff the hands. Work stab stitch on the hands to suggest fingers (see page 13). Turn in the top edges and overcast them together firmly.
☐Stitch and stuff the legs in basically the same way. When closing the top edges, make sure that the front and back seams are aligned — so that the top seam crosses them at a right angle.
☐Stitch the body pieces together in the same way, leaving the lower edge open. Fill it with stuffing; then turn in the opening edges and overcast them together. Using double thread, stitch the legs firmly to the body with overcasting. To attach the arms, bring one corner to each side of the shoulder, matching dots, and stab-stitch through the corner of the arm and the body and through the other corner, then back again until the arm is secure but still flexible.
For the head, stitch four darts on each of the head pieces, then pin the two pieces together, RS facing, and stitch around the edges, leaving a gap at the top of the head. Turn the head RS out and fill it firmly with stuffing; leave the gap open. Cut a small circle of muslin about ¾in in diameter; gather up the edge and fill it with stuffing. Push the muslin ball down into the head, positioning it to form a little lump for the nose. If you are using fabric paints which need to be sealed by ironing (see page 14), paint the doll's face at this stage. The features should be more subtle and detailed than those of a typical rag doll (see photograph). To iron the paint, remove the stuffing; then re-insert it. Slipstitch the edges of the gap together, and then attach the doll's head to the body, lapping the head over the neck edge slightly, so that the head rests securely on the neck and some effect of a chin is given to the doll. If you like, add a little color to the doll's face with a touch of powder-based rouge and eyeshadow.
☐Stitch the wig strip to the head as shown on page 37.

To make the clothes
On one blouse bodice piece cut a slit down the center from the neck for 3in. Roll under the raw edges and neatly slipstitch them in place. Work lines of gathering stitches at the lower edge of each sleeve, as marked, and gather until lower edge measures 6in. Topstitch pleated lace to the gathered edge of each sleeve. Join the sleeve seams, then join the shoulder and side seams of the main blouse. Turn the sleeves RS out and insert them into the bodice armholes, matching the sleeve seam to the side seam of the blouse. Gather the straight edge of ¾in-wide lace to fit the neck edge. Overcast it in place with tiny stitches. Sew a snap at the back.
☐Stitch the leg seam of each pantalet piece, then stitch the crotch seam. Press under ⅜in on each leg, and topstitch, attaching eyelet lace under the edge at the same time. Turn under the waist edge to form a casing; topstitch, leaving a gap. Insert elastic, pull it up to fit doll's waist and stitch ends together. Topstitch to close the gap.

☐Stitch the jacket darts, then join the two back pieces down the center back with a narrow French seam. Join the side and shoulder seams with plain seams and finish them together. Zigzag stitch around the outer edge of the jacket and around the sleeve edges.

☐Attach braid to the sleeve edges, covering the raw edges and joining the ends at the sleeve seam. Attach 2 more strips of braid above the lower edge of the jacket: one strip $1\frac{1}{4}$in from the cut edge and the other $\frac{5}{8}$in above the first; then attach braid all around the edge of the jacket. Sew the hook and eye just inside at waistline.

☐Using tailor's chalk or a colored pencil, mark 3 lines across the 24in width of the skirt base, on the RS, for ruffle placement lines. The lines should be spaced $3\frac{1}{4}$in apart, with the first line 3in down from one long edge. Placing RS together, join the two short sides, leaving 3in open at the top edge. Finish the raw edges and press the

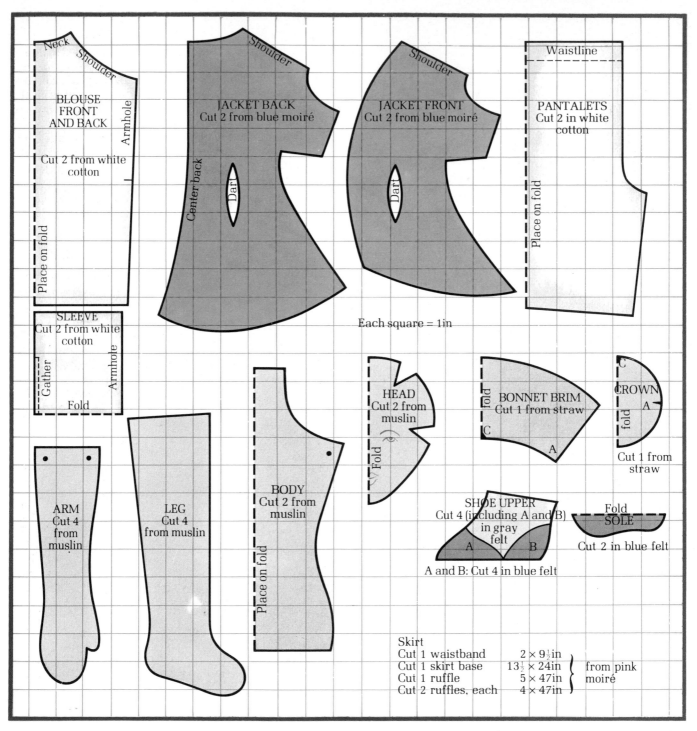

BLOUSE
FRONT
AND BACK

Cut 2 from white cotton

Neck Shoulder

Armhole

Place on fold

SLEEVE
Cut 2 from white cotton

Gather

Armhole

Fold

Shoulder

JACKET BACK
Cut 2 from blue moiré

Center back

Dart

Shoulder

JACKET FRONT
Cut 2 from blue moiré

Dart

Shoulder

Waistline

PANTALETS
Cut 2 in white cotton

Place on fold

Each square = 1in

ARM
Cut 4
from
muslin

LEG
Cut 4
from muslin

BODY
Cut 2 from
muslin

Place on fold

HEAD
Cut 2 from
muslin

Fold

Fold

C

BONNET BRIM
Cut 1 from straw

C

A

C

CROWN

A

fold

Cut 1 from
straw

SHOE UPPER
Cut 4 (including A and B)
in gray
felt

A   B

A and B: Cut 4 in blue felt

Fold

SOLE

Cut 2 in blue felt

Skirt
Cut 1 waistband $2 \times 9\frac{1}{2}$in
Cut 1 skirt base $13\frac{1}{2} \times 24$in   } from pink
Cut 1 ruffle 5×47in   moiré
Cut 2 ruffles, each 4×47in

seam open. Make a narrow hem on the lower edge. Prepare the ruffles by first stitching along one long raw edge of each ruffle, using a satin stitch and the blue thread used for the jacket. If you have a machine which can make a scalloped edge, this would look attractive, but otherwise make a straight edge.

□Next, make gathering stitches along the other long edge of each ruffle, then join the two short edges.

□Gather up each ruffle to measure $23\frac{1}{2}$in, then pin and stitch them to the skirt. Starting with the deepest ruffle, place it along the lowest placement line on the RS and zigzag stitch over the gathered edge. Turn the skirt WS out and fold it down so that it encloses the raw edge of the ruffle. Straight-stitch around the skirt, $\frac{3}{8}$in down from the fold, catching in the raw edge of the ruffle and the zigzag stitching.

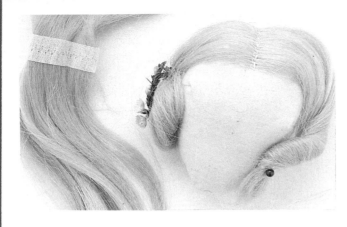

Hair

Hair for a costume doll should be more realistic than for a rag doll. Use a wig strip and arrange it on the head in a becoming style, stitching it in place inconspicuously. The wig for the Victorian doll is first attached to the head by backstitching over the center part. The hair at each side is twisted into coils and tied at the ends, then the ends are tucked underneath, forming buns. A bunch of artificial flowers makes a good hair ornament if the doll has no bonnet.

Bonnet

This photograph shows the back view of a bonnet similar to the one worn by the Victorian doll. The brim is first trimmed with three strips of braid: one just under the front edge, one just over it and one about ¾in from the inner edge. The inner raw edge of the brim and the edge of the circular crown are finished with zigzag stitch and then stitched together. The strip of lace is gathered and stitched to the lower edge, then covered with another strip of braid. Ribbon ties and a bunch of flowers complete the bonnet.

Shoes

The Victorian doll's boots are made as shown here. First topstitch the dark felt pieces to the light-colored shoe tops. The two top pieces are then stitched together along front and back edges, RS facing, then the soles are stitched to the tops. For a high heel, cut a piece of balsa wood to the shape shown, then cover it with felt, glued in place. Glue or stitch the heel to the boot. For laces, work a few straight stitches across the front of the boot.

Attach the remaining two ruffles in the same way.

☐ Gather the top edge of the skirt to measure 8in. Place the waistband on this edge with RS facing, and ⅜in extending at one end, ¾in on the other. Stitch it in place. Turn in ⅜in on short ends, fold waistband to WS, turn in raw edge and slipstitch over first line of stitching and along open end of overlap. Sew a snap to ends.

☐ For the bonnet, stitch or glue braid to the brim as described above. Zigzag stitch around the edge of the crown to prevent fraying, then stitch the crown to the brim from A to C. Trim the bonnet with cream lace, another strip of braid and the bunch of flowers. Cut the pink ribbon in half and sew it to the bonnet for ties.

☐ Make up the shoes as described above. The heels may be omitted, if you prefer.

Victorian bathers

Size
Approximately 27in tall

Materials
For each doll
1⅛yd of 36in-wide firmly-woven
    white cotton
⅛yd of 36in-wide brown corduroy
    for shoes
1lb of stuffing
Red crayon

For gentleman
Ball of dark brown bulky yarn
Piece of cardboard 9½ × 4¾in
Stranded embroidery floss in dark
    brown, light brown, pink and gray

For lady
2oz of honey-colored bulky yarn
Piece of cardboard 4 × 2¾in
Stranded embroidery floss in blue,
    beige, pink and red

Gentleman's clothes
⅝yd of 36in-wide striped fabric
¾yd of ⅝in-wide red velvet ribbon
3 red buttons
5 snaps
2 small white buttons
⅜yd of ¼in-wide elastic

Lady's clothes
1yd of ⅜in-wide blue velvet ribbon
2 small white buttons
2 snaps
1⅛yd of narrow lace edging
⅞yd of ⅜in-wide elastic and ⅜yd
    of cord elastic

Making the pattern — cutting out
Enlarge the pattern pieces as indicated on the graph and cut out the pieces for the body and clothes from the appropriate fabrics. Using dressmaker's carbon, transfer the markings to the fabric; a seam allowance of ¼in is included throughout.

To make the head
Embroider the faces first. (This is easier if you baste the face to a piece of lawn, mount it in an embroidery hoop and then cut away the lawn on the underside.) Cut 2 ⅜in felt circles for the eyes of each doll. Using a single strand of embroidery floss in the appropriate color, attach the eyes with short stitches around the edges. Using 2 strands, outline the eyes, man's eyebrows and lady's mouth in backstitch; work the mouths and nostrils in satin stitch and the eyelashes in short straight stitches.
☐Work small running stitches along the top edge of each head. Pull up the gathers slightly. Baste and stitch the front and back heads together, RS facing, leaving the neck open. Fill the head with stuffing, but do not close the neck opening.

Gentleman's hair and mustache Wind yarn around a 4 × 5½in piece of cardboard and sew the strands together along the top edge. Remove the stitched loops from the cardboard. Make another strip in the same way. Sew the stitched edge of each section to the center of the head, from forehead to center back. Gather each set of loops with one strand of yarn and stitch it securely to each side of the head. For the top hair wind yarn lengthwise around a 5½ × 1½in piece of cardboard, and cut the strands at one edge. Tie the strands in a bunch at the center and sew this to the top of the head.
☐For the mustache, wind yarn lengthwise around a 9½ × ¾in piece of cardboard; slip the loops from the cardboard and tie them in a bunch at the center. Stretch the mustache across the face and, twisting once at each side, sew the loops to each side of head.
Lady's hair For the bangs, wind yarn widthwise around a 4 × 2¾in piece of cardboard; stitch along one long edge and cut along the other. Place the stitched edge on the head seam, in the center, and stitch it in place. For the main part of hair, cut about 40 strands of yarn, 28in long. Lay them across the back of head and stitch along the seamline. Divide each side of hair into two bunches and braid it as shown. Wind the braids over the head as shown, and sew them firmly to head at several places.

To make the body
First checking that you have two matching pairs, place the top edge of each shoe side on the lower edge of each leg piece with RS facing, edges matching and straight edge of shoe to curved edge of leg. Baste and stitch the seam.
☐Place each pair of leg pieces together with RS facing and stitch each side edge. Baste and stitch each shoe sole to the foot opening and turn the legs RS out. Stuff the legs and shoes firmly and tie the top of each leg tightly with strong thread.
☐Place each pair of matching arm pieces together with RS facing. Stitch around the edges, leaving the top open. Push stuffing firmly into each hand section, fill the arms and bind the top of each arm tightly with strong thread.

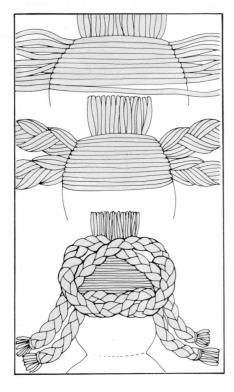

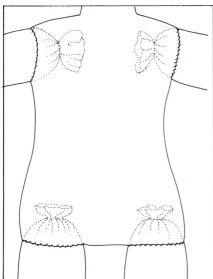

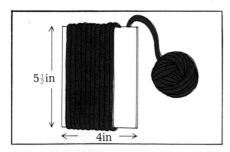

□Place the body pieces together with RS facing. Leaving gaps for inserting arms, legs and head, stitch around the edges. Turn the body RS out. Insert the arms and legs and slipstitch them in place. Fill the body firmly with stuffing, turn in the neck edge of the body and the head and slipstitch edges together neatly.

To make the gentleman's clothes
Place the shirt back and fronts together with RS facing and join the side and shoulder seams. Turn and stitch a narrow double hem around the neck edge. Fold each sleeve in half with RS facing and join the long seam. Turn and stitch a narrow hem on each wrist edge. Gather the top edge of each sleeve and pull up gathers to fit shirt armholes. Baste and stitch each sleeve in place. Stitch a $\frac{3}{8}$in hem around the lower edge of the shirt.
□Turn under $\frac{1}{4}$in, then another $\frac{5}{8}$in along each edge of the shirt front opening. Work 2 lines of topstitching, $\frac{3}{8}$in apart, to hold these hems in place. Sew a button at the neck opening of the overlapping center front edge, and sew the other two at $1\frac{3}{4}$in intervals below the first. Sew a snap behind each button.
□Place each pair of pants pieces together with RS facing and join the crotch seam. Place the two joined pieces together, RS facing, and stitch the side and inside leg seams. Turn and stitch a double hem around each leg and the waist of the pants. Zigzag stitch elastic to the wrong side of the waist edge.
□Cut the velvet ribbon in half, and stitch one end of each piece to form a miter. Sew a button to the mitered end of each velvet strap. Sew half a snap underneath each button and the other halves to the pants. Sew other end of suspenders inside back waist edge.

To make the lady's clothes
Place the tunic front and backs together with RS facing and join the side and shoulder seams. Turn under a narrow double hem on the neck edge and topstitch it in place, attaching lace edging to RS at same time. Fold each sleeve in half, RS facing, and stitch the long seam. Turn up and topstitch a narrow hem around each wrist edge attaching lace as on neck. Gather the top edge of each sleeve and pull up gathers to fit the armholes. Baste and stitch each sleeve in place. Turn up and topstitch a $\frac{3}{8}$in double hem around the lower edge of the tunic, attaching lace as on neck.
□Using a small zigzag, stitch a piece of elastic around the waist of the tunic on the WS. Cut the velvet ribbon in half, and sew the center of each to each side of the tunic waist. Work two $\frac{3}{4}$in thread loops (several strands of thread covered closely with blanket stitch) on the lower edge of the tunic, on each side. To gather up skirt for bathing, slip ribbon through loops and tie in bows.
□Turn and stitch a double $\frac{3}{8}$in hem on the back opening edges. Sew a small button to the neck and waist of the back opening. Sew a snap behind each button and to other edge of the tunic.
□Make pantalets as for gentleman's pants, but zigzag stitch elastic $\frac{3}{4}$in above the lower edge of each pant leg, and attach lace when topstitching hems.
□For the hat, turn under and press under $\frac{3}{8}$in on both long edges of the bias strip. Run a gathering thread around the edge of the circular hat piece, and pull up gathers to fit the bias strip. Fold the bias strip in half over the gathered edge. Leaving a small gap for elastic, topstitch all around edge through all thicknesses. Thread cord elastic through the bias casing; slipstitch the gap.
□Make the other strip into a bow and sew it securely to the hat.

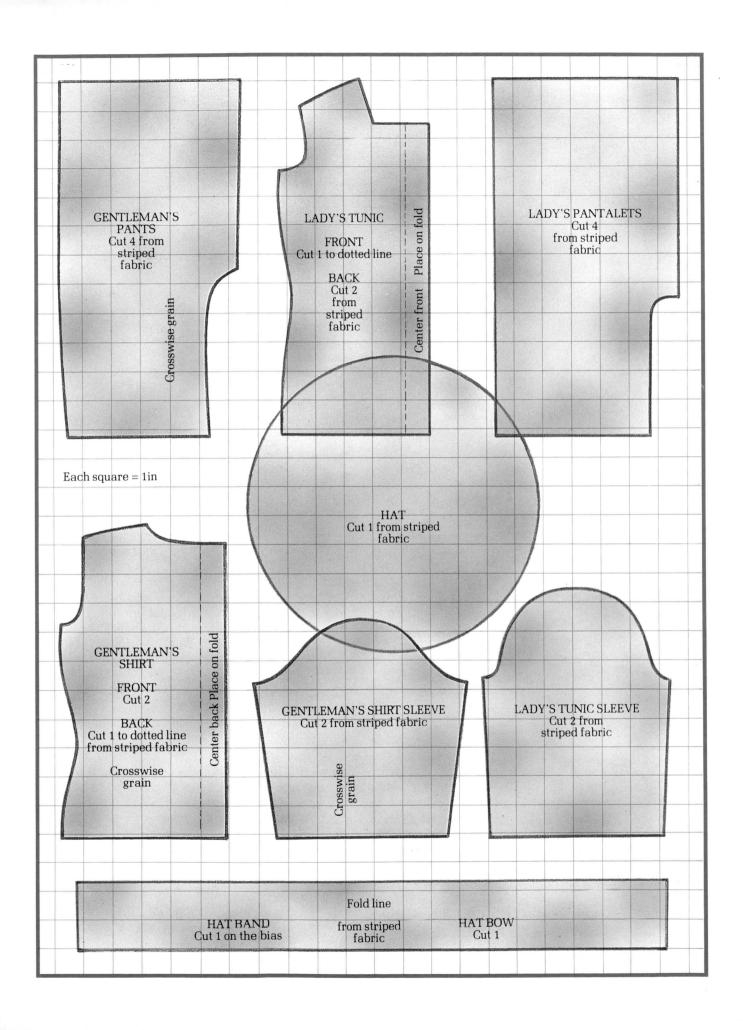

GENTLEMAN'S
PANTS
Cut 4 from
striped
fabric

Crosswise grain

LADY'S TUNIC

FRONT
Cut 1 to dotted line

BACK
Cut 2
from
striped
fabric

Center front   Place on fold

LADY'S PANTALETS
Cut 4
from striped
fabric

Each square = 1in

HAT
Cut 1 from striped
fabric

GENTLEMAN'S
SHIRT

FRONT
Cut 2

BACK
Cut 1 to dotted line
from striped fabric

Crosswise
grain

Center back Place on fold

GENTLEMAN'S SHIRT SLEEVE
Cut 2 from striped fabric

Crosswise
grain

LADY'S TUNIC SLEEVE
Cut 2 from
striped fabric

Fold line

HAT BAND
Cut 1 on the bias

from striped
fabric

HAT BOW
Cut 1

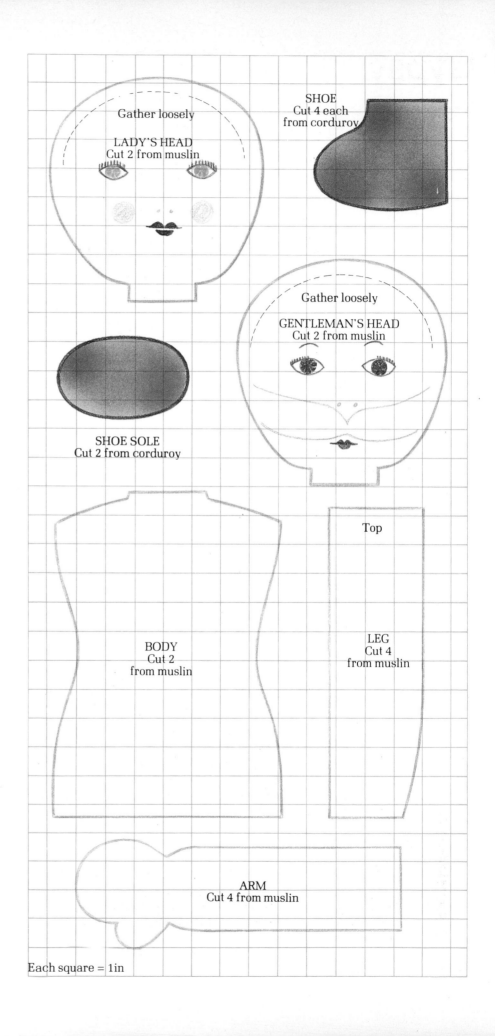

Gather loosely

SHOE
Cut 4 each
from corduroy

LADY'S HEAD
Cut 2 from muslin

Gather loosely

GENTLEMAN'S HEAD
Cut 2 from muslin

SHOE SOLE
Cut 2 from corduroy

Top

BODY
Cut 2
from muslin

LEG
Cut 4
from muslin

ARM
Cut 4 from muslin

Each square = 1in

Gypsy

Size
Approximately 10½in tall

Materials
½yd of 36in-wide cream terry cloth
3½oz of stuffing
Dark brown yarn for the hair
Dark brown felt for the eyes
Pink, brown and white matte
    embroidery cotton for the
    features
Piece of printed fabric
    5 × 20in for the skirt
⅞yd gathered eyelet lace edging
8in of ¼in-wide elastic
Piece of printed fabric 12in square
    for the scarf
2 small curtain rings for the
    earrings

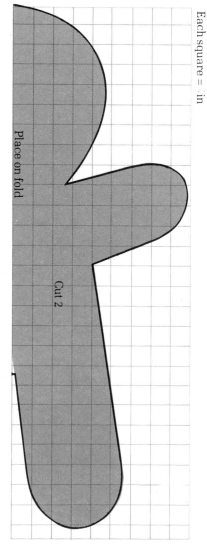

Each square = ½in

Place on fold

Cut 2

To make the doll

Enlarge the pattern as indicated on the graph and cut it out from terry cloth. A seam allowance of ⅜in is included.

☐ Place the two body pieces together, RS facing, and stitch all around the edges, leaving a gap in the side for turning.

☐ Turn the doll RS out, fill it with stuffing and slipstitch the opening edges together.

☐ Cut felt circles for the eyes, and glue in place. Embroider the features as shown. Stitch hair to head as described on page 18.

☐ Join the two short edges of the skirt, RS facing. Turn under ½in on one edge and topstitch ⅜in from fold to make a casing, leaving a small gap. Finger-press a hem on the other edge. Place eyelet lace under the edge and topstitch it in place. Thread elastic through casing; pull it up to fit the doll and stitch the ends together. Sew straps of eyelet lace to skirt as shown in photograph.

☐ Cut scarf fabric in half diagonally to form a triangle. Pink the edges or hem them. Sew earrings to the head.

Fairy godmother

Making the pattern — cutting out

Enlarge the pattern pieces as indicated on the graphs, and cut out the pieces for the body and clothes from the appropriate fabrics. Using dressmaker's carbon and tailor's tacks, as appropriate, transfer all markings to the fabrics. A seam allowance of $\frac{3}{8}$in is included where necessary.

To make the puppet

Body Fold top, RS facing, along fold line and stitch side seams. Turn body top RS out and stuff it firmly. Turn under lower edge and work gathering stitches around it. Pull up gathers and fasten thread securely.

☐ Fold each leg along fold line, RS together, and stitch back seam. Turn leg RS out and stuff it up to knee. Stitch across knee line from one side to the other, so that the seam is at center back. Finish stuffing the leg to the top.

☐ Place lower body sections together, RS facing, with legs sandwiched between, within markers, and extending upward through waist opening. Stitch layers together along side and lower edges. Turn lower body RS out and stuff. Turn under and gather top edge as for body top. Stitch body pieces together at waist, using faggot stitch for flexibility.

☐ Stitch arm pieces together, RS facing, leaving top open. Turn arms RS out. Topstitch fingers along lines indicated. Fill arms to elbow. Placing arm seams together (see photograph) stitch elbow line. Fill top arms, turn under edges and gather openings as for body top. Catchstitch arms to body.

Head and hair Work zigzag stitch around edge of ears; fold along brown dotted line. Join one head back and front, inserting an ear between marks. Repeat to form other side of face. Stitch both halves of head together, leaving an opening in back seam. Turn head RS out and stuff it. Slipstitch the opening edges together. Catch-stitch ears to sides of head.

☐ Work a few stitches vertically through nose to form nostrils. Cut black beads in half to form eyes (or ask someone with suitable equipment to do this for you), and glue one half in place for each eye. Glue eyelids over eyes. Color edges of eyes with felt-tip pen. Work stem stitch in beige under eye, and in brown over eye. Work lips in satin stitch, using dark peach for top lip and pale peach for bottom lip. Blush cheeks with peach pencil. Join short ends of neck with RS facing. Turn neck RS out. Turn in $\frac{1}{4}$in on one edge of neck and slipstitch it to head. Stuff the neck; turn under $\frac{1}{4}$in on remaining edge and work gathering stitches around it. Pull up gathers and slipstitch the neck to the body.

☐ Cut about 80 pieces of cotton yarn, 12in long. Stitch them through the center to a 2in piece of woven tape. Glue tape to center of head over back seam.

☐ Wire fabric flowers into a circlet and sew it to head. Loop front strands of yarn back behind ears and up to meet circlet. Twist a section from back of head into a bun and sew it in place. Trim remaining hair to shoulder length.

☐ Make braids from some of the remaining yarn. Braid them with pastel ribbon, loop them around circlet and sew them in place. Add flowers, beads and sequins or other ornaments to decorate hair as desired (see photograph).

Size

Approximately 16½in tall

Materials

$\frac{3}{8}$yd of 45in-wide fine beige knit fabric for body

$\frac{1}{4}$yd of 60in-wide silk tulle for overskirt

$\frac{1}{2}$yd of 36in-wide white silk georgette for dress

Fabric dye suitable for silk in 3 pastel colors

Piece of clear plastic 6in square for wings

Scraps of gray satin for shoes

1yd of $\frac{1}{4}$in-wide gray satin ribbon for shoe ties

Bits of $\frac{1}{4}$in-wide ribbon in pastel colors for hair

26 small crystal droplet beads

Assorted beads and sequins in pastel colors

Assorted small fabric flowers

Fine silver-colored wire

Ball of yellow cotton yarn for hair

Scraps of pale gray and beige fine leather for eyelids and shoe soles

$\frac{1}{4}$yd of $\frac{5}{8}$in-wide woven tape

Embroidery threads in dark peach, pale peach, beige and light brown for features

Silver thread

Transparent nylon sewing thread

Gray buttonhole twist

Soft peach pencil

2 black wooden beads for eyes

Black felt-tip pen

7oz of stuffing

2 pieces of $\frac{3}{4}$x$\frac{3}{8}$in wooden batten, 8in long

6 screw-in metal eyelets

1$\frac{1}{4}$in cotter pin

2 small washers

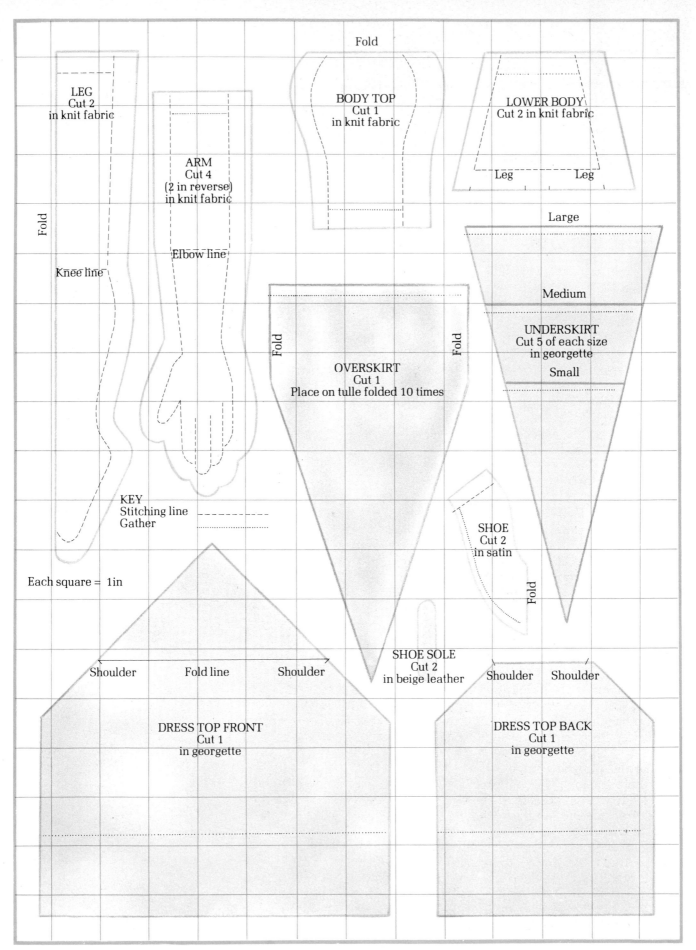

LEG
Cut 2
in knit fabric

Fold

Knee line

ARM
Cut 4
(2 in reverse)
in knit fabric

Elbow line

Fold

BODY TOP
Cut 1
in knit fabric

LOWER BODY
Cut 2 in knit fabric

Leg   Leg

Large

Medium

Fold

OVERSKIRT
Cut 1
Place on tulle folded 10 times

Fold

UNDERSKIRT
Cut 5 of each size
in georgette

Small

KEY
Stitching line   ― ― ― ―
Gather   . . . . . .

SHOE
Cut 2
in satin

Fold

Each square = 1in

Shoulder   Fold line   Shoulder

SHOE SOLE
Cut 2
in beige leather

Shoulder   Shoulder

DRESS TOP FRONT
Cut 1
in georgette

DRESS TOP BACK
Cut 1
in georgette

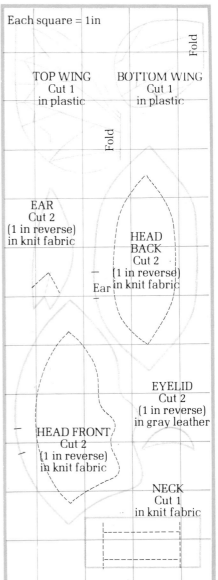

Fold

Fold

TOP WING
Cut 1
in plastic

BOTTOM WING
Cut 1
in plastic

Fold

EAR
Cut 2
(1 in reverse)
in knit fabric

HEAD
BACK
Cut 2
(1 in reverse)
in knit fabric

Ear

EYELID
Cut 2
(1 in reverse)
in gray leather

HEAD FRONT
Cut 2
(1 in reverse)
in knit fabric

NECK
Cut 1
in knit fabric

To make the costume

Dye the tulle and georgette: following the manufacturer's instructions, make a small quantity of each dye. Fold each piece of fabric several times. Dip a third of each fabric into the first color, rinse and repeat with the other two colors, overlapping each colour slightly. Rinse well, dry the fabric and press it.

☐ Zigzag stitch in silver around edges of underskirt pieces. Gather top edge of each piece. Sew 5 large pieces to one edge of a $2\frac{3}{4}$ in pieceof woven tape. Sew 5 medium pieces above these and 5 small pieces on top. Gather the overskirt and stitch it above underskirt pieces. Sew tape to body just below waist. Sew a crystal bead to each skirt point.

☐ Zigzag stitch in silver around edges of dress top pieces. Fold front forward along line indicated. Catch front and back pieces to shoulders at points indicated. Gather waist and catchstitch it to body just above middle, allowing fabric to blouse slightly. Sew a crystal to point. Decorate shoulders with flowers, strings of beads and sequins. Tie narrow strips of tulle around each elbow.

☐ Zigzag stitch in silver around top edge of each shoe piece. Join back seam of each shoe, RS facing. Turn shoe RS out, place on foot, gather bottom edge and sew to foot. Sew top edge to foot. Glue on soles. Glue a piece of gray ribbon to each side of shoe, wind it around leg and tie in a bow below knee.

☐ Using machine straight stitch work veins on wings in silver thread, following stitching lines. Place wings together with bottom wing overlapping top wing slightly. Sew wings in this position to center back, using transparent thread.

To make the puppet control

Drill a hole through the center of each batten. Push the cotter pin through both holes, placing a washer on each side. Open out the legs of the cotter pin and hammer them flat. Screw eyelets into battens as shown in drawing.

☐ Using gray buttonhole twist, thread strings for the puppet, as shown. Attach one string, 67in long, through A to arms, one $25\frac{1}{2}$in string through B to one side of head and another, the same length, through C to other side of head; attach a 195cm string through D and E to legs and one, 32in long, through F to bottom. Knot the strings firmly through the eyelets and sew them securely into fabric of puppet body.

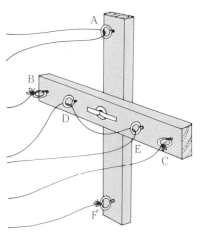

Needlepoint Russian doll

Size
Approximately 8in tall

Materials
$\frac{3}{8}$in of single-thread canvas with
  18 threads to 1in
Crewel yarn in the following colors
  and quantities: $5 \times \frac{1}{2}$oz (32yd)
  skeins of scarlet; 3 skeins of gold;
  2 skeins each of leaf green, royal
  blue and pale pink; 1 skein each
  of bright pink, cream, rust and
  black
Size 22 tapestry needle
Strong thread to match edges of doll
$\frac{3}{8}$yd of 36in-wide unbleached muslin
3oz of stuffing
Waterproof canvas marking pen
Masking tape
Thumbtacks
Board for blocking
Piece of blotting paper.

To work the embroidery
Bind the canvas edges to prevent snagging. Trace the outline of the doll twice onto canvas with marking pen, marking vertical centers. On front side of doll, count 13 horizontal threads down from top of head and mark 14th thread.
☐Work hair and face in tent stitch, following chart and using 2 strands of yarn.
☐Work remainder of design, following chart, beginning with scarf, and using 2 strands throughout. Work in straight stitches (except for hands, which are in tent stitch), following the directions of the stitches as shown on chart.
☐Work the other side of the doll, omitting face, hands and arms. (Or work it to match the front, if you prefer.)

To finish
Block the work: place it face down on the board (covered with blotting paper) and fix it to the board with thumbtacks, making sure that the corners are square. Dampen the work thoroughly and leave it to dry.
☐Trim the excess canvas from each doll section, leaving a margin of $\frac{5}{8}$in. Turn the edges to the WS and baste them in place.
☐Place the sections together, WS facing. Using a single strand of strong thread, overcast the edges (changing colors to match the embroidery). Leave lower edges open.
☐Trace the outline of the doll twice onto unbleached muslin. Add $\frac{5}{8}$in seam allowances all around. Stitch the sections together along the seamline, leaving a gap. Turn RS out and stuff firmly. Close the gap with slipstitching.
☐Insert the muslin shape into the doll. Overcast the lower edges together with strong thread.

Strongman

Size
Approximately 14in tall

Materials
1oz of sport yarn sport yarn in main color A (pink)
Small amounts in contrasting colors B (black), C (brown) and D (orange)
Pair of size 3 knitting needles
Bits of fine yarn red and black for the features
5½oz of stuffing

Gauge
28 sts and 36 rows to 4in in st st on size 3 needles

Front
* Beg at feet, with B, cast on 30 sts. Cont in g st (every row K), work 10 rows.
Dec 1 st at each end of next and 2 foll alt rows. 24 sts. Work 1 row.
Bind off 6 sts at beg of next 2 rows. 12 sts.
Beg with a K row, cont in st st, inc 1 st at each end of the 5th and every foll 4th row until there are 20 sts, ending with a P row.
Change to A. Inc 1 st at each end of foll 4th row. 22 sts.
Work 8 rows, dec 1 st at each end of next and foll alt row, ending with a P row.
Inc 1 st at each end of 3rd and every foll 4th row until there are 26 sts, ending with a P row.
Change to stripe sequence of 2 rows C, 2 rows D, *at the same time*, inc 1 st at each end of every 4th row until there are 30 sts. Work 14 rows straight. Change to A.*
Next row (K1, K2 tog) 3 times, K2 tog, sl next 8 sts onto a safety pin for bib of trunks, cast on 8 sts, K2 tog, (K2 tog, K1) 3 times. 22 sts.
Beg with a P row, work 10 rows. Leave these sts on a spare needle.
With RS of work facing return to sts for bib. Join in D, work 12 rows in stripe sequence as set.
Bind off.

Right arm
Back section
**With A, cast on 3 sts. Beg with a K row, cont in st st, inc 1 st at each end of 3rd and every foll alt row until there are 9 sts. Work 21 rows straight, ending with a P row.

Shape elbow
Next 2 rows K1, turn, P1.

Next 2 rows, K2, turn, P2.
Cont in this way until the rows "K6, turn, P6" have been worked.
Next row K twice into first st, K6, turn, P8.
Next 2 rows K twice into first st, K7, turn, P9. 11 sts.**
Work 3 rows across all sts, ending with a K row. Leave these sts on a spare needle.

Front section
Work as for back section from ** to **, reversing elbow shaping. Work 2 rows across all sts, ending with a K row. Leave these sts on a spare needle.

Left arm
Work back and front sections to match right arm.

To work front shoulders
With WS of work facing and with A, P across 11 sts of right front arm, across 22 sts of front, then P across 11 sts of left front arm. 44 sts.
***Beg with a K row, cont in st st,

dec 1 st at each end of 9th row.
Next row P.
Next row (K2 tog) twice, K to last 4 sts (K2 tog) twice. 38 sts.
Next row (P2 tog) to end. 19 sts.

Shape shoulders and head
Bind off 5 sts at beg of next 2 rows. 9 sts. Work 2 rows.
Next row (K twice into next st) to end. 18 sts.
Inc 1 st at each end of every foll alt row until there are 26 sts. *** Work 11 rows, ending with a P row.
Change to B and cont in g st. Work 10 rows.
Next row (K2 tog, K4) 4 times, K2 tog. 21 sts.
Work 1 row.
Next row (K2 tog, K3) 3 times, K2 tog, K2, K2 tog. 16 sts.
Work 1 row.
Next row (K2 tog, K2) 4 times. 12 sts.
Next row (K2 tog) to end. 6 sts.
Next row (K2 tog) to end. 3 sts.
K3 tog and fasten off.

Back
Work as for front from * to *.
Next row (K2 tog, K1) to end. 20 sts.
Beg with a P row, work 10 rows st st. Leave these sts on a spare needle.

To work back shoulders
With WS of work facing and with A, P across 11 sts of left back arm, across 20 sts of back, then P across 11 sts of right back arm. 42 sts.
Work as for front shoulders from *** to ***.
Change to B, and complete as for front but work in g st throughout.

To finish up
Catch down cast-on sts behind bib and sew bib to chest along top edge. With RS tog, join back to front, leaving opening at top of head. Turn work RS out. Fill body with stuffing, emphasizing "muscles." Close top of head. With B, backstitch between boots, and with A, between legs. With stab stitches define the elbows and wrists. Sew hands to hips. With D, thread "laces" through boots and tie in bow. With C double, make 2 braids 5in long, knot both ends to secure. Sew to top of bib, take over each shoulder, cross over on back and sew to trunks. Embroider features, using stem stitch, satin stitch and French knots. Using B, stitch hairline and sideburns.

Oriental dolls

Size
Approximately 16in tall

Materials
4oz of firmly-twisted fingering yarn in white and pale gold for girl and boy respectively

1lb of stuffing

1 pair each size 0 and 3 knitting needles

For the girl
3 oz of firmly-twisted fingering yarn in main color A (green)

Small amounts in three contrasting colors: B (yellow), C (red) and D (blue)

Pair of size 2 knitting needles

$\frac{1}{2}$yd of $\frac{5}{8}$in-wide velvet ribbon

$\frac{1}{2}$yd of $\frac{1}{4}$in -diameter filler cord

Piece of printed fabric 8 × 12in for sash

Scrap of red leather for mouth

Black and red embroidery thread for features

Skein of black raffia for hair

4in of $\frac{5}{8}$in-wide woven white tape

Small amount of corrugated cardboard

Dark brown gummed paper for sandals

2 hooks and eyes

Beads, ribbons, artificial flowers, tooth picks for hair decorations

For the boy
2oz of firmly-twisted fingering yarn in each of two colors, A (wine) and B (blue)

Small amount of black leather for shoe soles

Small amount of black felt for shoe tops

1yd of bias binding

1yd of fine gold braid

3 oval beads for toggles

Scrap of brown leather for mouth

1yd of 4in-deep black fringe for hair

3 skeins of yellow raffia

8in of $\frac{3}{8}$in -wide elastic

6in of black shirring elastic

Black and brown embroidery thread for features

To make the basic doll
Gauge
26 sts and 36 rows to 4in in st st on size 3 needles

Body
Using size 3 needles, cast on 16 sts. Work 8 rows st st (1 row K, 1 row P).

* Dec 1 st at each end of next row. Work 7 rows st st.
Rep last 8 rows once more. Inc 1 st at each end of next row. Work 7 rows st st. Rep last 8 rows once more.*
Work 16 rows st st.
Rep from * to *.
Bind off.

Arms
Using size O needles, cast on 16 sts.
1st row (RS) (P1, K1) 4 times, (K1, P1) 4 times.
2nd row (K1, P1) 4 times, (P1, K1) 4 times.
Rep these 2 rows twice more.
Next row (P1, K1) 4 times, cast on 4 sts, (K1, P1) 4 times. 20 sts.
Next row (K1, P1) 5 times, (P1, K1) 5 times.
Next row (P1, K1) 5 times, (K1, P1) 5 times.
Change to size 3 needles.
Next row P8, K1, P2, K1, P8.
Next row K8, P1, K2, P1, K8.
Rep the last 2 rows once more.
Work 5 rows st st, beg with a P row.
Next row (Sl 1, K1, psso, K6, K2 tog) twice. 16 sts.
Work 39 rows st st.
Next row (Sl 1, K1, psso) 8 times. 8 sts.
Next row (P2 tog) 4 times. 4 sts.
Break yarn, thread through sts on needle and pull up tightly.

Legs
Using size 3 needles, cast on 6 sts.
Work 18 rows st st, inc 1 st at each end of 3rd row and dec 1 st at each end of 18th row.
Shape foot
Cast on 13 sts at beg of next 2 rows.
Next row K12, K2 tog, K4, sl 1, K1, psso, K12.
Next and every foll alt row P.
Next row K11, K2 tog, K4, sl 1, K1, psso, K11.
Next alt row K10, K2 tog, K4, sl 1, K1, psso, K10.
Next alt row K7, sl 1, K1, psso, K2 tog, K4, sl 1, K1, psso, K2 tog, K7.
Next alt row K6, K3 tog, K4, sl 1, K1, K2 tog, psso, K6.
Next alt row Sl 1, K1, psso, K14, K2 tog. 16 sts.
Work 63 rows st st. Bind off.

Head
Using size 3 needles, cast on 8 sts.
Work 2 rows st st.
Next row (K1, pick up and K tbl loop between last st and next st to make 1, K1) 4 times. 12 sts.
Next row P.
Next row (K1, make 1, K1, make 1, K1) 4 times.
Next row P.
Next row (K2, make 1, K1, make 1, K2) 4 times.
Next row P.
Next row (K3, make 1, K4) 4 times.
Work 7 row st st.
Shape nose
Next row K15, make 1, K2, make 1, turn, P4, turn, K4, turn, P4, turn, sl 1, K1, psso, K2 tog, K15.
Work 11 rows st st.
Next row (K2, K2 tog, sl 1, K1, psso, K2) 4 times.
Next row P.
Next row (K1, K2 tog, sl 1, K1, psso, K1) 4 times.
Next row P.
Next row (Sl 1, K1, psso) 8 times.
Next row (P2 tog) 4 times.
Break yarn, thread through sts on needle and pull up tightly.

Neck
Using size 3 needles, cast on 10 sts.
Work 6 rows st st. Bind off.

To finish
Fold body in half widthwise and join side seams, leaving cast-on and bound-off edges open. Fill firmly with stuffing. Join opening. Join back head seam, leaving an opening. Fill with stuffing and close opening. Make neck into a tube and sew to head. Stuff firmly and sew neck and head to body.
Join leg seams. Sew sole flaps to feet. Fill to knees then stitch across legs at knees. Fill upper legs. Sew legs to body.
Sew arm seams. Stitch along purl stitches on hands through both

thicknesses to define fingers and thumbs. Fill hands and gather wrists on inside of hands. Fill lower arms and stitch across elbow. Fill upper arms. Join opening. Sew arms to body.

To make the girl's costume
Gauge
26 sts and 36 rows to 4in in st st on size 3 needles.

Kimono back
Using size 3 needles and A, cast on 42 sts. Work 86 rows st st, marking beg and end of 69th row. Bind off.

Kimono fronts
Right front Using size 3 needles and A, cast on 26 sts. Work 58 rows st st. Cont in st st, dec 1 st at beg of next and every foll alt row until 15 sts rem, placing a marker at end of 69th row. Cont straight until 86 rows have been worked. Bind off.
Left front Work as for right front, but working 59 rows before dec, placing marker at beg of 69th row.
Kimono sleeves and sleeve edgings
Using size 3 needles and A, cast on 17 sts. Work 88 rows st st, placing marker threads at beg of 27th and 63rd rows. Bind off.
Using size 2 needles and B, with RS of work facing, pick up and K 70 sts from side of sleeve without marker threads.
Work 4 rows st st, beg with a P row.
Next row Bind off 21 sts, K to end.
Next row Bind off 21 sts, K to end.
Work 3 rows st st, beg with a P row. Bind off.

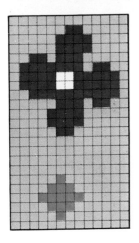

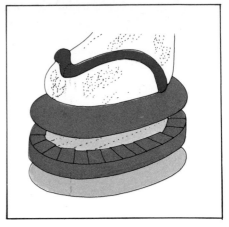

Fold over hem and sew neatly to picked-up edge.

Kimono neckband
Join shoulder seams. Using size 2 needles and B, with RS of work facing, pick up and K 29 sts up right front neck, 15 sts across back neck and 29 sts down left front neck. 73 sts.
Work 4 rows st st, beg with a P row.
Next row K.
Work 4 rows st st, beg with a K row.
Bind off.
Fold hem under and sew neatly to picked-up edge.

Hem band
Using size 3 needles and C, cast on 20 sts, K 3 rows.
* K 2 rows in C, 2 rows in B, 2 rows in C, 2 rows in D.*
Rep from * to * until band measures 13½in.
Bind off.

To finish kimono
Following graph, Swiss darn flowers on back, sleeves and front of kimono (see page 000 for Swiss darning). Sew sleeves to body between markers. Join side and sleeve seams. Sew hem bands to lower edge of kimono.

Face and hair
Embroider eyes and eyebrows in black as shown in photograph. Cut mouth shape from leather and fix in place with glue and straight stitch embroidery.
Spread out ends of raffia, without unwinding skein, to width of 4in. Stitch one end of skein to woven tape. Glue tape to front of head with raffia forward over face. Fold raffia over to back of head and bind into

pony tail.
Sew bound point to back of head. Roll tail under to form bun and sew in place.

Color toothpicks with felt-tip pens or paints. Glue beads to one end of toothpicks for hairpins. Make additional hair ornaments from tiny beads and artificial flowers.

Sash
Cut a 4 × 7½in strip and a 6¼ × 7½in rectangle from printed fabric. Fold strip in half lengthwise, RS tog, and stitch down long side and across one end, taking ⅝in seam allowance. Turn RS out and stitch open end. Fold rectangle in half widthwise, RS facing, and stitch 6¼in edges tog. Turn RS out and fill half of tube with stuffing. Bring ends of tube tog and tuck one end inside the other, folding under cut edge to form pad. Sew pad to one end of sash. Sew hooks and eyes to ends of sash.

Sandals
Cover two 6¼in pieces of filler cord with velvet ribbon. Sew to foot at "big toe" point. Glue cords to feet. Cut sole shapes from corrugated cardboard and cover with gummed paper. Glue to soles of feet.

To make the boy's costume
Gauge
26 sts and 36 rows to 4in in st st on size 3 needles

Pants
Using size 3 needles and A, cast on 43 sts. Work 3 rows st st beg with a K row.
Next row K.
Work 68 rows st st, beg with a K row. Bind off 3 sts at beg of next 2

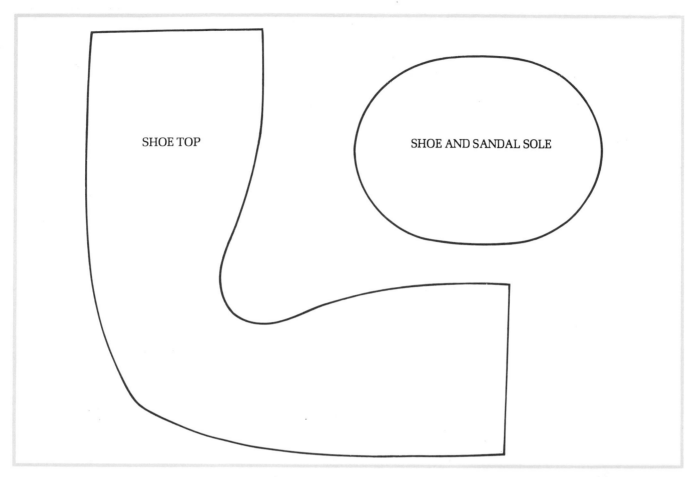

SHOE TOP

SHOE AND SANDAL SOLE

rows. Dec 1 st at beg of every row until 25 sts rem.
Work 9 rows st st.
Next row K.

Work 4 rows st st, beg with a K row.
Bind off.
Make other leg in the same way.
Join inside leg seams, then crotch seam.
Turn under hems at top and bottom and slipstitch in place. Thread ⅜in -wide elastic through waist hem.

Jacket back
Using size 3 needles and B, cast on 28 sts. Work 46 rows st st, marking each end of 23rd row. Bind off.

Jacket fronts
Using size 3 needles and B, cast on 16 sts, work 40 rows st st for right front (41 rows for left front), marking beg of 23rd row. Bind off 2 sts at beg of next and foll 2 alt rows. Bind off.

Jacket sleeves and collar
For sleeves, using size 3 needles and B, cast on 35 sts. Work 34 rows st st. Bind off.

Join shoulder seams. Pick up and K 25 sts around neck edge for collar. Work 5 row st st. Bind off.

To finish jacket
Set in sleeves between markers. Join side and sleeve seams. Use bias binding to bind all edges. Stitch gold braid to fronts for frogging, gluing braid around beads to make toggles.

Hat, hair and features
Braid raffia, and coil and stitch it to form hat, beginning at point. Sew shirring elastic to inside of crown to fit under chin.
Glue a length of fringe around hairline, then fill in with more lengths in gradually decreasing circles. Braid a few strands of fringe and sew to nape of neck. Trim ends. Embroider eyes and eyebrows with black thread as shown in photograph. Cut mouth from brown leather; glue in place. Work a few brown stitches across middle.

Shoes
Cut sole shapes from black leather and tops from black felt. Join back seam. Stitch tops to soles.

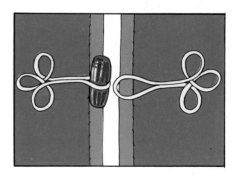

Animals

All manner of beasts inhabit these pages: a grizzly bear who's really a softie, a flamboyant feathered creature unknown to Audubon or Attenborough, a pink spider that even arachniphobes could love — and, of course, a selection of pussycats and puppies.

Cuddly basset and puppy

Sizes
Basset, approximately 19in tall
Puppy, approximately 9½in tall

Materials
For both toys
1⅛yd of 52in-wide medium-brown velveteen (fabric A)
¾yd of 52in-wide dark brown velveteen (fabric B)
½yd of 52in-wide light brown velveteen (fabric C)
1½lb of stuffing
About 1lb of lentils or beans
⅝yd of 36in-wide unbleached muslin
Scraps of felt in white, black, dark brown and pink

Making the pattern — cutting out
The basset and puppy are both made in the same way from the same pattern. Enlarge the patterns to the two different sizes as indicated on the graphs. Cut out the pieces from the appropriate fabrics, following the cutting guide so that the pile runs in the correct direction on each piece. A seam allowance of ⅜in is included throughout. Trace the actual-size patterns for the nose and tongue and cut them from pink felt. Transfer all the pattern markings to the velveteen using tailor's tacks.

To make the basset and puppy
In joining sections, always baste them together first, following the direction of the pile where possible; this prevents the velveteen from slipping when it is stitched.
☐ Join the jaw gusset to one body piece, RS facing, matching points A and B. Repeat to join the gusset to the other body piece.
☐ Place the body pieces together, RS facing, and join them from point A to C. Join four feet to body.
☐ Place inside leg pieces together, RS facing, and then join them from E to F. Join feet to legs.
☐ Join inside legs to body, RS facing, matching points E to B and F to G. Stitch body pieces together between points G and D. Turn body RS out through the opening.
☐ To weight the paws, for each dog make 4 small bags, about 2½in square, from the unbleached muslin. Fill each bag with lentils or beans and sew up the top. The bags fill the puppy's paws, but only partly fill the basset's. (The puppy could have its legs completely filled with lentils for a floppy effect.)
☐ Fill the head firmly with stuffing. Put a bag of lentils in each foot, sewing the bag to bottom foot seam to secure it. Stuff the body and legs.
☐ Placing RS together, sew tail pieces together, leaving the wide end open. Turn tail RS out and fill it. Turn under the raw edges and slipstitch tail to body at C and D. Sew ears together, leaving them unstuffed, so that they remain floppy in contrast to the body.
☐ For the basset's eyes, cut 2 2¾in-diameter circles of white felt, and 2 circles each of brown and black felt, making them pro-portionately smaller. For the puppy's eyes, cut 2in-wide white circles and smaller ones in brown and black. Slipstitch eyes to head in the positions shown. Slipstitch the nose and tongue to the head.

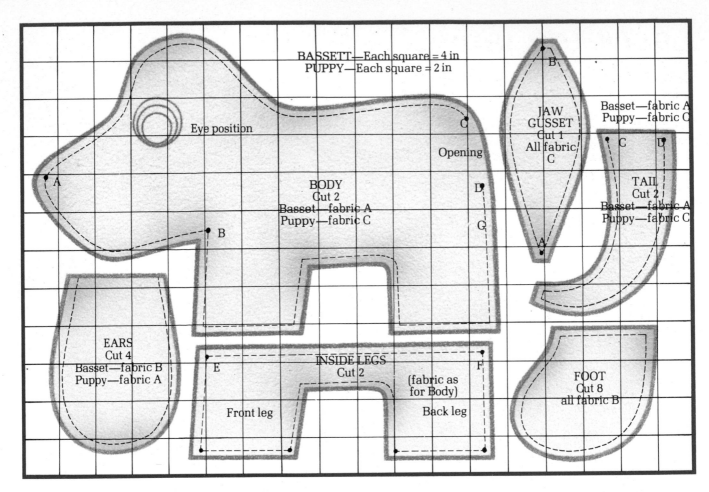

BASSETT—Each square = 4 in
PUPPY—Each square = 2 in

Eye position

C

Opening

B

BODY
Cut 2
Basset—fabric A
Puppy—fabric C

D

G

JAW
GUSSET
Cut 1
All fabric
C

B

A

Basset—fabric A
Puppy—fabric C

C   D

TAIL
Cut 2
Basset—fabric A
Puppy—fabric C

A

EARS
Cut 4
Basset—fabric B
Puppy—fabric A

E

INSIDE LEGS
Cut 2

(fabric as
for Body)

F

Front leg

Back leg

FOOT
Cut 8
all fabric B

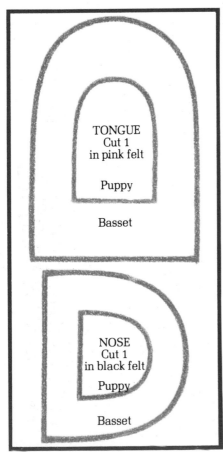

TONGUE
Cut 1
in pink felt

Puppy

Basset

NOSE
Cut 1
in black felt

Puppy

Basset

Cutting guide

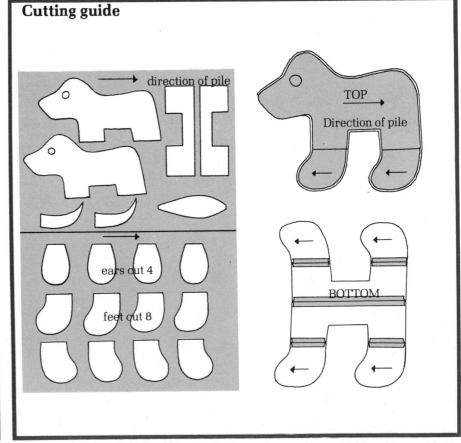

direction of pile

ears cut 4

feet cut 8

TOP

Direction of pile

BOTTOM

Larry the lamb

Making the pattern — cutting out

Enlarge the pattern pieces as indicated on the graph, adding $\frac{3}{8}$in seam allowance to all edges (except those placed on a fold). Cut out the pieces in fabrics as follows: from fur fabric, cut one main body piece (on fold), one gusset (on fold), one top of head, 2 sides of head, 2 ears and 2 tails; from black felt, cut 8 feet, 2 ears and 2 nose pieces; from red felt, cut one tongue — the same shape as the tail but much smaller.

To make the lamb

For the head, first close the dart on the top section, placing points G together, RS facing, and stitching the edges to the inner corner. Place one side head piece on the top head piece, RS facing, matching points H and I. Baste and stitch the seam. Repeat to join the other side head. Join side heads together along lower straight edges. On the nose, stitch the curved dart, joining points K. Turn the nose RS out and slip it into the front of the head (still WS out), so that the two darts are aligned. Stitch the nose in place. Hand-sew the eyes to the head at the points marked +. Turn the head RS out.

☐ Stitch the two tail pieces together, leaving the straight end open, and turn tail RS out. Fill it lightly with stuffing.

☐ Fold the main body piece RS together, and stitch the back seam between the two dots. Place the gusset and main body piece together, RS facing, and baste and stitch the seams, inserting the tail at the mark and leaving the feet edges and one underside seam open.

☐ Stitch the foot pieces together in pairs and turn them RS out. Slip them into the leg openings (still WS out) and stitch them in place.

☐ Slip the head into neck opening, RS facing. Baste and stitch.

☐ Fill the feet and legs with stuffing, pushing it well down so that the lamb will stand up. Fill the head and the rest of the body. Slipstitch the edges of the opening together.

☐ Stitch a felt ear to each fur ear, RS facing, turn ears RS out, turn in the raw edges and slipstitch the edges together. Fold each ear as shown and stitch them firmly to the head in the positions shown in the photograph. Sew the tongue to the nose.

☐ Attach the bell to the ribbon and tie ribbon around lamb's neck.

Size

Approximately 12in long

Materials

$\frac{5}{8}$yd of washable white fur fabric
Piece of black felt approximately 8in square
Scrap of red felt
2 safety eyes or buttons
7oz of stuffing
$\frac{1}{2}$yd of $\frac{3}{4}$in-wide blue ribbon
Small bell

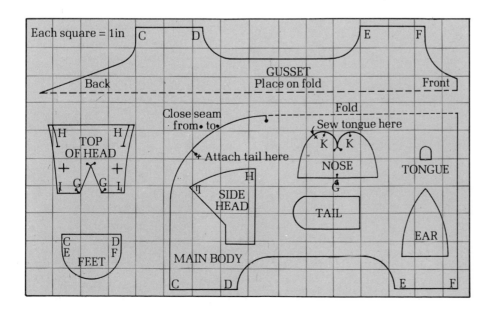

Mother cat and kittens

Size

Mother cat is approximately 16in long, excluding tail.
Kitten is approximately 9in long.

Materials

For mother cat and one black and one white kitten

¾yd of 36in-wide black fur fabric
⅜yd of 36in-wide white fur fabric
3 pairs of safety eyes
Plastic string
Pink pearl cotton
1lb of stuffing

Making the pattern — cutting out

Make the pattern for the mother cat in two stages: first enlarge the drawing as given, to the size indicated. Then trace the individual pieces, some of which overlap. Trace the shapes contained within solid lines, cutting them off at double broken lines but ignoring the single broken lines. Next, trace the smaller shapes contained within the larger ones, as follows: cut a lower inside back leg/foot from the single broken line to the end and an outer back foot from the double line to the end. Cut patterns for the upper inside back leg/foot and outer foot in the same way. Cut both front legs from the broken line downward. Cut the side head piece. Label each piece on the side shown on the graph pattern.

☐ Cut the pattern pieces from black and white fur fabric as specified on the pattern, cutting from a single layer of fabric placed WS upward. Place the pieces with the labeled side upward, except where pattern states that one or more should be cut in reverse. Make sure that the pile runs correctly for each piece, as indicated by the arrows on the pattern.

☐ Enlarge the pattern pieces for the kitten as indicated on the graph and cut them from one color of fur fabric, making sure that the pile runs correctly.

☐ Transfer all pattern markings. Label the pieces for easy reference. A seam allowance of ⅜in is included.

To make the mother cat

Stitch the two tail pieces together, RS facing, leaving the straight end open. Turn the tail RS out and fill it firmly with stuffing. Close the opening edges with running stitch across the seamline.

☐ Stitch a paw piece to each separate front leg and to the front legs on the under body. Stitch each back foot to the corresponding back leg on the top body and underbody.

☐ Stitch the tummy gusset to the chest, matching notches, then stitch the back gusset to the other side of the chest.

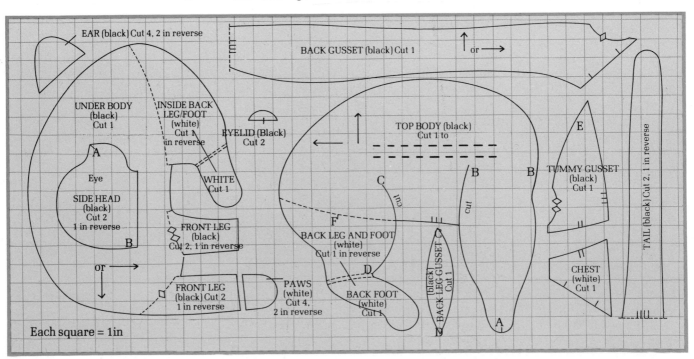

Each square = 1in

60

☐Stitch the front legs to the tummy and back gussets, matching the triangular notches. Stitch the tail to the free end of the back gusset.

☐Cut the top body piece along the curved lines leading to points B and C. Stitch the back leg gusset to the back leg of the top body, matching points C and D. Stitch each inside back leg to the corresponding back leg on the under body and top body, matching the outer edges (and, in the case of the top back leg, matching it to the leg gusset for part of its length).

☐Insert the safety eyes in the side heads in the positions marked. Stitch the side head pieces to the top body, matching points A and B. Join the side head pieces from the nose (point A) down to the straight neck edges.

☐Join the neck edge of the left side head to the top body (the edge formed by cutting to point B) and to the chest. Join the neck edge of the right side head to the chest and back gusset.

☐Join the tummy gusset to the top body (matching notches) and to the under body. Join the lower part of the chest to the under body. Join the back gusset to the top body and under body, leaving a gap of about 8in in one seam for turning and stuffing.

☐Turn the cat RS out. Fill it firmly with stuffing, beginning with the head and feet. Slipstitch the opening edges together.

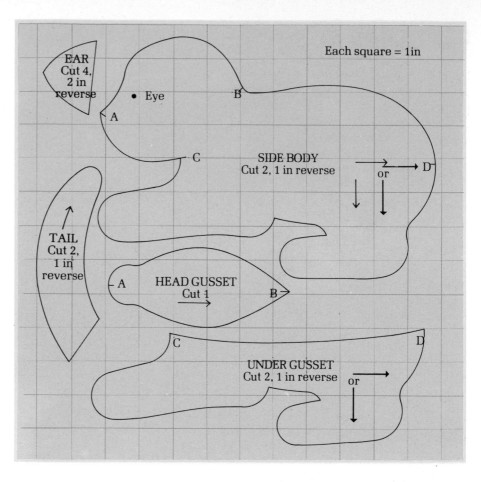

□Stitch each pair of ear pieces together, RS facing, leaving the straight edges open. Turn ears RS out. Turn in opening edges and baste them in place. Form a small tuck in this edge and hand-sew the ears firmly to the head.

□Embroider a triangular nose in pink pearl cotton using satin stitch. For the mouth work 3 straight stitches as shown in the photograph, using a double strand of thread.

□Slipstitch the eyelids to the face, positioning them slightly over the eyes for a contented "purring" expression. For whiskers and "eyebrows" unravel some plastic string and sew several strands through front of face as shown in the photograph. To hold the tail in a curved position, attach it to the lower back leg with a few stitches, using matching thread.

To make the kitten

Join the tail pieces, RS facing, and fill tail with stuffing. Close the opening edges with running stitch.

□Insert the safety eyes into the head in the position shown. Stitch the under body gussets to the body pieces, matching points C and D. Baste the tail to RS of one body piece, just above point D, so that tail curves upward. Place the two body pieces together, RS facing, and baste and stitch from B to D, catching in the tail.

□Join the head gusset to each side of head, matching points A and B. Join the sides of the head between points A and C. Join the two under body gussets for about 2in from each end.

□Turn kitten RS out and fill it firmly with stuffing, beginning with the head and legs. Slipstitch the opening edges together.

□Make and attach ears and embroider features as for the mother cat.

62

Grizzly bear

Making the pattern — cutting out
Enlarge the pattern pieces as indicated on the graph. Cut out the pieces in fabrics as follows: from dark brown fabric cut 2 main body pieces, 2 outer front legs, 2 ears and one head gusset (on fold); from light brown fabric cut one muzzle and one inner body (both on fold) and 2 each of front and back pads and ears. Cut the nose from black felt. A seam allowance of ⅛in is included throughout. Transfer the markings to the WS of fabric.
☐ Clip the fur on the foot pads and light brown ear pieces until the fibers are approximately ⅜in long.

To make the bear
When joining sections, first baste them together, to prevent the fabric from slipping. Or work all stitching by hand.
☐ Stitch all the darts on the main body pieces. Join the head gusset to the main body pieces on each side from point A to E. Join the main pieces down the back seam, from E to F.
☐ Join the muzzle to the main body from B around and back to B, then complete the muzzle by stitching its remaining edges (B-L) together. Mark the positions of the eyes and fit them in.

Size
Approximately 16½in tall (sitting down) excluding the ears

Materials
¾yd of 54in-wide thick, dark brown fur fabric
Piece of thick, light brown fur fabric 16in square
Scrap of black felt for nose and paws
Black buttonhole twist
Small amount of black yarn for mouth and claws
2 dark brown safety eyes.
14oz of stuffing

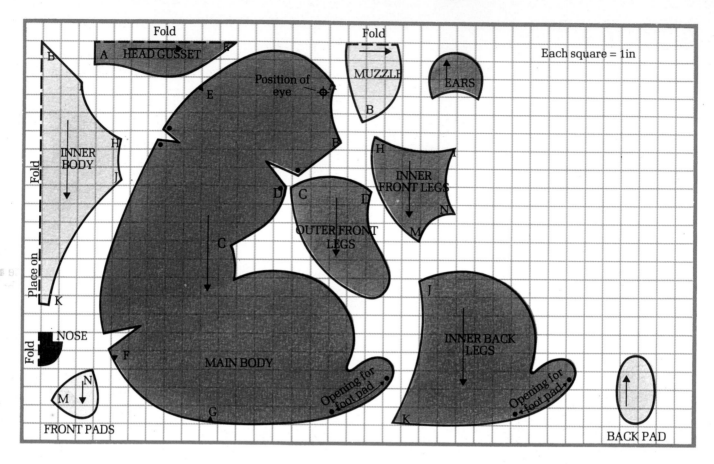

Fold
A HEAD GUSSET F
B

Fold
MUZZLE
B

EARS

Each square = 1in

Position of eye

INNER BODY

Fold

Place on

H

J

E

INNER FRONT LEGS

H

N

Position of eye

D

C

D

OUTER FRONT LEGS

M

N

C

NOSE

Fold

F

MAIN BODY

G

INNER BACK LEGS

J

Opening for foot pad

K

Opening for foot pad

BACK PAD

M N

FRONT PADS

☐Join the outer front legs to the main body from C to D. Join the front pads to the inner front legs from M to N. Join the inner front legs to the inner body from H to I and the inner back legs to the inner body from J to K.

☐Cut all these pieces with the pile lying in the direction of the straight grain arrows.

☐Join the inner body to the outer body, matching up the arms and legs and the points marked on the pattern. Leave the seam open between points F and G. Also leave open the marked section underneath the back feet. Insert the back foot pads into the gaps under the feet and stitch. Turn the bear RS out.

☐Using a piece of dowel, or other blunt stick, push the stuffing through the remaining gap at the back of the bear. Fill the extremities first — the muzzle and paws — then stuff the rest of the body. Slipstitch the gap with strong thread.

☐Make the nose from black felt as described on page 65. Sew it on with buttonhole twist, putting the flatter edge uppermost.

☐To make the ears, put a dark brown and a light brown piece together with RS facing, and stitch around the long, rounded edge. Turn the ear RS out, overcast the remaining raw edges together, then gather that edge a little. Repeat for the other ear. Position the ears on the head, making adjustments as necessary. Stitch the ears to the head with a double strand of strong thread.

☐Cut out small ovals of black felt and stitch them to the foot pads. Using black yarn, work five long stitches on each paw to suggest claws.

☐Also using black yarn, work stem stitch down from the center bottom of the nose for about $\frac{5}{8}$in and then out to each side for about $\frac{3}{4}$in to create an inverted "T" shape for the mouth, as shown in the photograph.

64

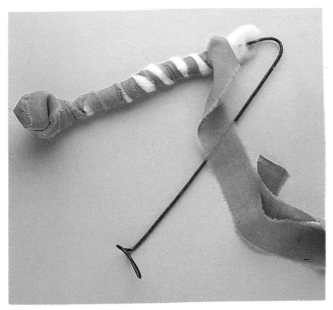

Support wire
To prevent long legs or a long neck from sagging, use a wire coat hanger. Straighten out the hanger and cut off the required length with wire cutters, then bend in the ends for safety (also to strengthen feet if required). Pad the whole length of the wire with stuffing and wrap a strip of fabric around it like a bandage. Secure the loose ends with a few stitches, then insert the wire into the toy, adding more padding as necessary to bury the wire.

Eyes
The position of the eyes should be marked either when you cut out the pattern or when the toy has been stitched but not stuffed. Push the point of a sharp pair of scissors through the fabric, making the hole just large enough to accommodate the shank of the plastic eye, then fix the eye. It is important to be very sure that you have positioned the eye correctly before you fit the metal washer onto the shank, because it cannot be removed afterward.

Noses
Fabric noses can be made from felt or — for a shiny, healthy look — from satin. Cut a circle of fabric, work gathering stitches around the edges, and stuff it with a little absorbent cotton or stuffing, then pull up the gathers slightly; sew it to the toy with small slipstitches. A squat, mushroom-like shape makes a good nose for a dog or bear. Join the two adjacent sides on each side of the longer (bottom) straight edge, as if stitching a dart. Gather the edges and stuff the shape as for a round nose. If a nose is too rounded it can often be manipulated into a suitable shape.

Family of ducks

Size
Ducks, approximately 10in tall
Duckling, approximately 5in tall

For all three ducks' bodies
$\frac{5}{8}$yd of 36in-wide white stretch
 terry cloth
$\frac{3}{8}$yd of 36in-wide yellow stretch
 velour
Scraps of blue and pink felt for the
 eyes and tongue
12oz of stuffing
3 squeakers (optional)

For clothes
$\frac{3}{8}$yd of 36in-wide blue fabric for
 jacket
$\frac{3}{8}$yd of 36in-wide white fabric for
 jacket lining
$\frac{3}{8}$yd of 36in-wide red printed fabric
 for dress and necktie
$\frac{3}{4}$yd of $\frac{5}{8}$in-wide white eyelet lace
 edging
$\frac{1}{4}$yd of $1\frac{1}{4}$in-wide white gathered
 eyelet lace edging
5in of $\frac{3}{8}$in-wide lace edging
$\frac{3}{8}$yd of narrow white ribbon
$\frac{3}{8}$yd of narrow blue ribbon
Piece of blue knit fabric, 12in
 square, for the head scarf
12in of red bias binding
Scraps of red, white and blue fabric
 for bib, cap and handkerchiefs
2 buttons for jacket
Artificial flower

Making the pattern — cutting out
Enlarge the pattern pieces for the body and clothes as indicated on
the graphs. Note that the scale is different for ducks and duckling
bodies, but the same for the clothes. Cut out the pieces from the
appropriate fabrics. Cut the beaks, feet and the duckling's tail from
yellow velour; all other body pieces from white terry cloth. For the
dress, cut 2 pieces of printed fabric, each $5\frac{1}{2} \times 6\frac{1}{4}$in , for the back and
one piece $10 \times 6\frac{1}{4}$in for the front. Cut 2 pockets from printed fabric,
using the jacket pocket pattern but making them shallower. Transfer
markings to fabric. A seam allowance of $\frac{3}{8}$in is included.

To make the ducks
Place each pair of wings together with RS facing, and stitch around
seamlines, leaving straight edge open. Clip curves and turn wings RS
out. Fill wing lightly and baste opening edges together. Make the feet
and duckling's tail in the same way.
☐Join the two upper outside beak pieces along the center (inward-
curving) seam. Join this piece to the upper inside beak. Turn beak RS
out, and topstitch $\frac{1}{4}$in from edge. Join lower inside and outside beak
pieces. Turn lower beak RS out. Join inside lower beak to inside
upper beak, inserting the tongue in the seam. Stuff upper beak lightly.
☐Stitch the dart in each head section. Insert the wing pieces into
slits and stitch along seamlines.
☐Stitch the gusset to the top of head between points A and B. Join
the body pieces down center back and front. Insert the duckling's tail
into the lower back seam. A squeaker may be inserted, if desired;
sew it into a small fabric bag, and include bag in center back seam.
☐With the body still WS out, insert beak into head, matching the
center seam on upper beak with gusset at point A. Baste and stitch
beak in place.
☐Baste the feet in the position indicated on the pattern, so that they
point inward, with raw edges matching. Stitch the base to the body,
leaving an opening at the back for stuffing.
☐Fill the body firmly, and overcast the opening edges together. Cut
out $\frac{3}{8}$in-diameter circles of blue felt. Glue or stitch eyes to the head.

To make the clothes
Place the two jacket pieces together with RS facing and join the
center back seam. Join the two lining pieces in the same way. Place
jacket and lining together with RS facing and stitch around the
seamline, leaving an opening for turning RS out. Clip the curved
edges. Turn jacket RS out and press. Slipstitch the opening edges
together. Topstitch around the edge. Finish armhole edges with
zigzag stitch. Press under the pocket edges, topstitch the straight
edge and topstitch pocket to jacket front.
☐For the handkerchief, machine stitch $\frac{1}{4}$in from the edge of a 4in
square of fabric; fray the fabric to the stitching. Sew the two buttons
to the jacket front, $1\frac{1}{4}$in apart. Sew on flower.
☐For the necktie, place a lining piece on each end of the main piece,
RS facing; stitch. Turn tie ends RS out and press under the seam
allowance on the remaining raw edges. Fold tie along crease lines;
press. Slipstitch the folded edges together.
☐For the cap, join red and blue triangles together alternately. Stitch
bias binding to the edge, turn it to the WS and slipstitch it in place.
☐For the dress, place the two back pieces together with RS facing

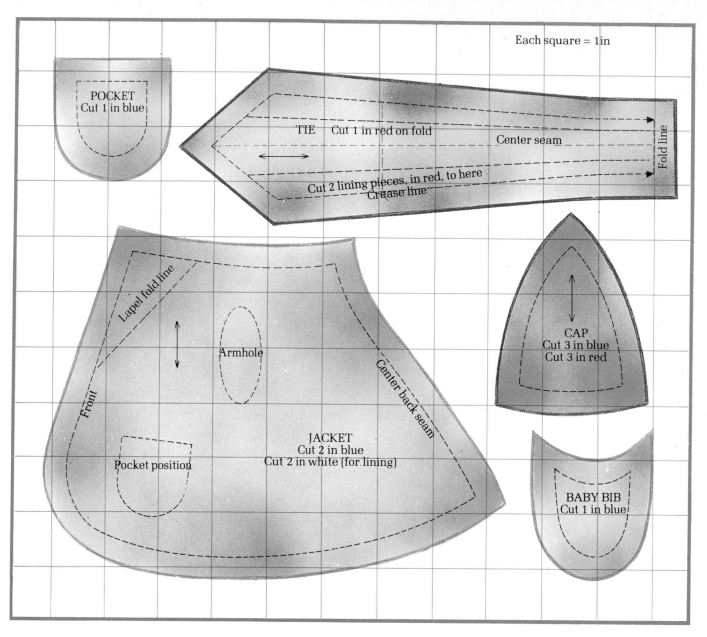

Each square = 1in

POCKET
Cut 1 in blue

TIE   Cut 1 in red on fold   Center seam

Fold line

Cut 2 lining pieces, in red, to here
Crease line

Lapel fold line

Armhole

Front

Center back seam

Pocket position

JACKET
Cut 2 in blue
Cut 2 in white (for lining)

CAP
Cut 3 in blue
Cut 3 in red

BABY BIB
Cut 1 in blue

and stitch along one 6¼in edge, leaving 2¼in open at one end. Join the back and front pieces, leaving 5in open, ¾in from the top edges, for armholes. Turn under and topstitch edges of armholes and back opening. Turn up and topstitch a ⅜in hem on lower edge, attaching narrow eyelet lace at the same time.

☐Gather up the neck edge to measure 6½in, and distribute gathers evenly. Baste the gathered eyelet lace to the neck and stitch it in place. Cut the white ribbon into two 6in pieces. Sew them to each side of back neckline opening.

☐Finish pocket edges and stitch them to front of dress as for the jacket pocket. Cut a 4in square of white fabric for the handkerchief; trim it with wide eyelet lace.

☐For the head scarf, cut the square of knit fabric in half diagonally. Turn under and topstitch narrow hems.

☐Edge the bib with ⅜in-wide lace trim. Sew the center section of the blue ribbon along the top of the bib.

☐Cut a 1½ × 5in strip of red printed fabric. Fold it in half and stitch the long side and one short end. Turn it RS out and finish open end. Tie the strip in a bow and sew it to duckling's head.

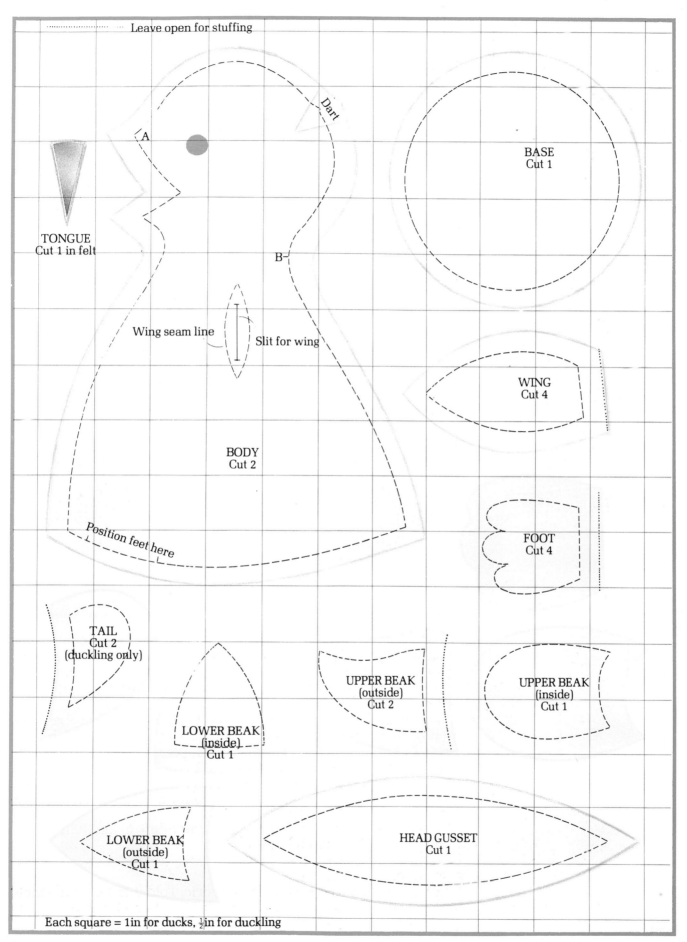

Leave open for stuffing

TONGUE
Cut 1 in felt

A

Dart

BASE
Cut 1

B

Wing seam line

Slit for wing

WING
Cut 4

BODY
Cut 2

FOOT
Cut 4

Position feet here

TAIL
Cut 2
(duckling only)

UPPER BEAK
(outside)
Cut 2

UPPER BEAK
(inside)
Cut 1

LOWER BEAK
(inside)
Cut 1

LOWER BEAK
(outside)
Cut 1

HEAD GUSSET
Cut 1

Each square = 1in for ducks, ½in for duckling

Sammy spider

Size
Approximately 18in wide, including legs, and 10in tall

Materials
1⅜yd of 58in-wide deep-pile fur fabric
2 cubic ft of polystyrene beads
2 toy safety eyes
Small amount of stuffing

Making the pattern — cutting out
Enlarge the pattern pieces as indicated on the graph and cut them from fur fabric, following the cutting layout and placing the pieces on the WS of a single layer of fabric. Make sure that the leg pieces are correctly aligned with the pile. Note, also, that one of each pair of leg pieces is cut in reverse. A seam allowance of ⅜in is included throughout.

To make the spider
Insert the eyes in the side body strip 5in apart and 2½in from the top as shown.
☐When joining seams, baste first, to prevent the fabric from slipping; or hand sew. Work, where possible, in the direction of the pile. Join the upper and lower body sections to the side body strip, turning back the ends as shown. Turn the body RS out.
☐Fill the body with polystyrene beads — but not too full, or the seat will have no "give". Turn in the seam allowances and slipstitch the side seam.
☐Placing RS together, join each pair of leg pieces, leaving the straight ends open. Turn each leg RS out and fill it firmly with stuffing. Turn in and slipstitch the top edges of each leg.
☐Place four legs evenly around each side of the spider's body, and stitch them securely to the lower seam.

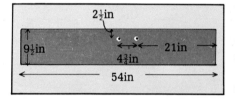

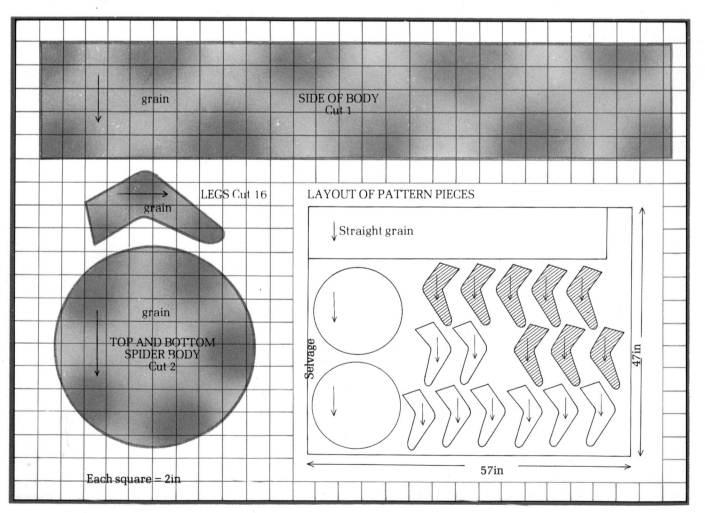

grain
SIDE OF BODY
Cut 1

grain
LEGS Cut 16

LAYOUT OF PATTERN PIECES

grain
TOP AND BOTTOM
SPIDER BODY
Cut 2

↓Straight grain

Selvage

47in

57in

Each square = 2in

Rabbit family

Size
Adult rabbit, approximately 12½in tall
Baby rabbit, approximately 6in tall

Materials
For each adult rabbit
⅔yd of 36in-wide light brown fur fabric
Piece of beige felt 6in square
2 safety eyes ⅜in diameter
Small amount of black yarn for nose
7oz of stuffing

For the baby rabbit
¼yd of 36in-wide light brown fur fabric
Scraps of beige felt
2 ⅜in in diameter safety eyes
Small amount of black yarn
3½in oz of stuffing

For the clothes
⅔yd of 36in-wide printed fabric for dress
Piece of white cotton fabric 8in square for apron
¾yd of ⅝in-wide lace edging
⅝yd of ⅝in-wide eyelet lace edging
1⅛yd of ⅜in-wide white woven tape
¾yd of ¼in-wide white elastic
Piece of navy blue corduroy 24 × 8in for pants
Piece of fabric 25cm square for father's neckerchief
Leather scraps and 2 small buttons for suspenders
Scrap of felt or suede for vest
2 small buttons
Piece of fabric 7in square for baby's neckerchief

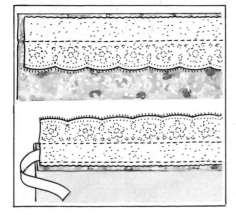

Making the pattern — cutting out
Enlarge the pattern pieces as indicated on the graph and cut them from the appropriate fabrics. Cut all body pieces from fur fabric with the pile running downward. Also cut two leather straps, ⅜ × 10in, for suspenders. A seam allowance of ⅜in is included throughout.

To make the rabbits
Place the two body pieces together with RS facing, and stitch around the edges, leaving the neck edge open. Double stitch the inside leg seams, as shown on the pattern. Cut the fabric between the legs of each rabbit and clip the seam allowances. Turn the bodies RS out and fill them with stuffing. Leave the neck edge open.Work a line of running stitch across each arm as indicated on the pattern.

☐Join the head gusset to the curved edge of one side head piece, RS facing. Repeat to attach the other side head. Clip the seam allowances and turn the head RS out. Push the safety eyes through the head at the points marked and secure them with washers on the WS. Fill the heads firmly with stuffing and embroider noses with black yarn, working a "Y" shape in stem stitch. Turn under the neck edge of the head; making sure it faces directly forward, stitch it securely to the neck of the body.

☐Place a furry ear piece and a felt piece together, RS facing, and stitch around the curved edge. Turn ear RS out. Turn in the raw edges and slipstitch them together. Take a small tuck in the center front of each ear and sew it in place.

☐On the tail piece, work a line of gathering stitches about ¼in from the edge. Place a small amount of stuffing in the center of the tail, tuck in the seam allowance, and pull up the gathering thread. Fasten off securely and sew the tail in place.

To make the clothes
For the mother rabbit's clothes Place the dress pieces together with RS facing and stitch the side and shoulder seams. Clip the curved edges. Turn under and topstitch a narrow hem on the lower edge of the dress. Leaving a small gap near each underarm seam for threading elastic, turn under and topstitch a ⅜in hem to form a casing around each armhole. Thread each casing with elastic, pull it up to fit arm and stitch the ends together. Topstitch the openings.

☐Placing RS together, stitch lace around the neck edge of the dress. Turn under and topstitch the neck edge through lace and fabric, to form a casing. Thread casing with elastic; finish as for armholes.

☐For the apron, cut the woven tape into one 20in and two 9in pieces. Finish the edges of the apron skirt with a medium-size zig-zag stitch or a narrow rolled hem. Gather the top edge of the apron skirt to measure 3¾in. Center the long piece of tape over the gathered edge and zigzag stitch it in place. Zigzag stitch a piece of eyelet lace along the top (wider) edge of the apron bib. Turn under one end of each 9in piece of tape and zigzag stitch it in place. At the other end, lap one side of the tape over the apron bib side edge and zigzag stitch it in place. Trim the other long side of the strap with eyelet lace. Fold over and stitch the free end of each strap to form a ⅝in loop. Slip the lower edge of the bib under the waistband and zigzag stitch it in place. Thread the ends of the waistband tape through the loops of straps.

For the father rabbit's clothes Place the two pants pieces together with RS facing. Join the crotch seam, leaving a gap in the back for the tail as indicated on pattern. Join the two straight leg seams. Turn under and press $\frac{3}{8}$in on the waist edge of the pants. Baste a $10\frac{1}{4}$in length of elastic to the WS of waistband, stretching it to fit, and stitch the hem and elastic in place with a medium-size zigzag stitch. Turn and stitch a hem on the lower edge of each pant leg.

☐Stitch one end of each leather strap inside the back waistband of the pants. Curve the other end of each strap and attach it to the front waistband of the pants with a small button as shown.

☐Cut the 10in square of fabric in half diagonally to make triangular neckerchief. Work a rolled hem along each edge.

For the baby rabbit's clothes Topstitch around the outer edges of the vest about $\frac{1}{8}$in from the raw edge. Sew on the buttons in the positions marked.

☐Cut the 7in square of fabric in half diagonally to make a triangular neckerchief and work a rolled hem along each edge.

73

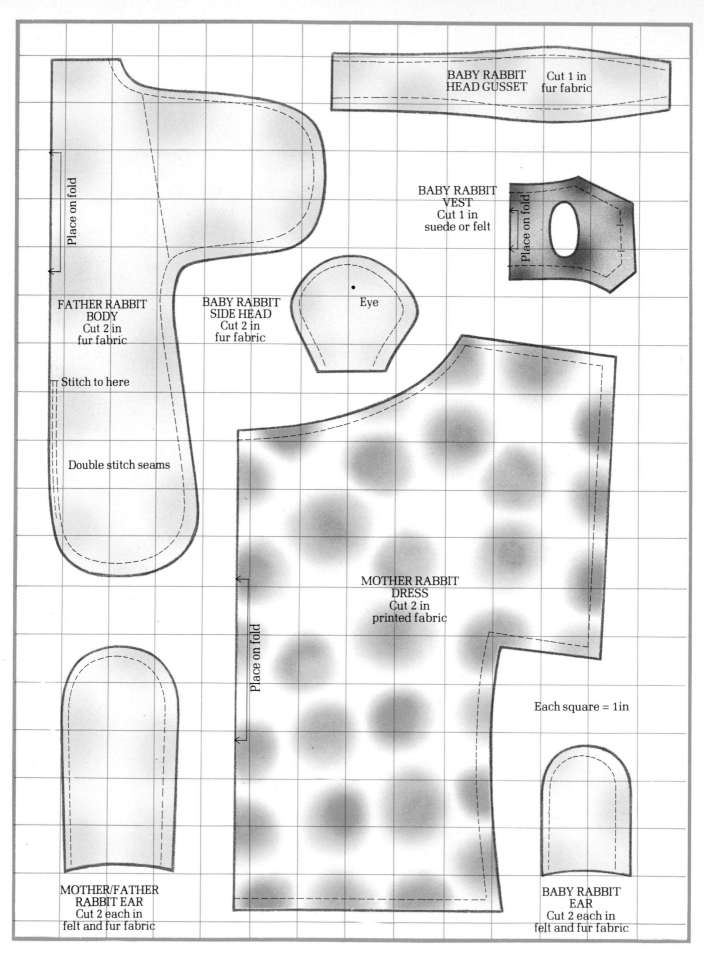

BABY RABBIT
HEAD GUSSET   Cut 1 in
fur fabric

BABY RABBIT
VEST
Cut 1 in
suede or felt

Place on fold

Place on fold

FATHER RABBIT
BODY
Cut 2 in
fur fabric

BABY RABBIT
SIDE HEAD
Cut 2 in
fur fabric

Eye

Stitch to here

Double stitch seams

MOTHER RABBIT
DRESS
Cut 2 in
printed fabric

Place on fold

Each square = 1in

MOTHER/FATHER
RABBIT EAR
Cut 2 each in
felt and fur fabric

BABY RABBIT
EAR
Cut 2 each in
felt and fur fabric

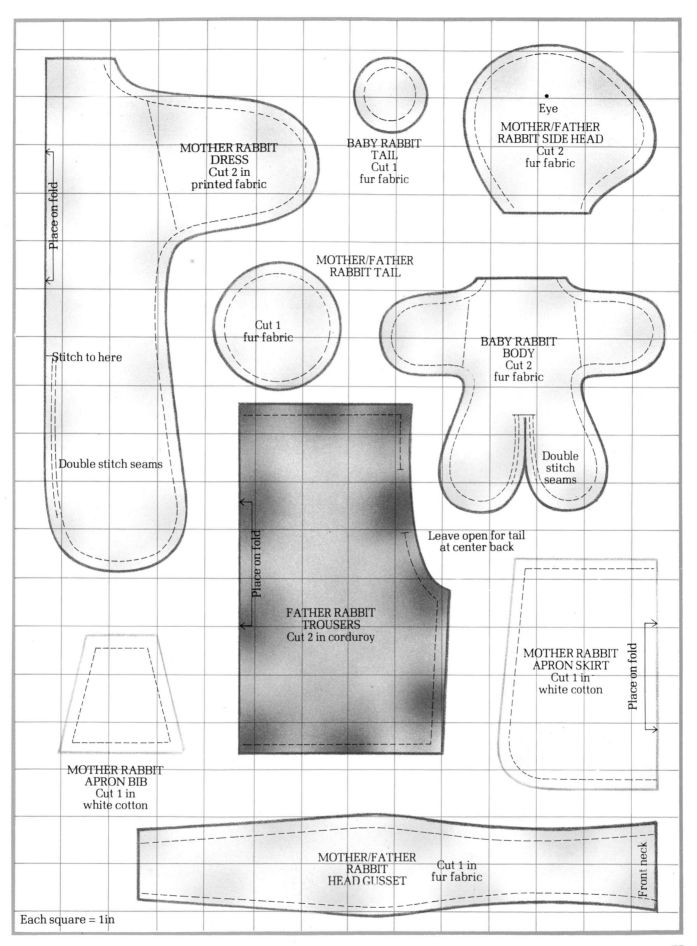

MOTHER RABBIT
DRESS
Cut 2 in
printed fabric

Place on fold

Stitch to here

Double stitch seams

BABY RABBIT
TAIL
Cut 1
fur fabric

Eye
MOTHER/FATHER
RABBIT SIDE HEAD
Cut 2
fur fabric

MOTHER/FATHER
RABBIT TAIL

Cut 1
fur fabric

BABY RABBIT
BODY
Cut 2
fur fabric

Double
stitch
seams

Leave open for tail
at center back

FATHER RABBIT
TROUSERS
Cut 2 in corduroy

Place on fold

MOTHER RABBIT
APRON SKIRT
Cut 1 in
white cotton

Place on fold

MOTHER RABBIT
APRON BIB
Cut 1 in
white cotton

MOTHER/FATHER
RABBIT
HEAD GUSSET

Cut 1 in
fur fabric

Front neck

Each square = 1in

75

Crocodile and giraffe

Size
Crocodile, approximately 27½in long
Giraffe, approximately 19in tall

Materials
For the crocodile
¾yd of 36in-wide white cotton
  fabric
1 tin each of pale green and dark
  green cold water dye
String
Black and red felt-tip pens
1lb of stuffing

For the giraffe
¾yd of 36in-wide white cotton
  fabric
Piece of brown felt 4 × 16in
1 tin each of orange and brown cold
  water dye
String
Black felt-tip pen
Piece of stiff orange paper for horns
11oz of stuffing

Dyeing the fabric
Pleat the piece of fabric lengthwise, twist it and tie it with string at 1¼in intervals. For the crocodile body, mix up pale green dye according to the manufacturer's instructions. Immerse the fabric in dye and leave it for the recommended period of time. Remove the fabric from the dye, allow it to dry thoroughly and untie the string. Pleat the cloth in the opposite direction and tie it with string as before. Prepare the dark green dye, re-dye the fabric and let it dry. Press it on both sides. For the giraffe body, dye the fabric first orange then brown.

Making the pattern —cutting out
Enlarge the pattern pieces as indicated on the graph, adding ⅜in seam allowance to all edges, except mane, hoof, sole and tassel. Note that the giraffe's body pattern includes the whole shape; the gusset, only the lower part. Cut the pattern pieces from the appropriate fabrics. For the crocodile also cut 22 squares of green-dyed fabric, each 2¾in square.

To make the crocodile
Form the scales by placing the fabric squares together in pairs, RS facing, and stitching across one end in zigzag lines, making each side of the zigzag about ¾in long. Trim close to stitching, clip and turn scales RS out.
☐Starting about 12in from the tail end, pin and stitch each scale piece to the RS of gusset, with scales pointing backward as shown. Turn under the top edge of the last piece before stitching.
☐Placing RS together, stitch the gusset to each of the top side pieces. Stitch the top and under body pieces together, RS facing, leaving a gap in one side. Turn the body RS out and fill it with stuffing. Close the gap with slipstitching.
☐Using felt-tip pens, draw the eyes, nostrils and claws on the crocodile.

To make the giraffe
Stitch a gusset piece to each body piece with RS facing, leaving foot edges open. Clip curves and turn each side RS out. Cut slashes in the tassel and mane as shown. Place the tail pieces together with RS facing and the tassel sandwiched between at one end, cut edge inward. Stitch, leaving top open. Turn tail RS out and stuff it.
☐Place the two sides of the body together with RS facing (gussets on outside). Insert the tail between the edges at center back, raw edges matching. Insert the mane with cut edge inward. Stitch around the upper part of the body. Turn the body RS out.
☐Join the short, straight edges of each hoof with overcasting. Overcast a sole to each hoof. Slipstitch a hoof to each leg opening.
☐Fill the legs, head, neck and the rest of the body with stuffing. Turn in the edges of the gusset opening and slipstitch them together.
☐Place the ear pieces together with RS facing and stitch all around, leaving the straight edges open. Turn the ears RS out, fold them in half along the length and slipstitch them to each side of the head.
☐Using felt-tip pen, draw the eyes, mouth and nostrils on the head. Cut 2 quarter circles of orange paper with a radius of about 2¼in and roll them into cone shapes. Glue edges in place. Slipstitch a horn to each side of the head.

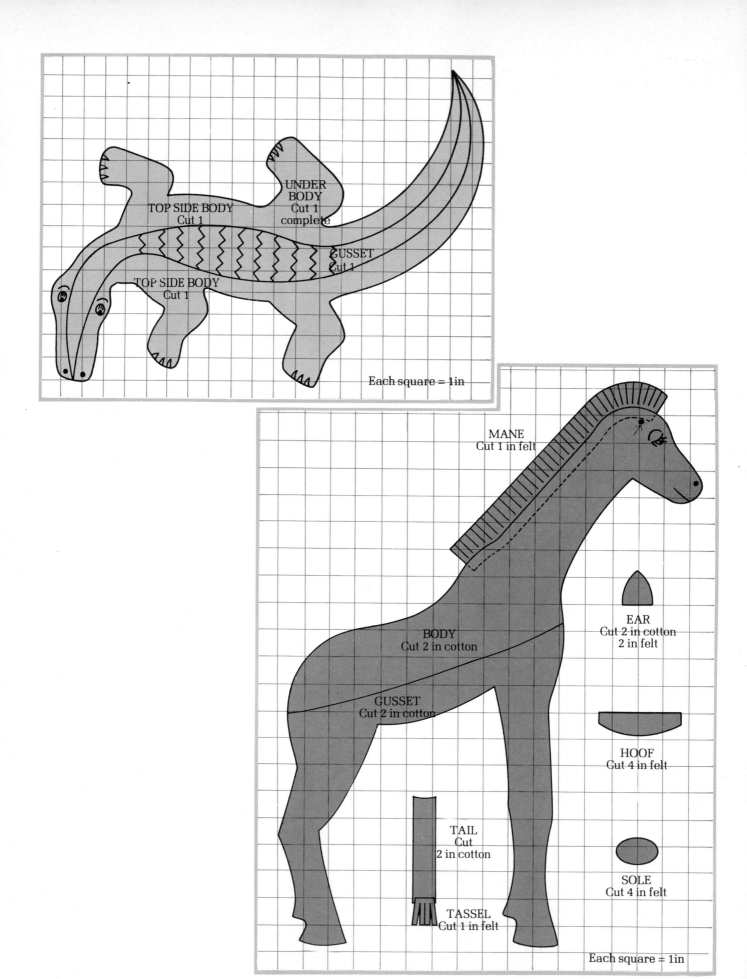

TOP SIDE BODY
Cut 1

UNDER
BODY
Cut 1
complete

TOP SIDE BODY
Cut 1

GUSSET
Cut 1

Each square = 1in

MANE
Cut 1 in felt

EAR
Cut 2 in cotton
2 in felt

BODY
Cut 2 in cotton

GUSSET
Cut 2 in cotton

HOOF
Cut 4 in felt

TAIL
Cut
2 in cotton

SOLE
Cut 4 in felt

TASSEL
Cut 1 in felt

Each square = 1in

Tropical birds

Size
Approximately 8in long

Materials
For each bird
2 pieces of felt 7 × 3in in green
    and white
Scrap of yellow felt
Small amount of stuffing
Pipe cleaner
Black felt-tip pen

Making the pattern — cutting out
Enlarge the pattern pieces as indicated on the graph. Cut the pieces from felt as follows: from green felt cut 2 body pieces and the upper beak; from white felt cut 2 upper body/wing pieces; from yellow felt cut the lower beak. Transfer all pattern markings to the fabric. A seam allowance of ¼in is included throughout.

To make the bird
Stitch an under wing to each upper body piece, matching points C and D and leaving open the straight edge between them. Turn wings RS out. Stitch a main body piece to each upper body and wing, matching points A, B, C and D.
☐Place the two halves of the bird together, with wings sandwiched between, and stitch around the edges of the body, leaving a gap in the back as shown on the pattern. Fill the bird with stuffing, starting with the wing tips, then filling the lower part of the main body, and finally filling the top. Slipstitch the opening edges together.
☐Sew the two parts of the beak together. Curve the sides inward and slipstitch beak to head.
☐For claws, cut two 2¾in of pipe cleaner and fold each piece double. Pierce the body in two places with a bodkin or scissor points and insert the bent ends of pipe cleaners into each hole. Sew claws in place and curve them as shown. Draw the eyes and feathers on the bird with felt-tip pen.

Giant panda pals

Size
Mother panda, approximately 30in from nose to bottom
Baby panda, approximately 18in

Materials
For the mother panda
$\frac{7}{8}$yd of 54in-wide white fur fabric
$\frac{5}{8}$yd of 54in-wide black fur fabric
2 amber safety eyes
$2\frac{1}{4}$lb of stuffing
Scraps of black felt
Strong linen thread
Black tapestry yarn

For the baby panda
$\frac{5}{8}$yd of 54in-wide white fur fabric
$\frac{3}{8}$yd of 54in-wide black fur fabric
$1\frac{3}{4}$lb of stuffing
Scraps of black felt
Strong linen thread
Black tapestry yarn

Making the pattern — cutting out
Enlarge the pattern pieces as indicated on the graph, using the appropriate scale for each panda and adding $\frac{3}{8}$in seam allowance to all edges. Cut the pieces from the appropriate fabrics, making sure that the pieces are correctly aligned with the direction of the pile (indicated by the arrows). Cut from a single layer, reversing the pieces as necessary.

To make the pandas
In joining seams, baste edges first to prevent the fabric from slipping, or stitch seams by hand. Work in the direction of the pile where possible.

☐ On the eye patches clip the fur shorter. Stitch eye patches to the front head pieces. Join the front and back head pieces between points P and R. Join head and chin gussets at point M. Join one edge of the combined gusset to one side head from L to M to N. Repeat on opposite side of head. Clip curves of the seams to ease, if necessary. Insert the safety eyes through the eye patches, placing them to give a lifelike expression.

Join the neck to the collar, RS facing, between points B and K, and collar to center body between C and H. Join rear body to center body from D to G, and join outer back leg from G to F. Match the inner leg to the outer leg with RS facing, and stitch down the long sides. Join the parts of the other side of the body in the same way.

☐ Join the neck gusset to the collar gusset from K to K. Join the collar gusset to the body gusset from H to H. Join the body gusset to the rear gusset from F to F. Make sure stitching is fastened off securely.

☐ Now join one edge of gusset strip to one body unit from L to K to J, and from H to G, then across inner back leg to F. Leave the space between J and H open. Join it to rear body between points F and E. Join body units between points E and A. Join other seam E-F.

☐ Join the front paw sections, leaving open the top and edges and a space on the lower edges large enough for paw pads. Insert a pad into each foot, RS facing, so that pile on pad runs forward. Turn paws RS out and insert them into body opening from J to H. Fit pads into the back legs with the pile running forward as before.

☐ Stuff the legs, rear body and head firmly. Use linen thread to stitch the head to the body securely, matching center points A on body and

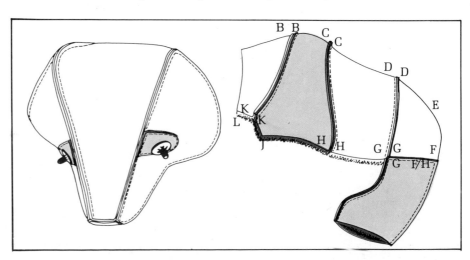

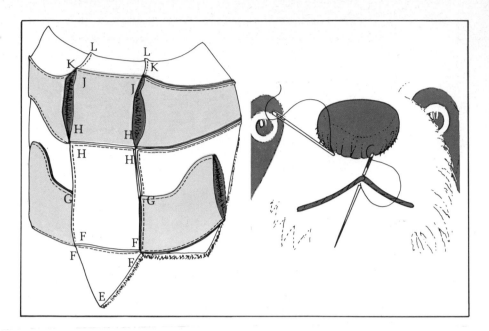

head gusset. Stuffing the rest of body; slipstitch opening edges.

☐Join each pair of ear pieces around the curved edges; turn ears RS out. Gather the straight edges and overcast them together. Use linen thread to stitch the ears to point P on the gusset-side head seams.

☐Stitch, turn and fill the tail with stuffing; overcast the straight edges and ladder stitch them, using linen thread, to the rear gusset below point E. Catch the tail base to the main body.

☐Using a double strand of tapestry yarn, make a straight stitch from cheek to cheek for the mouth. Pull it upward at the center and catch it in place. Use a double strand of the sewing thread to gather the edge of the nose. Stuff nose lightly, draw up the gathers and secure them. Ladder stitch nose to head.

☐Hold the back legs in a natural position and ladder stitch between inner leg and underbody for the appropriate distance, using linen thread. Brush the panda to raise the pile.

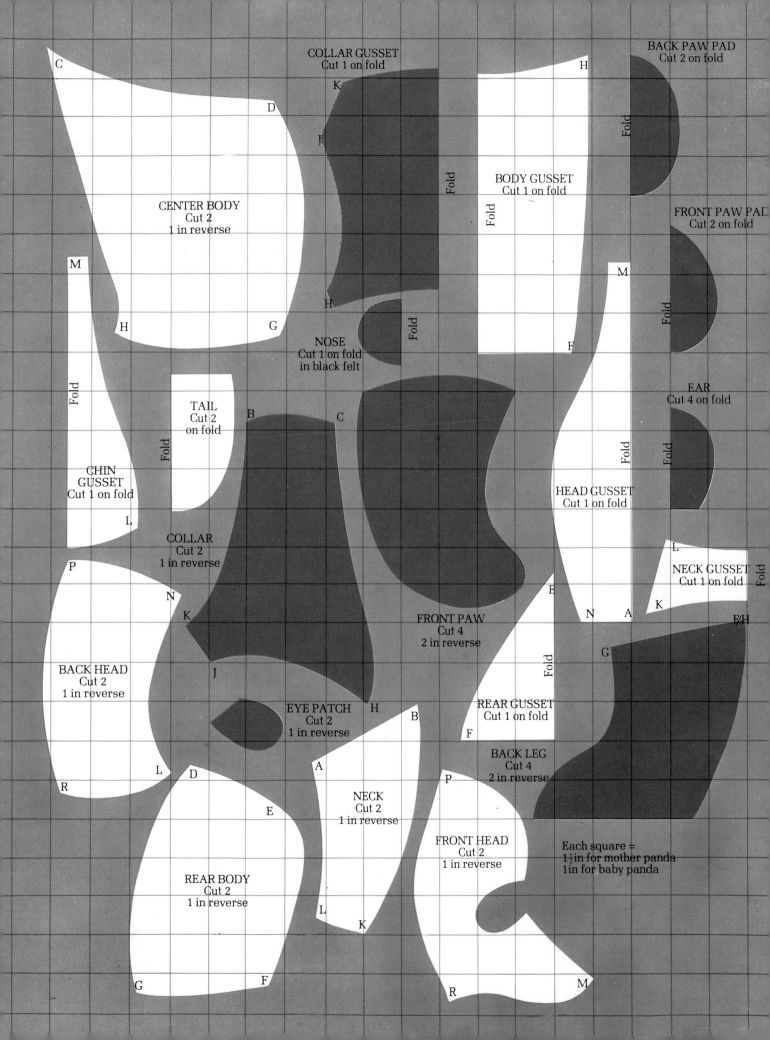

Danny the dragon

Size
Approximately 16in long

Materials
Piece of green felt 20in square

⅛in of 36in-wide red fabric

Pearl cotton in orange, green, yellow, black and white

4 pipe cleaners

7oz of stuffing

Small beads and sequins

Making the pattern — cutting out
Enlarge the pattern pieces as indicated on the graph, adding ⅜in seam allowance to all edges. Cut them from the appropriate fabrics and transfer all pattern markings.

To make the dragon
Place each pair of ruffle pieces together with RS facing and stitch the scalloped edges. Clip curves and turn ruffles RS out.

☐Place each pair of leg pieces together with WS facing, sandwiching ruffles in the back leg seams. Leaving the feet open, topstitch each leg around the edges. Fill the legs firmly with stuffing and slipstitch the soles of the feet to the leg openings.

☐Place a felt ear and a fabric ear together, RS facing, and stitch around the edges, leaving a small gap for turning. Turn ears RS out. Join the tail pieces in the same way.

☐Place a felt wing and a fabric wing together, RS facing; stitch around edges, leaving narrow end open. Turn wings RS out. Work 2 lines of topstitching along wings, as shown; insert pipe cleaner into front and back edges. Turn in and slipstitch open ends.

☐Using yellow pearl, work a row of feather stitch along the center panel of each wing. Stitch sequins and beads along the center of each front panel as shown in the photograph.

☐Baste each wing in place along the top edge of each side of body.

☐Fold the gusset strip in half lengthwise. Cut along the fold line, leaving 8in uncut at one end. Slip the ruffle between the two layers

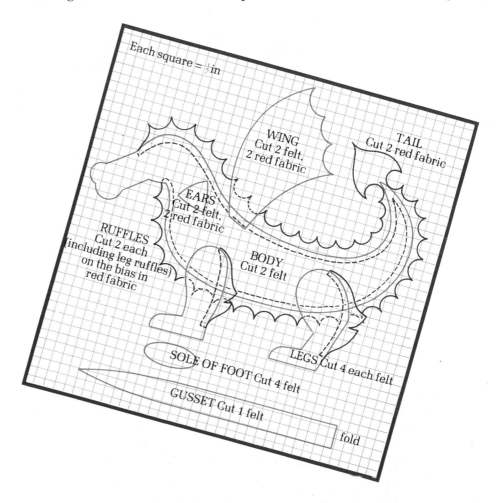

of gusset, with scalloped edge inside and raw edges even, and stitch the seam, as close as possible to the raw edges. Open out the gusset strip and place one long edge on one top side of head/body, WS matching, from throat to tail. Topstitch the seam. Repeat to join gusset to the other side; trim the seam allowances.

☐ Join the under body seam with topstitching, sandwiching the other ruffle between the edges, scalloped edge outward, and leaving a gap for stuffing. Trim the seam allowance.

☐ Fill the body firmly with stuffing; slipstitch the opening edges together. Fill the end of the tail piece with a small amount of stuffing, turn in the raw edges and slipstitch tail to the body.

☐ Using satin stitch and pearl in black, orange and white, embroider the features. Slipstitch the ears in place. Position legs on body and, using green pearl cotton, buttonhole stitch them in place.

Lorna the lioness

Making the pattern — cutting out
Enlarge the pattern pieces as indicated on the graph and cut them from the appropriate fabrics, cutting through a single layer of fur fabric, placed RS down. Take care to cut the pieces with the pile running correctly, as indicated by the arrows on the pattern pieces, and avoid cutting the pile. Reverse the pattern pieces that are cut twice. Transfer all pattern markings. A seam allowance of $\frac{5}{8}$in is included.

To make the lioness
Stitch the nose to the head gusset, RS facing, along the straight seam A-B. Clip into the corners. Then stitch the curved sides of the nose to the sides of gusset, matching points A and P on one side, B and P on the other.

☐Placing RS together, stitch one of the head side pieces to one curved side of the nose, matching points P and Q. Repeat to join the other head side. Stitch the head sides to the remainder of the gusset, along the seamlines between points U and P on each side. Leave the neck seam open.

☐Stitch the mane to the head, RS facing, matching points D and U on each side and M at center top of head.

☐Stitch the neck seam from point G on the nose, through Q and D, to point X on the mane.

☐Working from the WS, fold the neck seam on the nose pattern piece to the center, matching the three points at F. Match the neck seam to center of gusset. Stitch straight across the resulting triangle shape as shown. Clip the curves on the head seams and turn the head RS out.

☐Make a small cut in the center of each felt eye, and slip a safety-eye shank through it. Then push the safety-eye shank through the fur fabric in the position marked. Push the washer onto the safety-eye shank from the WS, with the raised side of the prongs uppermost. Take care to line up the washer correctly at the base of the shank for a secure fit. Make tiny stitches around the edge of each felt eye to hold it in place.

☐Stitch the left underbody to the left body, RS facing, from point X, around the two legs, to point Z. Repeat for the right underbody and right body. Then stitch the two body sections together, from the neck at point Y, along the center back seam, to point Z. Clip curves on all the body seams.

☐Stitch the head to the body with RS facing, matching the seamlines on the body and mane from point X on the neck, up to Y on the top back seam, and back down to point X at the neck. Stitch the underbody seam with RS together, leaving the opening marked for stuffing. Turn the lioness RS out.

☐Fill the front legs with stuffing up to the position marked. Cut 2 circles of unbleached muslin measuring 8in in diameter, to cover the exposed top of the legs. Working from the inside of the lioness, catch-stitch a circle of muslin to the fur fabric around the top of each front leg. Repeat for the back legs, but cut each muslin circle to measure $8\frac{3}{4}$in in diameter.

☐Stuff the head firmly. Cut a circle of unbleached muslin measuring $12\frac{1}{2}$in in diameter, and sew this to the inside neck in the same way as for stuffing the legs.

☐Fill the body through the center underbody seam, and firmly

Size
Approximately 35in long, excluding tail

Materials
$3\frac{7}{8}$yd of 54in-wide short-pile gold colored fur fabric
$\frac{1}{2}$yd of 54in-wide long-pile gold colored fur fabric
$\frac{1}{2}$yd of 36in-wide unbleached muslin
Small scraps of brown felt
2 large brown plastic safety eyes
3yd of bulky brown yarn
10lb of stuffing

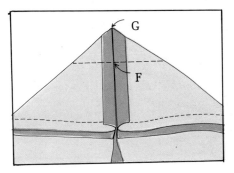

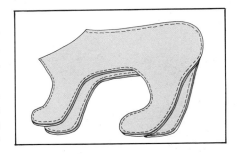

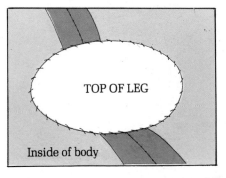

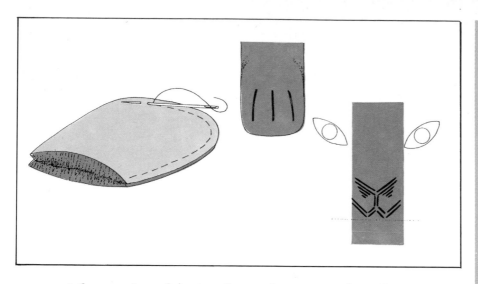

overcast the opening edges together using strong thread.

☐For the tail, cut a length of short-pile fabric 23in long and 6in wide, with the pile running lengthwise. Cut a 6in square of long-pile fabric for the tail tip.

☐Stitch the tail tip to the end of the tail, RS facing, with the pile running in the same direction. Fold the tail lengthwise, RS facing, and stitch the long edges together. Turn the tail RS out.

☐Turn in the raw edges of the tail at both ends, and stipstitch them neatly together. Stitch the top end of the tail to the body at point Z.

☐Stitch each pair of ear pieces together around the curved edges, with RS facing. Clip the seam and turn ears RS out. Turn in the raw edges and overcast them together. Stitch the ears to the head in the positions marked, curving them slightly.

☐Using brown yarn, embroider 3 claws at the top of each paw with 2in-long stitches. Embroider the mouth and nose with straight stitches as shown. To make the whiskers, cut 6 pieces of yarn, each 4in long. Attach 3 whiskers to each side of the nose with two backstitches.

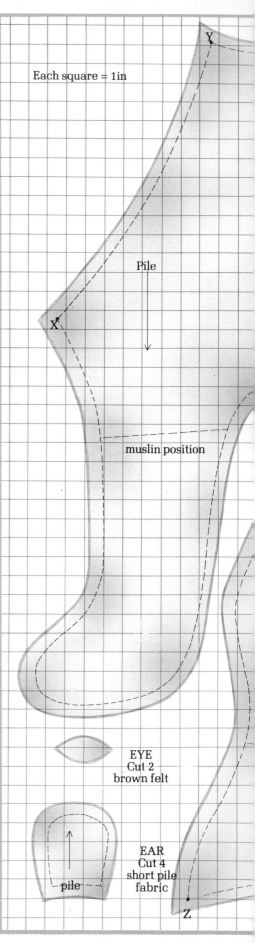

Each square = 1in

Pile

X

muslin position

EYE
Cut 2
brown felt

EAR
Cut 4
short pile
fabric

pile

Y

Z

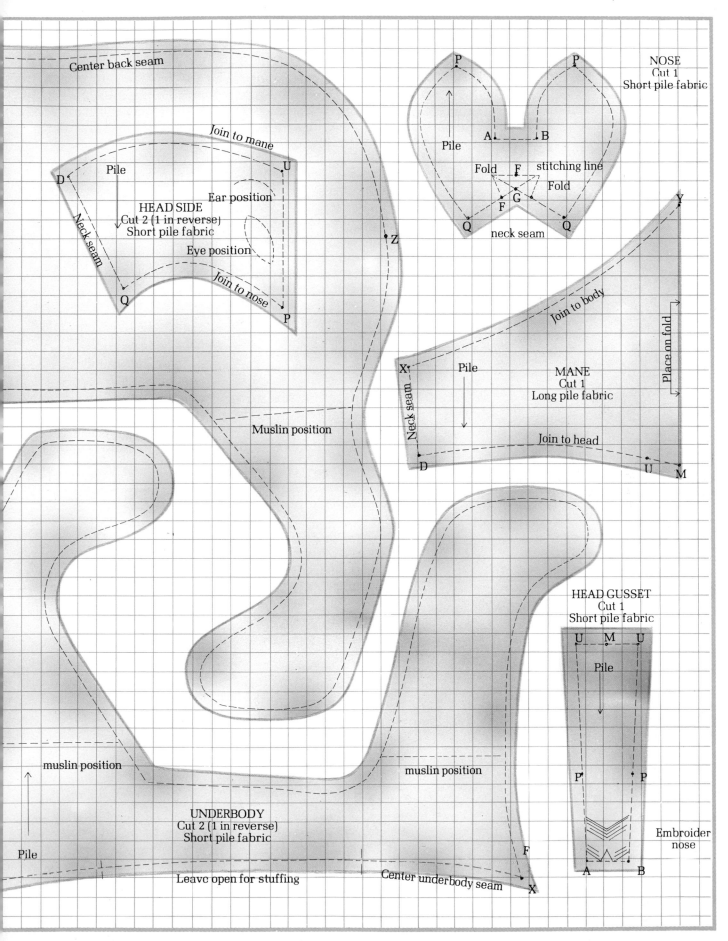

Center back seam

Join to mane

P   P   NOSE
Cut 1
Short pile fabric

Pile

A   B

D

Pile

HEAD SIDE
Cut 2 (1 in reverse)
Short pile fabric

U

Ear position

Eye position

Neck seam

Fold   F   stitching line
Fold

F   G

Z

Q   Q

neck seam

Y

Join to body

Join to nose

Q

P

X

Pile

Neck seam

MANE
Cut 1
Long pile fabric

Place on fold

Muslin position

Join to head

D   U M

HEAD GUSSET
Cut 1
Short pile fabric

U M U

Pile

muslin position   muslin position

P   P

UNDERBODY
Cut 2 (1 in reverse)
Short pile fabric

Embroider
nose

Pile

F

Leave open for stuffing   Center underbody seam X

A   B

Feathered friend

Size
Approximately 43in tall

Materials
1yd of 60in-wide shaggy pink fur
fabric
½yd of 36in-wide green and black
striped knit fabric
½yd of 36in-wide yellow satin
Scrap of purple fabric for eyes
2 large safety eyes
Feather duster
10oz of stuffing
Piece of polyester batting 16in
square

Making the pattern — cutting out
Enlarge the pattern pieces as indicated on the graph, and cut them from the appropriate fabrics and batting, cutting fur fabric pieces from a single layer and making sure that the pile is aligned correctly. Transfer all pattern markings. A seam allowance of ⅜in is included.

To make the bird
Stitch the four body pieces together, RS facing, leaving the lower edges open. Clip the curves and turn body RS out. Fill the body firmly with stuffing. Turn in the opening edges and slipstitch them together, with two opposite seams aligned.

□Cut tail hole in one body section where indicated. Overcast or blanket stitch the edges to finish them. Cut the handle of the feather duster to 4in and insert it downward into the opening so that it lies between fur fabric and inner pocket.

□Place a batting foot piece between two satin pieces (placed RS outward) and baste layers together. Topstitch along the marked lines in red, then work close zigzag stitch around the edges. Trim the edges close to stitching. Make the other foot in the same way.

□Fold each leg piece lengthwise, RS facing, and stitch long edges together. Turn legs RS out and fill them firmly with stuffing. Turn in edges on one end and slipstitch them to the foot; turn in and slipstitch the other end to the base of the body, making sure that feet point forward.

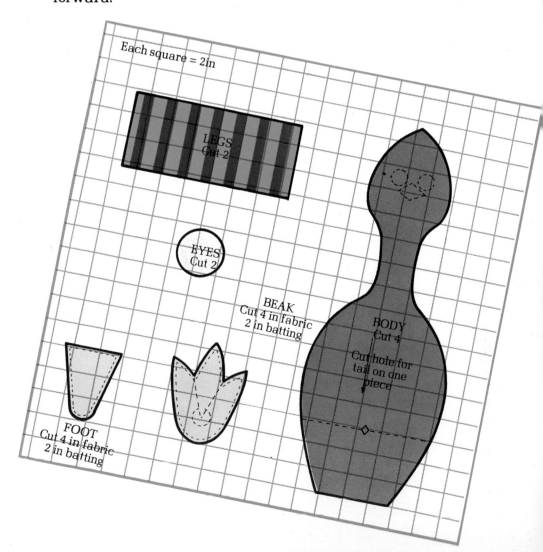

☐Join and quilt beak pieces as for feet, leaving straight edges open. Place the two beak pieces together and stitch along the two adjacent straight edges. Pad the lower beak wih a little stuffing. Slipstitch the beak to the head.

☐Attach a safety eye to each purple fabric circle. Work gathering stitches around the edge of each circle. Draw up gathers, fill circles with stuffing and fasten gathering thread securely. Sew the eyes to the head.

Hilda hippo

Size
Approximately 16½in long

Materials
⅝yd of 36in-wide printed fabric
1⅜yd of ¼in-wide pink ribbon
⅝yd of 1½in-wide wide lace edging
Piece of pink felt 8in square
Scraps of black felt
Black stranded embroidery floss
11oz of stuffing
Artificial flowers

Making the pattern — cutting out

Enlarge the pattern pieces as indicated on the graph, and cut them from printed fabric and felt. Transfer all pattern markings to the fabric. A seam allowance of ⅝in is included.

To make the hippo

Sew a printed ear to each felt ear, RS facing, leaving the straight edges open. Clip the curves and turn ears RS out. Make a fold in the straight edge, and baste it in place. On the head, cut along the center line of the dart, nearly to the point. Insert the ear, with the felt side facing forward, and stitch it in place, forming the dart at the same time.

☐ Fold the tail section in half, RS facing, and stitch the outer sides together. Trim the seam and turn tail RS out. Fill tail firmly with stuffing. Work running stitch along the open edges to secure the stuffing. Put tail aside.

☐ Placing RS together, stitch the left-hand under-gusset to the left side of body, along the lower edge, from C to D. Repeat for right-hand side of body. Make sure the ends of the under-gusset are pointed.

☐ Placing RS together, stitch the head gusset to the left side of the body, A to B. Take care to follow the contours of the head. Then stitch the other side of head gusset to the right side of the body. Stitch body sections together from B to C. Stitch seam A to D, inserting the tail between the seam between points E and F.

☐ With the hippo still inside-out, stitch the four foot pads to the leg openings.

☐ Clip around the seams, and turn the hippo RS out. Cut out 2 circles of black felt, ⅝in in diameter, for the nostrils. Stitch them to the nose as shown in the photograph.

☐ Cut out 2 circles of black felt 1in in diameter for the eyes. Stitch them in place. For eyelashes, work 5 long straight stitches above the eyes.

☐ Fill the hippo firmly with stuffing, beginning with the head, then filling the legs, and finally the main body section. Take care to follow the contours of the body, pushing the stuffing well into the curves. Turn in raw edges on the under-gusset and overcast them together.

☐ For the hat, cut a 3in-diameter circle of pink felt. Join the ends of the lace and gather the straight edge until it fits the edge of the felt. Stitch lace to hat. Cut a piece of ribbon 35in long. Fold this in half, and sew the middle to the underside of the hat. Make a bow with the remaining ribbon and sew this to the top of the hat. Sew artificial flowers next to the bow.

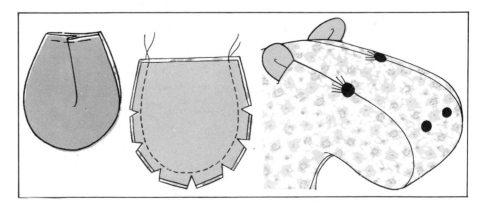

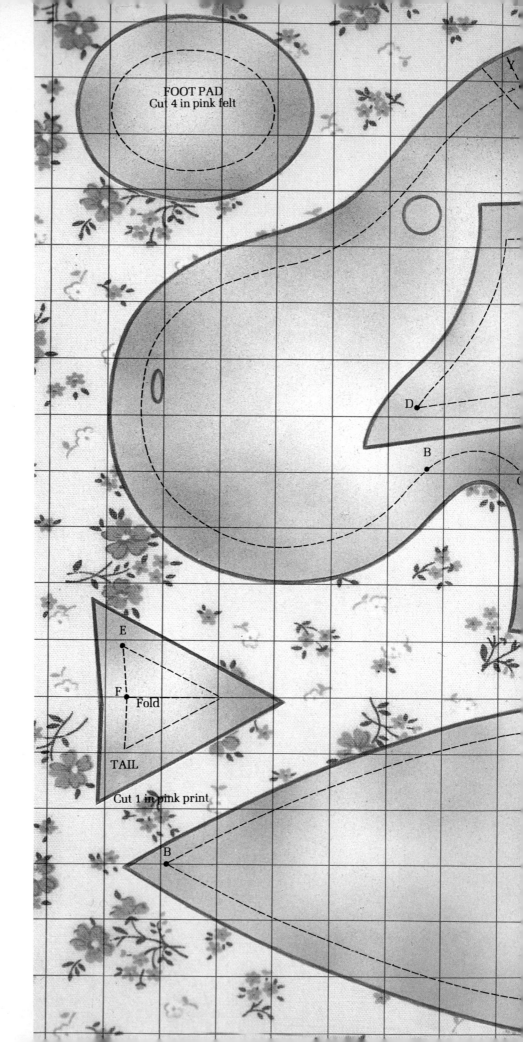

FOOT PAD
Cut 4 in pink felt

D

B

C

E

F Fold

TAIL

Cut 1 in pink print

B

94

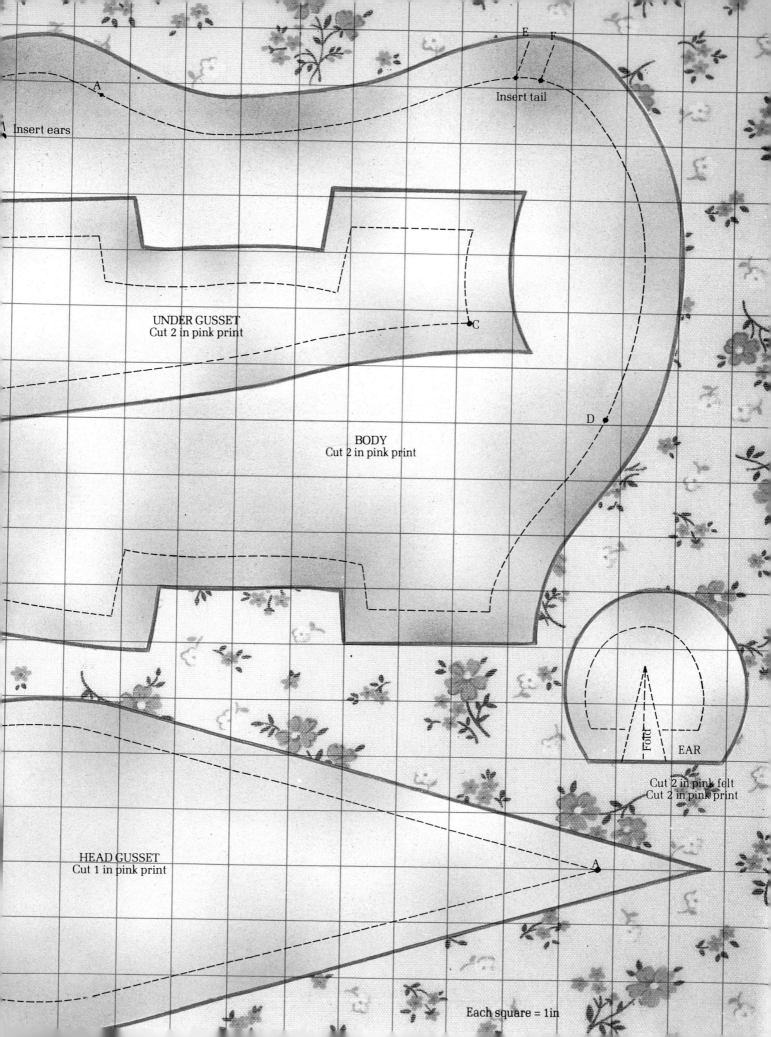

A

Insert ears

E F

Insert tail

UNDER GUSSET
Cut 2 in pink print

C

D

BODY
Cut 2 in pink print

Fold

EAR

Cut 2 in pink felt
Cut 2 in pink print

HEAD GUSSET
Cut 1 in pink print

A

Each square = 1in

Happy family

Sizes
Pig, approximately 18in long.
Piglet, approximately 10½in long

Materials
Pig
5oz of a knitting worsted yarn in main color A
Small amount in contrasting color B
3 piglets
5oz of a knitting worsted yarn in main color A
Small amount in contrasting color B
1 pair each size 2 and 8 knitting needles
1½ib of stuffing
6 large snaps
Small amount of dark pink yarn for embroidery

Gauge
12 sts and 23 rows to 4in in g st on size 8 needles
22 sts and 42 rows to 4in in g st on size 2 needles

Pigs
Use size 8 needles and yarn double.

Body (make 2 pieces).
Using A, cast on 10 sts. Cont in g st (every row K) inc 1 st at beg of every row until there 20 sts.
Cast on 10 sts at beg of next row.
Work 11 rows.
Next row Bind off 10 sts, K to end.
Work 39 rows.
Cast on 8 sts at beg of next row.
Work 11 rows.
Next row Bind off 8 sts, K to end.
Dec 1 st at beg of next 6 rows. Work 16 rows.
Next row Bind off 3 sts, K to end.
Dec 1 st at beg of next 4 rows. Work 4 rows. Bind off.

Underbody
*Using A, cast on 1 st. Cont in g st inc 1 st at beg of every row until there are 11 sts. *
Cast on 10 sts at beg of next 2 rows.
Work 11 rows.
Bind off 10 sts at beg of next 2 rows.
Work 39 rows.
Cast on 8 sts at beg of next 2 rows.
Work 11 rows.
Cast on 8 sts at beg of next 2 rows.
Dec 1 st at beg of next 4 rows. Work 22 rows.
Dec 1 st at beg of every row until 1 st rem. Fasten off.

Upper gusset
Beg at back of body, work as for underbody from * to *.
Cont in g st and A, work 86 rows.
Dec 1 st at beg of next 4 rows. Work 6 rows. Dec 1 st at beg of every row until 1 st rem. Fasten off.

Ears (make 2)
Using A, cast on 12 sts. Cont in g st, work 12 rows.
Dec 1 st at beg of every row until 1 st rem. Fasten off.
Inner ears (make 2)
Work as for ears using B.

Tail
Using A, cast on 20 sts. K 1 row.
Bind off.

Footpads and muzzle (make 5)
Using B, cast on 3 sts. Cont in g st, inc 1 st at each end of next 2 rows.
Work 5 rows.
Dec 1 st at each end of next 2 rows.
Bind off.

Piglets
Work as given for pig, using size 2 needles and one strand of yarn throughout.

To finish
Sew upper gusset between body sections, beg at shaped edge of back.
Sew underbody in position, leaving an opening for stuffing.
Sew muzzle to snout and footpads to legs.
Sew "knob" section of snaps inside muzzle of each piglet so that knob protrudes to outside. Fill bodies and close openings. Sew ears and inner ears tog, then sew to head. Fold tail lengthwise and overcast, tightening sewing to curl. Make a small tassel for mother pig's tail. Sew tail to body. Embroider eyes and mouth. To fasten piglets to pig, sew corresponding halves of snaps to underbody of pig.

Charlie caterpillar

Underbody With A, cast on 16 sts.
1st row (RS) K.
Beg with a K row work in reverse st
st (1 row P, 1 row K) for 5 rows.
Rep these 6 rows 25 times more.
**Next row With A, K.
Next Row With A, P.
Next row With C, K.
Next row With C, P.
Next row With B, K.
Next row With B, K.
Rep these 6 rows once more. Bind
off.**

Back With C, cast on 21 sts. Join in
A and work in patt as foll:
1st row (WS) With C and A tog, K.
2nd row With A, K.
3rd row With A, P.
4th row *K1A, (K1C, P1C) twice into
next st sl 2nd, 3rd and 4th sts over
first st on RH needle, rep from * to
last st, K1A.
5th row With C, P.

6th row With C, K.
Rep last 6 rows 25 times more, then
first row again.
Now work as for underbody from **
to **.

To finish

Join one long seam. Lay knitting flat,
WS uppermost. Place batting over
entire knitted area.
With B, stab stitch through both
layers along every second ridge.
Attach elastic to inside of
underbody from the 5th to 10th
ridge.
Join remaining seam. Gather each
end and secure firmly.
With A, embroider mouth. Catch-
stitch 5th ridge from head to 11th
ridge over center 8 sts on back.

Feelers With B, cast on 18 sts. K1
row. Bind off. Thread feelers
through head and stitch in place.

Size
Approximately 21in long

Materials
2oz of a medium-weight mohair
blend yarn in three colors: A
(gold), B (brown) and C (green)
Piece of synthetic batting
21 × 12in
4in of 2in-wide elastic
Pair of size 5 knitting needles

Gauge
9sts and 16 rows to 1½in in patt on
size 5 needles

Pompon animals

Size
Approximately 1½ to 2¼in diameter

Materials
Small amounts of yarn in brown,
    beige, red, black, white, yellow,
    gray, rust and reddish brown
Scraps of felt in gold, gray and beige
Beads for eyes
Brown twine for mice's tails and
    whiskers
Black poster paint for ladybug's
    spots
Black string for ladybug's feelers
Small piece of cardboard

To make the pompons
For each animal make one or two pompons using the method shown
here — which is easier than the disk method (page 150) when making
very small pompons. Cut 2 rectangles of cardboard, each about
2 × 3in. In the center of one long edge, draw and cut out a semicircle
using a coin (penny or quarter) as a pattern. Trim each rectangle to
the bridge shape shown; the outer curved edge is the radius of the
finished pompon.

☐ Place the two cardboard patterns together and lay a piece of yarn
over them as shown below. Wind yarn over the patterns, keeping the
tension firm and even, until the arch is covered with yarn. Do not cut
the winding yarn, but pull the short length of yarn to the inside edge
and continue winding until the center is well filled; the pompons
must be very dense. Slide scissors or a sharp craft knife between the
patterns and cut the yarn (the double layer of cardboard serves as a
guide in cutting evenly). Tie the piece of yarn firmly around the
center of the pompon. Trim the pompon to make it smooth, if
necessary, or to make the desired shape.

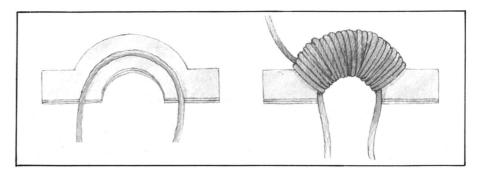

To make the chicks
Make a pompon about 2in in diameter and trim it to shape. Cut 2
triangular pieces of yellow felt, sew them together along one side
and sew them to the head part of the pompon. Sew bead eyes above
the beak, securing the thread well inside the pompon.

To make a porcupine
Make a pompon about 2in in diameter, using a ball of brown yarn
and one of beige yarn and mixing them well over the patterns. Trim
the pompon to shape and sew bead eyes to the head.

To make the rabbits
Make a pompon about 2¼in in diameter for the mother, 1½in in
diameter for the baby rabbits. Trim them to shape. Cut triangular
ears from gray felt, make a small tuck in the base of each ear and
sew ears firmly to top of head. Sew bead eyes in place.

To make the robins
For the adult robin make two pompons: one 1¼in in diameter in
reddish brown for the head and one 2in in diameter, using reddish
brown and adding some rust in the center of the arch. Tie or sew the
pompoms together firmly. Sew a beige felt beak and bead eyes to the
head pompon. For the baby, make a 1½in-diameter pompon in reddish
brown, inserting a small amount of rust in the center. Add beak and
eyes.

To make the mice

Make a pompon about $2\frac{1}{4}$in in diameter for the mother, $1\frac{1}{2}$in in diameter for the baby mouse. Trim them to shape. Make round felt ears and sew them and bead eyes to the head. Thread pieces of brown twine through the pompon for tail and whiskers.

To make the ladybug

Make a pompon about 2in in diameter, using a little white yarn in the center of the arch, a little black yarn to each side of it and red yarn over the rest of the template. Sew black string "feelers" to the head; knot and trim the ends. Paint black spots on the red body.

Games and costumes

Some games have rules — some are made up as you go along. This section contains toys for both kinds of game. Among them are a checkerboard rug and a colorful variation of chutes and ladders. For games of make-believe there is a selection of costumes for both boys and girls, a climbing net ideal for Tarzan-Jane adventures and a circus tent to provide a setting for stunts and theatricals.

Snakes and ladders playmat

Size
$33\frac{1}{2} \times 43$in

Materials
2 pieces of red felt $33\frac{1}{2} \times 43$in
Piece of light gray and dark gray felt, each 20×30in
Piece of pink, yellow, purple, green and blue felt, each 24in square
Piece of green and red felt, each $8\frac{1}{2} \times 5\frac{1}{2}$in
5yd of 36in-wide iron-on interfacing
Small round wooden beads and gold beads, gold sequins and blue bugle beads for markings on snakes and dice
Flat red and black buttons for counters
Small amount of stuffing
Piece of thin cardboard 3×4in
Pinking shears

Making the pattern — cutting out
Iron interfacing to one side of the light and dark gray and the 24in squares of felt. Enlarge the pattern pieces for the snakes, ladders, numbers and starting and finishing points as indicated on the graph. Cut them from the appropriate fabrics the required number of times (see photograph).
☐ Using the piece of cardboard as a template, cut 50 rectangles each of light and dark gray felt.
☐ Trim the template to measure $2\frac{3}{4}$in square, and use this to cut 6 squares of red and 6 of green felt, using the smaller pieces of felt.

Each square = 1½in

To make the playmat

Pin the light and dark gray patches alternately over one piece of red felt, leaving ¼in between them and a border of ¾in around all four edges. Using a closely-spaced zigzag stitch and matching thread, appliqué each gray patch in place.

☐Position the snakes, ladders, numbers and starting and finishing points on the mat as shown in the photograph and zigzag stitch them in place.

☐Sew sequins and small gold beads to the snakes' heads, for eyes. Use blue bugle beads for fangs and wooden beads for markings.

☐Place the appliquéd piece on top of the other piece of red felt and stitch them together ¾in from the edges. Trim the edges of the mat with pinking shears, cutting through both layers of felt.

To make the dice

Sew four felt squares together to form a ring, taking ¾in seam allowance. Sew a square to one end, then stitch two sides of the remaining square to the other end.

☐Turn the cube RS out. Fill it firmly with stuffing. Slipstitch the opening edges together. Sew sequins and small gold beads to each face of the cube to form numbers 1 to 6.

Roadway rug

Size
Approximately 24 × 32in

Materials

¾yd of 36in-wide medium-weight
   gray fabric
¾yd of 36in-wide unbleached muslin
Scraps of fabric in several different
   shades of green, brown and blue
   (see pattern)

Piece of beige terry cloth 16in
   square
Scraps of felt and patterned fabric
   for houses and gardens
Green bouclé knitting yarn
Crochet hook

Making the pattern — cutting out

Enlarge the pattern pieces as indicated on the graph and cut them
from the appropriate fabrics. No seam allowance is required.
☐Trim the gray fabric to measure $25\frac{1}{2} \times 34\frac{1}{2}$in and round the
corners.

To make the rug

Following the graph for positioning, baste the shapes that touch the
edge of the design onto the gray fabric. Using matching thread and a
wide zigzag, stitch them in place.
☐Trim the muslin to the same size as the gray fabric. Place the two
together, RS facing. Stitch around the edges taking $\frac{3}{4}$in seam
allowance and leaving 10in open on one side. Trim seam and clip
corners. Turn rug RS out, slipstitch opening edges together.
☐Baste the main pieces to the background, following the pattern,
and zigzag stitch around the edges.
☐Using green bouclé yarn, crochet lengths of chain stitch to go
around the edge of the fields, to represent hedges. Zigzag stitch each
length of chain in place. Baste the remaining small pieces to the
background and stitch them in place using satin stitch. Draw in the
gates with felt-tip pen and work satin stitch over the drawn lines.
gates with felt-tip pen and work satin stitch over the drawn lines.

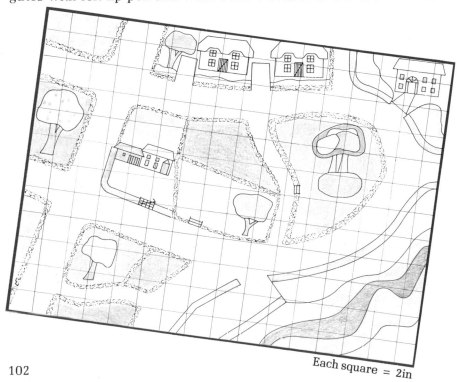

Each square = 2in

Checkerboard rug

Size
52½in square

Materials
4⅜yd of 36in-wide gray felt
1yd of 36in-wide royal blue felt
1yd of 36in-wide pale blue felt
1⅛yd of 36in-wide red felt
1⅛yd of 36in-wide green felt
¼yd of 36in-wide yellow felt
Scraps of orange, turquoise, light
    gray and purple felt
1⅛yd of medium-weight iron-on
    interfacing
Fabric glue stick
Pinking shears
Latex glue (optional)

To make the rug
Cut the gray felt into 3 lengths, each 52½in long. Cut one piece in half lengthwise. Join one wide piece and one narrow piece along the long edge, taking ⅜in seam allowance. Repeat with the remaining two pieces. Press seams open.

☐Cut out 16 royal blue squares and 16 of pale blue, all measuring 5½in square. Cut 32 squares of iron-on interfacing to back the felt pieces, and press them in place.

☐Trace each of the 5 small shapes onto tracing paper and cut them out. Use the tracing paper patterns to cut 64 circles, 64 squares and 32 each of the other shapes from different colors of felt. Use fabric glue stick to apply 7 shapes to each pale blue square, as shown in the photograph. Stitch each shape in place; tie off ends on the WS.

☐Lay one piece of gray felt, right side up, on a large flat surface. Place pale and royal blue squares alternately in rows of eight, leaving a ¾in gap between each one and placing the outer squares 1⅜in from the edges of the gray square. Pin and baste, then machine stitch each square in place with a medium-size zigzag. Use red thread on the pale blue squares and yellow thread on the royal blue ones. Tie off ends.

☐Lay the appliquéd felt section on top of the other gray felt piece, WS together. Check with a right-angled triangle and yardstick that the felt edges are exactly square. Pin and straight stitch ¾in in from the edges of the two gray squares. Using pinking shears, trim ¼in from the edges to straighten and finish them.

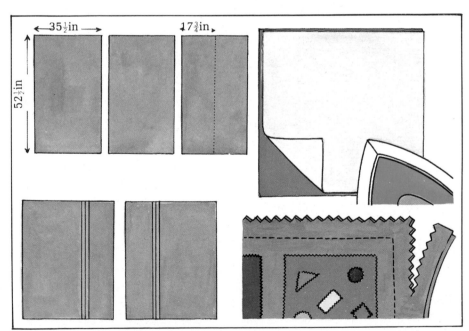

To make the counters
Make a tracing of the large circle (green and red are the same size), and cut out this pattern. Use it to cut 12 circles of red felt and 12 of green. With fabric glue stick, apply red circles to a double layer of green felt and green circles to a double layer of red felt. Pin through circles to hold lower layer in place, then cut fabric into squares (about 5in). Zigzag stitch around circle edges with blue thread. Trim the edges to make circles about 4¾in in diameter.

□Make a tracing of the yellow square and triangle and cut 12 each from yellow felt. Use fabric glue to apply the shapes to the center of the prepared circles. Zigzag stitch the triangles to the red circles and the squares to the green circles, using green and red thread respectively. Tie off all ends on the WS.

□Lightly steam press the circles to bring them back into shape (felt has a tendency to stretch), then pink around the edges.

□If the rug is to be used on a bare floor, coat part or all of the underside with latex glue to prevent slipping.

Rescue helicopter

Size
Approximately 12in long

Materials
12in of 36in-wide dark red fabric
8in of 36in-wide white fabric
Piece of gray felt 8 × 12in
Piece of brown felt 6½ × 12in
Scraps of felt in blue, navy blue, white and pale pink
Piece of cardboard 10in square
Stranded embroidery floss in brown and gold
Small amount of stuffing
12in of narrow cord for hanging
Scrap of nylon tape

Making the pattern — cutting out
Enlarge the pattern pieces for the helicopter as indicated on the graph, and cut them from the appropriate fabrics and cardboard (adjusting the sizes of the cardboard shapes as instructed). A seam allowance of ⅜in is included. Trace the full-size patterns for the ladder and figures onto tracing paper, then trace the individual sections onto the appropriate colors of felt, using dressmaker's carbon. Trace the whole outline of the rescuer onto gray felt to provide a base for the smaller pieces.
☐Cut two ¼in-wide strips of navy blue felt, each 9in long.
☐From brown felt cut 4 rectangles, 2 measuring 2¾ × 6¼in and 2 measuring 2¼in × 5in. Cut letters and insignia, if desired, from white, gray and navy felt.

To make the helicopter
Sew the pilot and the passenger to the windshield pieces (the passenger is to the right), using slipstitch or stab stitch and matching thread and positioning the pieces carefully. Embroider the features using 2 strands of brown floss and straight stitch and stem stitch as appropriate. Embroider the microphone in brown using satin stitch. Embroider gold braid using chain stitch; for the button work a French knot.
☐Placing RS together, join the right-hand windshield to the right-hand helicopter body and cabin base (longer curve of base is toward the back). Join the left-hand pieces in the same way. Stitch letters and insignia to the sides in the positions shown. Place the two sides together, RS facing, and stitch around the edges, leaving an opening along the cabin base. Turn the helicopter RS out.
☐Stitch navy blue borders around the windshield, trimming them as necessary. Fill the helicopter firmly with stuffing. Slipstitch the opening edges together.
☐Fold each brown felt rectangle in half lengthwise and stitch along long edges and across one end. Turn tubes RS out and fill them with stuffing. Close the ends. Stitch them together as shown, with the longer ones extending ⅝in at each end. Sew the center of each crosswise tube to the underside of the helicopter.
☐Slip the cardboard tail rotor blades between the two felt blade pieces. Stab stitch around the edges. Assemble the top rotor blades in the same way. Thread the cord through a small circle cut from felt and sew the circle to the top of the blades. Sew the blades firmly to the top and end of the helicopter.
☐Sew the individual sections of the rescuer onto the gray felt shape. Embroider the eyes using 2 strands of floss. Sew half of the nylon tape to the top rung of the ladder and the other half to the landing gear. Sew the rescuer to the ladder in the position shown.

TOP ROTOR BLADES

Cut 4 in gray felt,
2 in cardboard ⅛ in smaller
all round

Each square = 1in

WINDSCREEN
Cut 2, 1 in reverse,
in white fabric

HELICOPTER BODY
Cut 2, 1 in reverse,
in red fabric

CABIN BASE
Cut 2, 1 in reverse,
in red fabric

TAIL ROTOR BLADES
Cut 2 in felt,
1 in cardboard ⅛ in smaller

Ninepins

Size
Each ninepin is approximately $14\frac{1}{2}$in tall.

Materials
For 9 ninepins and ball
$\frac{7}{8}$in of 36in-wide felt in each of pink, pale blue, burgundy, lilac and peach
$\frac{3}{8}$yd of 36in-wide light gray felt
$\frac{1}{8}$yd of 36in-wide white felt
$\frac{1}{8}$yd of 36in-wide turquoise felt
Piece of cardboard about 12×36in
9 ready-made doll's faces
$3\frac{1}{2}$lb of stuffing
Scraps of yarn and fur fabric for hair
$2\frac{3}{4}$yd of gathered eyelet lace edging
24 small plain buttons
1 fancy button
Ribbons in colors matching and contrasting with the felt
Flower motifs

For the shoe
$1\frac{3}{8}$yd of 36in-wide turquoise felt
Scraps of peach and brown felt for windows and door
$\frac{3}{4}$yd of 36in-wide polyester batting
Piece of thick cardboard 12×36in
Small amount of black yarn and white lace edging
6 eyelets and eyelet pliers

Making the pattern — cutting out
Enlarge the pattern pieces for the ninepins as indicated on the graph, adding $\frac{3}{8}$in seam allowance to each piece. Cut them from the various pieces of felt, omitting the bonnet pieces for the boy ninepins. For each ninepin also cut 9 cardboard circles, $3\frac{3}{4}$in in diameter and 9 circles, in matching felt, 4in in diameter. Use the trace pattern, with $\frac{3}{8}$in seam allowance added, to cut 12 pieces of felt for the ball.
☐For the shoe, cut a pattern for the sole measuring $11\frac{3}{4} \times 24\frac{1}{2}$in .
☐Cut the pattern once from cardboard and twice from turquoise felt. For the side pieces cut 2 pieces of batting and 2 pieces of cardboard, each $31\frac{1}{2} \times 5$in. Cut 2 windows, $4\frac{3}{4} \times 3\frac{1}{4}$in , from peach felt and a door, $4\frac{3}{4} \times 4\frac{1}{4}$in, from brown felt. A seam allowance of $\frac{3}{8}$in is included.

To make the ninepins
Join the four main pieces of each ninepin along the side edges and turn them RS out. Clip the seam allowance around the edge of each felt circle and place each one over a cardboard base. Glue the clipped edges to the WS. Fill each ninepin firmly with stuffing, turn in the seam allowance around the lower edge and slipstitch it neatly to the base.
☐Make hair from yarn or fur fabric and glue it to the head of each ninepin. Use yarn for the old lady and four girls, fur fabric for the four boys. Glue one face to each skittle (match the chin to the center line of one panel).
☐Stitch a 12in-long piece of eyelet lace edging to the longest edge of each bonnet brim.
☐Pin, baste and stitch the back pieces to the bonnet sides, placing RS together and easing the curved edge to fit. Stitch an 7in piece of matching ribbon to the underside of each end of eyelet lace. Decorate each girl with 3 small buttons and a few flower motifs.
☐Place bonnets on ninepins and tie the ribbons under their chins.
☐Catch-stitch three short pieces of eyelet lace to the neck of the old lady to make a bodice. For the old lady's shawl, cut a triangle of gray felt measuring $10\frac{1}{2} \times 10\frac{1}{2} \times 15\frac{1}{4}$in . Wrap the shawl around the old lady, fold over the ends and fasten them with a small fancy button.

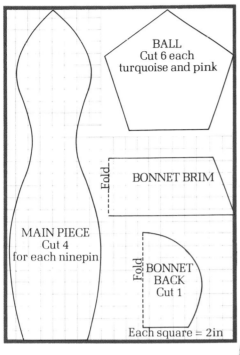

MAIN PIECE
Cut 4
for each ninepin

BALL
Cut 6 each
turquoise and pink

Fold

BONNET BRIM

Fold

BONNET
BACK
Cut 1

Each square = 2in

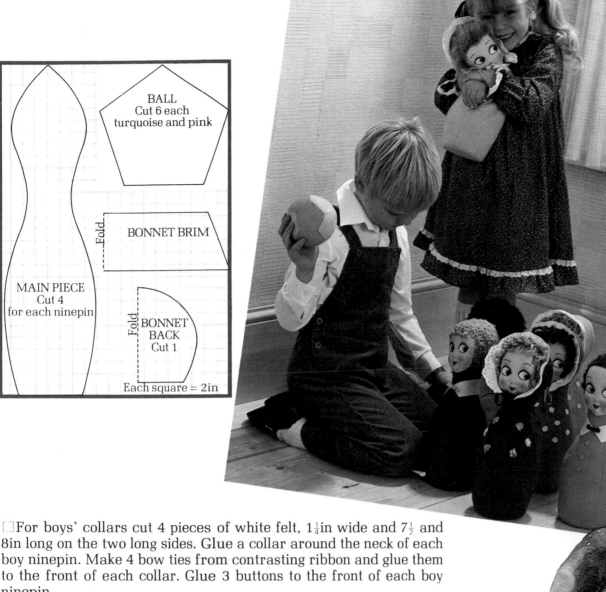

☐For boys' collars cut 4 pieces of white felt, $1\frac{1}{4}$in wide and $7\frac{1}{2}$ and 8in long on the two long sides. Glue a collar around the neck of each boy ninepin. Make 4 bow ties from contrasting ribbon and glue them to the front of each collar. Glue 3 buttons to the front of each boy ninepin.

To make the shoe
Clip the seam allowance on the edge of one felt sole and press it to the WS. Using fabric glue fix the turned edges to the WS of the cardboard sole.
☐Place a batting side piece on a cardboard piece and a felt piece on top.
☐Glue the felt seam allowances to the WS of cardboard. Slipstitch the side to the sole with cardboard sides facing. Assemble and attach the other side piece in the same way. Slipstitch the side pieces together at the heel. Glue remaining felt pieces to the inside of shoe.
☐Using an eyelet pliers, make 3 holes $\frac{3}{8}$in from the front edge of each side piece. Make a braid from 6 strands of black yarn and use this to lace the front edges together. Glue the door and windows to one side of the shoe shape and decorate them with scraps of yarn and lace as shown in the photograph.

To make the ball
Stitch all the patchwork shapes together, RS facing, to form a ball, leaving one seam open. Turn the ball RS out, fill it with stuffing and slipstitch the opening edges together.

Climbing net

Size
Approximately 1 × 2yd

Materials
33yd of flax hemp rope, 1¼in thick

To make the net
Cut the rope into 3 7¾yd lengths and one 9¾yd length. Use the latter as the top and sides of the frame. Tie the 7¾yd lengths to the center of the 9¾yd length using lark's head knots (Diagram **1**).

☐Construct the rest of the net using overhand knots (Diagram **2**); position the knots as you like, but remember to keep all holes large enough so that children's heads can slip in and out of them easily.

☐Attach the net to a tree or a metal swing frame with lengths of rope or metal karabiners (available from mountaineering suppliers).

1

2

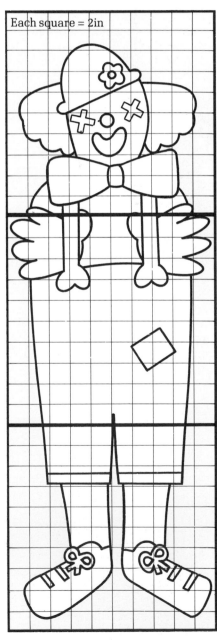

Each square = 2in

Materials
3 blocks of plastic foam, each
    $20 \times 20 \times 4$in
$2\frac{3}{4}$yd of 50in-wide dark blue
    poplin
Scraps of white and yellow felt for
    face, hands and head
Assorted printed fabrics for
    costume and features
$1\frac{5}{8}$yd of $\frac{5}{8}$in-wide nylon tape

Clown cushions

Making the pattern — cutting out
Enlarge the pieces for the appliqué as indicated on the graphs, and cut them from the appropriate fabrics. Add $\frac{3}{8}$in seam allowance to each edge along the dark lines. From poplin cut 3 $20\frac{3}{4}$in squares, 3 pieces $20 \times 20\frac{3}{4}$in, 12 strips $4\frac{3}{4} \times 20\frac{3}{4}$in and 3 strips $2\frac{1}{4} \times 20\frac{3}{4}$in. A seam allowance of $\frac{3}{8}$in is included.

To make the cushions
First stitch the appliqué pieces to the three $20\frac{3}{4}$in squares of poplin. Baste them in place, then work close zigzag stitch over the edges. Stitch a $4\frac{3}{4}$in-wide strip to each edge of each square, RS facing.
☐ Lay each piece RS up with upper edge at the top. Pin a $2\frac{1}{4}$in strip to the free edge of the $4\frac{3}{4}$in strip at the top of each cover, RS facing. Pin a $20 \times 20\frac{3}{4}$in piece to the bottom strip. Stitch all six seams.
☐ Turn under and press $\frac{3}{8}$in along the top edge of each $2\frac{1}{4}$in-wide strip. Turn and press $\frac{3}{8}$in to RS along the remaining $20\frac{3}{4}$in edge of the bottom piece. Cut a 20in length of nylon tape and stitch one half over the turned edge on strip and bottom piece, leaving $\frac{3}{8}$in of fabric free at each end.
☐ Fit the covers onto the foam blocks with WS out, and baste the corner seams. Baste the bottom piece to the remaining side edges. Lap the bottom piece over the strip, fasten the lengths of nylon tape and baste the side edges of the strip in place. Remove the covers and stitch the seams. Remove the basting, turn covers RS out and fit them to the foam blocks. Slipstitch the edges.

Ice-cream games

Size
Approximately 7in tall

Materials
For 2 sundaes and a cone
3 cardboard cones, 7in long with
2¾in diameters (from machine
knitting yarn, or made as
described below)
3 polystyrene balls with 2¼in
diameters
2⅞yd of medium thickness filler
cord, cut into 3 equal lengths
⅜yd of 36in-wide flannelette
3 large eyelets
Compass
For the knickerbocker glory
Piece of pink satin 12in square
Piece of white stretch terry cloth
6½in square
Scrap of white felt
Multicolored bugle beads
1 red wooden bead
Star-shaped sequins
Pale blue thread
Piece of cardboard 2¾in square
For the strawberry sundae
Piece of pale gray satin
12in square
Piece of pink fleecy fabric
6½in square
Piece of red printed fabric
12in square
Scrap of green felt
Small amount of cotton absorbent
Pale gray thread
Piece of cardboard 2¾in square
For the ice-cream cone
Piece of tan cotton satin 12in
square
Piece of white stretch terry cloth
6½in square
Scrap of brown felt
Tan thread
Brown bugle beads
1 red wooden bead

Making the pattern — cutting out
Enlarge the pattern pieces as indicated on the graph. If you are unable to obtain cones from machine knitting yarn, make them from thin cardboard, using the cone pattern given. Bend the cardboard to find the direction in which it bends more easily and position the pattern accordingly. Overlap the seam allowances and glue the long edges together. Trim off ⅜in at the lower end.

☐ Cut the pattern pieces from the appropriate fabrics. Cut a circle 2¾in in diameter from top fabric (satin and cotton satin), flannelette and felt for each ice cream. From ice cream fabric pieces (white terry cloth and pink fleece) cut circles measuring 6½in in diameter, using the compass. From the cardboard squares cut circles measuring 2½in in diameter.

☐ A seam allowance of ⅜in (⅛in on strawberries) is included.

To make the basic ice cream shapes
If you are using ready-made knitting yarn cones, snip off 1¼in from the end for the sundaes, so that the circular bases can be attached more easily.

☐ On each top fabric cone piece draw quilting lines, using a fabric marking pen and ruler. Place the lines diagonally, ⅝in apart. On the knickbocker glory and the ice cream cone, draw more lines in the other drection to form diamond shapes.

☐ Baste the top fabric shape, RS upward, to the flannelette piece, Work the quilting by machine, using straight stitch, or by hand, using small running stitches.

☐ Use matching thread to quilt the gray satin and the tan cotton, and use blue thread to quilt the pink satin. To avoid puckering the fabric, start stitching from the center and work outward.

☐ Stitch the top fabric and flannelette circles together around the edge with a close zigzag stitch to form the base.

☐ Wrap the quilted fabric around the cardboard cone, with flannelette side outward, and pin edges together along the seamline. Remove the cone and stitch the seam. Press the seam open and turn shape RS out. Slip the cone into the fabric cover and push the excess fabric through the hole in the pointed end. Clip the upper edge of the cover at frequent intervals and glue this to the inside of the cone with a little fabric glue. Fix a large eyelet through the center of each circular base; secure the circle to the base of the cone with a few firm stitches on the underside. Make a hole in the center of each cardboard circle, and glue these to the lower edge of each sundae base. Glue a circle of felt to the underside of the cardboard circle, first cutting a hole in the felt.

☐ Thread one end of the filler cord through the base of the cone, and make a large knot to prevent the cord from slipping through. Insert the other end of the cord as far as it will go into the hole on the polystyrene ball, and secure it with fabric glue.

☐ Work two rows of gathering stitches around the edge of each ice cream fabric circle. Place circle over ball and draw up stitches around filler cord. Fasten off securely.

To complete the knickerbocker glory
Sew bugle beads at random over the surface of the ice cream and top with a red bead cherry. Glue the melted ice cream shape to the edge of the cone. Sew a star sequin to each alternate diamond.

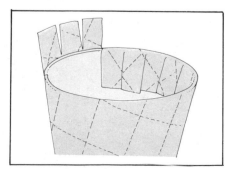

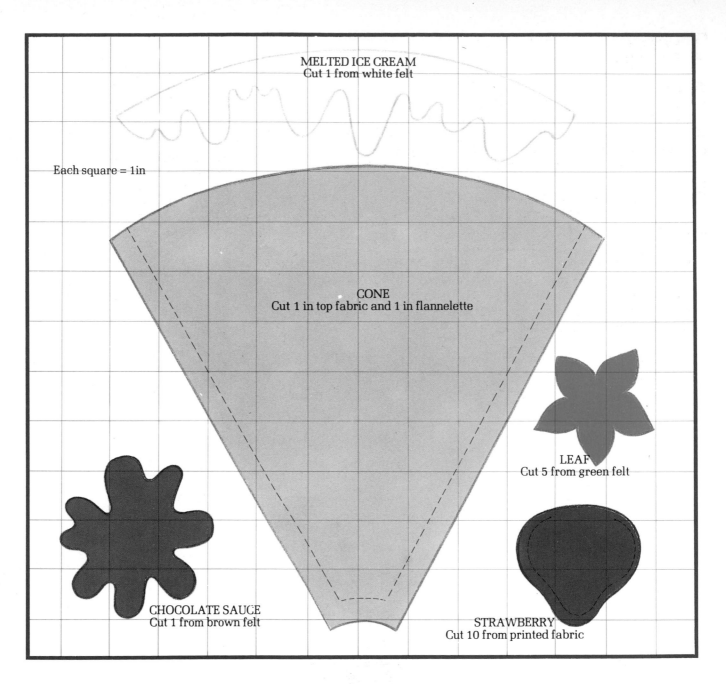

MELTED ICE CREAM
Cut 1 from white felt

Each square = 1in

CONE
Cut 1 in top fabric and 1 in flannelette

LEAF
Cut 5 from green felt

CHOCOLATE SAUCE
Cut 1 from brown felt

STRAWBERRY
Cut 10 from printed fabric

To complete the ice cream cone
Glue the chocolate sauce shape to the top of the ice cream. Sew brown bugle beads at random over the brown felt, and sew a red bead on top. If desired, a few felt chocolate sauce drops can be cut and glued to the cone.

To complete the strawberry sundae
Sew each pair of strawberry shapes together, RS facing, leaving a gap at the top. Turn strawberries RS out and fill them with absorbent cotton. Close the gap with a few stitches, pulling them to gather up fabric. Sew a leaf shape to the top of each strawberry. Glue the points to the strawberry with fabric glue. Sew the strawberries around the top of the sundae glass, varying the angle of the fruits for a natural effect.

116

Tutu

To make the tutu

Cut the net lengthwise into 3 equal pieces.

☐Using fabric marking pen, trace the horse design 8 times onto one strip of net, spacing them equally. Using 3 strands of floss, work the outline of the horses in chain stitch. For the saddles, reins and plumes, sew sequins and other trimmings to the net as shown in the photograph.

☐Place the net strips on top of one another, with the embroidered piece on top. Stitch them together along both short edges, ending the stitching 2¼in below the top edge. Stitch the layers together ¼in from the top edge, then 2in below the first stitching, to form a casing for elastic. Insert elastic through the casing, and try the skirt on the child. Cut off elastic to fit and sew the ends together firmly. Adjust the gathers.

☐For a sash, place ribbon around the waist, over the casing, and slipstitch it in place. Tie the long ends in a bow at the back.

Size
To fit a 6-7 year old

Materials
2¾yd of 54in-wide net
¾yd of ¾in-wide elastic
1 skein of black stranded
　embroidery floss
Sequins, feathers and other
　trimmings for the horse motif
1⅝yd of 1in-wide satin ribbon
　(optional)

Knitted cape

Size
To fit a 4-5 year old
Length: 21in

Materials
2oz of a silver metallic fingering
  yarn
23yd of silver tinsel (B)
Pair of size 17 knitting needles
Size H crochet hook
1⅝yd of 1½in-wide ribbon

Gauge
10 sts and 8 rows to 4in in g st on
Size 17

To make
Beg at neck edge, with A, cast on 40
sts.
Cont in g st (every row K). Work 2
rows.
**Tinsel row (WS) K to end,
weaving in B on every alt st.
Alternatively K to end with A and
then thread B through ridges of alt
sts on RS of work.
Work 1 row.**
Next row *K3, pick up loop between
last st worked and next st on LH
needle and K tbl — called "make 1"
—, K1, rep from * to end.
Work 1 row. Rep from ** to **
again.
Next row *K4, make 1, K1, rep from
* to end.
Work 1 row. Rep from ** to **
again.
Next row *K5, make 1, K1, rep from
* to end.
Cont to inc in this way on every foll
4th row until the row "*K13, make
1, K1, rep from * to end" has been
worked. 150 sts.
Work 1 row, then work the tinsel
row again.
Bind off.
Fold 2¼in at neck edge to WS and
catch down. Thread ribbon through
neckline casing, leaving long ends
to tie.

Front edgings
Using crochet hook and A, work into
front edge as foll:
Next row 1sc into first row end, (ch
4, 1sc into next row end) to end.

Horned hat

Size
To fit a 4-5 year old

Materials
Piece of blue felt 18in square
Piece of yellow felt 8½in square
¾yd-diameter button-covering form
¾in of 1in-wide grosgrain ribbon
Scrap of heavyweight interfacing
Small amount of stuffing

Making the pattern — cutting out
Enlarge the pattern pieces as indicated on the graph and cut
them from the appropriate fabrics. A seam allowance of
¼in is included.

To make the hat
Stitch the six blue panels together to form the crown. Turn
the crown RS out.
☐Cover the button form with yellow felt and it sew to the center
top of the cap.
☐Sandwich the interfacing visor piece between the two felt
pieces and topstitch round the outside edge. Place the center
of the visor on the center of one panel with RS together
and raw edges matching. Baste and stitch it in place. With the
visor turned upward, baste the ribbon around the lower edge; stitch
it in place. Turn the ribbon to the inside and slipstitch it to the WS
of cap.
☐Stitch each pair of horn pieces together, leaving the base open.
Stuff each horn firmly, turn under the raw edges and slipstitch horns
to each side of the cap.

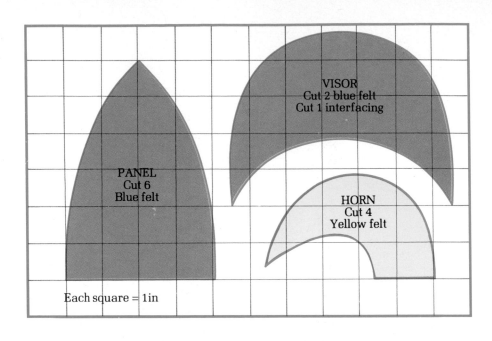

PANEL
Cut 6
Blue felt

VISOR
Cut 2 blue felt
Cut 1 interfacing

HORN
Cut 4
Yellow felt

Each square = 1in

Robin Hood costume

Size
To fit a 5-6 year old

Materials
⅞yd of 36in-wide green felt
Piece of red felt 10 × 18in
1⅞yd of 2in-wide red braid
⅞yd of 1in-wide red braid
1 green and 4 red pipe cleaners
2 red buttons

Making the pattern — cutting out
Enlarge the pattern pieces as indicated on the graph and cut them from the appropriate fabrics. Transfer all pattern markings. A seam allowance of ⅜in is included.

To make the outfit
Stitch the shoulder and side seams of the tunic. Press seams open and, using red thread, topstitch to each side of the seam. Topstitch around armholes and neck slit. Stitch the collar seams. Topstitch around scalloped edge of collar. Place WS of collar to RS of tunic and topstitch the collar in place around the neck.

☐Topstitch around the curved edge of the pocket flap. Make a buttonhole in the flap. Sew the pocket flap to the front of tunic in the position marked. Stitch along the fold of the pocket. Position the pocket just under the flap, and topstitch along the remaining three sides.

☐Topstitch around hem of tunic. Sew one button to the pocket. Sew another to the front opening of collar, and work a button loop on the other edge to correspond.

☐Cut a 28½in length of 1in-wide braid and topstitch it to the tunic in the position marked.

☐Topstitch along the scalloped edge of each armband. Stitch short ends together and topstitch to each side of the seam.

☐For the hat, stitch the two hat pieces together around the curved edge, starting and ending at the second fold line. Trim seam, clip curve and turn hat RS out. Stitch the remainder of the curved seam from the RS.

☐Turn up straight edge at first fold line, press and then topstitch along lower edge. Turn up at second fold line and press to form brim. Glue green pipe cleaner to center of feather; cut slits as shown on the pattern and glue feather to hat.

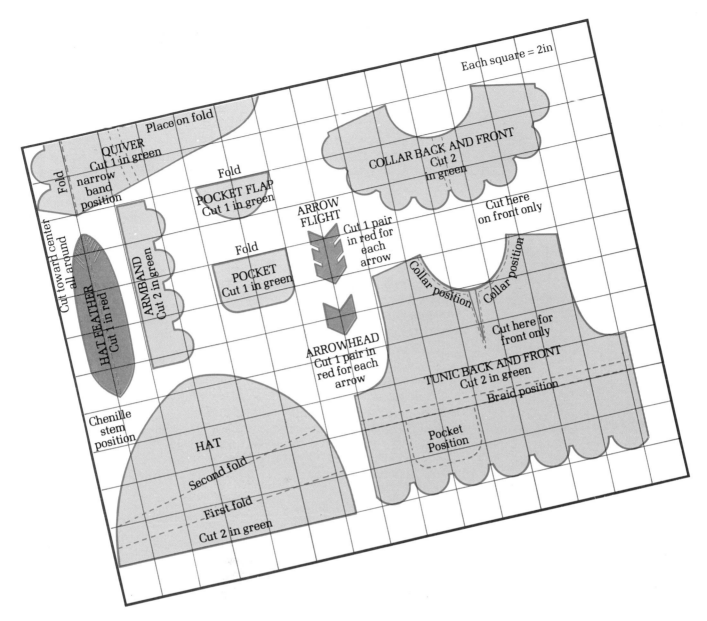

Each square = 2in

QUIVER
Cut 1 in green
narrow band position
Place on fold
Fold

Fold
POCKET FLAP
Cut 1 in green

ARROW FLIGHT
Cut 1 pair in red for each arrow

COLLAR BACK AND FRONT
Cut 2 in green

Cut here on front only

Cut toward center all around

HAT FEATHER
Cut 1 in red

ARMBAND
Cut 2 in green

Fold
POCKET
Cut 1 in green

ARROWHEAD
Cut 1 pair in red for each arrow

Collar position
Collar position

Cut here for front only

TUNIC BACK AND FRONT
Cut 2 in green

Braid position

Chenille stem position

HAT
Second fold
First fold
Cut 2 in green

Pocket Position

☐To make the quiver, topstitch along the scalloped edge and fold edge to RS. Stitch the narrower braid to the position marked. Fold the quiver in half lengthwise, RS facing, and stitch the long edges together.

☐Join the ends of the wide braid to make a ring. Sew this diagonally across the quiver, so that it can be hung around the chest.

☐To make an arrow, glue an arrowhead and flight to opposite ends of a red pipe cleaner. Spread fabric glue over one side of the arrowhead and flight. Place another arrowhead and flight over the first to enclose the ends of the wire. Stitch along each side of the wire before the glue dries. Make three more arrows in the same way.

Astronaut suit

Size
To fit any size child

Materials
Child's track suit
½yd of silver lamé, any width
½yd of 36in-wide red felt
Small amount of stuffing
Red rubber boots
Rhinestones to decorate boots
Cardboard box large enough to fit over head
Silver paper (preferably self-adhesive) to cover box
2 blocks of polystyrene packing
Plastic tubing about 32in long
2in strip of nylon tape

Cutting out
From silver lamé, cut 10 strips, each 3in wide and the appropriate length to go over shoulders and around sleeves and boots. From red felt cut one strip 2¼in wide and long enough to go around polystyrene blocks and overlap slightly. Use pinking shears for a decorative edge. Cut another strip, also 2¼in wide and long enough to go around front of body and fasten onto the space pack, plus a little extra for fastening.
☐ Cut small shapes as desired from lamé and felt to decorate the suit. Use the trace patterns provided below, or make your own.

To make the outfit
Fold each silver lamé strip in half lengthwise, RS facing, and stitch along the long edges and one end, taking ⅜in seam allowance. Turn tubes RS out and fill them — not too tightly — with stuffing. Turn in and slipstitch the ends. Sew tubes over the shoulders of the track suit and around the cuffs as shown in the photograph on page 119. Glue a tube around the top edge of each boot.
☐ Stitch the decorations to the track suit as shown in the photograph, or as desired. Glue rhinestones to the boots.
☐ Glue the two polystyrene blocks together. Wrap the red felt strip around the blocks and glue it in place.
☐ Cut the belt piece into two lengths — one short and one long (see the photograph). Stitch one end of each to the pack strap. Stitch fastening tape to the free ends for the belt closing.
☐ Cut a hole in the polystyrene and insert one end of plastic tubing into it.
☐ For the helmet, remove opening flaps of the cardboard box, then cut a hole about 7in in diameter in one adjacent side. Use the cut-out circle as a pattern to draw a circle the same size on red felt. Draw another circle about ¾in outside the first one, forming a ring; cut out the ring.
☐ Cover the box with silver paper, gluing it in place if it is not self-adhesive. Glue the red felt ring to the opening edges. Punch a small hole in one side of the box for inserting the other end of the plastic tubing when helmet is worn.

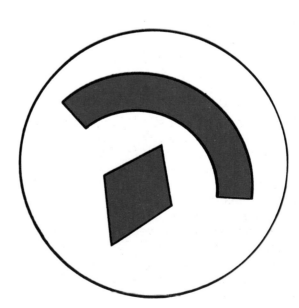

Kimono

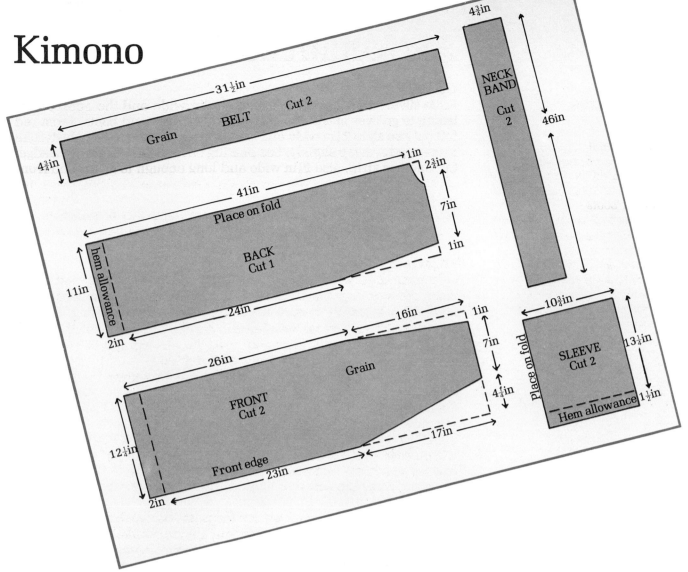

Making the pattern — cutting out

Following the measurement diagram, draw the pattern pieces. A seam allowance of ⅜in is included. Cut the pieces from the main fabric and fronts, back and sleeves from lining fabric.

To make the kimono

Join the shoulder seams, RS facing, on the main kimono pieces. Match the center of each sleeve to the shoulder seam and stitch the sleeves to the front and back. Stitch the underarm and side seams.
□Join the main lining pieces in the same way.
□Press 2in to the WS on the hem and 1½in on the lower edge of sleeve on both kimono and lining. Place the lining inside the kimono, WS facing, and slipstitch them together at hem and sleeve edges.
□Join the two sections of the neckband to make one long piece. Press ⅜in to WS on all edges. Fold band in half, WS facing; press.
□With RS together, place the center of one of the long edges of the neckband at the center back neck. Baste the band to the front and neck edges. Stitch it in place, beginning at the hem on one side and working around to the hem on the other side. Fold the band to the inside and slipstitch over the first stitching. Slipstitch ends together.
□Join the sections of the belt to make one long piece. Fold the band in half lengthwise with RS together, and stitch along the length. Turn belt RS out. Trim the ends into "V" shapes, turn in the raw edges and slipstitch them together. Sew a tassel to each end.

Size
To fit a 7-12 year old

Materials
3¼yd of 36in-wide silky fabric
3¼yd of 36in-wide lining fabric in a
  contrasting color
2 decorative tassels

Big Top

Size
Approximately 47in high

Materials
$3\frac{1}{4}$yd of 57in-wide ticking
$3\frac{5}{8}$yd of 36in-wide unbleached
  muslin
$\frac{1}{4}$yd of 54in-wide fabric in each of
  red, blue, green and yellow
11 curtain rings 1in in diameter
13yd of thin, strong rope
1yd of woven tape
$1\frac{3}{8}$yd length of 1in-diameter dowel
12in length of $\frac{1}{4}$in -diameter dowel
8 skewers or tent pegs

Making the pattern — cutting out
Make a pattern for the roof sections: draw a horizontal line 20in long and, at its center, a vertical line $38\frac{3}{4}$in long, forming an inverted "T" shape. Join the ends of the lines to form a triangle. In the same way, make a triangular pattern for the flags, with a base and height of $7\frac{1}{2}$in .
☐Cut the large triangle 8 times from ticking, aligning the center line with a stripe of the fabric. Using the small pattern, cut 6 pairs of triangles from each piece of red, blue, green and yellow felt.
☐Cut the unbleached muslin crosswise into 5 $25\frac{1}{2}$in strips.

To make the tent
Stitch the muslin pieces together along their 2in edges, taking $\frac{3}{8}$in seam allowance, to form one long strip. Turn and stitch a $\frac{3}{8}$in hem on one long and one short side of the strip.
☐Join the triangular sections, RS facing, along all the long sides, to form the roof.
☐Pin the unhemmed long edge of the muslin side piece to the raw edge of the roof, RS facing and with the hemmed short edge of the muslin at the center of one triangular section. Cut off the excess muslin at the other end, leaving $\frac{3}{8}$in for turning under. Stitch this side hem, then turn up and stitch the lower hem of the side piece.
☐Stitch each pair of flag pieces together, RS facing, along their longer sides. Turn flags RS out. Insert each flag between the side and roof of the tent, 3 to each triangular section, with raw edges matching. Baste and stitch the seam, taking $\frac{3}{8}$in seam allowance.
☐Pull the top of the roof into a point where the seams meet and cut off $\frac{3}{8}$in to make a hole. Place a curtain ring on the WS of the fabric, encircling the hole. Clip the edges of the fabric as necessary and turn them over the ring; overcast them firmly in place.
☐Sew a curtain ring to each side of the tent entrance, about 9in in from the edge and 15in up from the bottom. Cut the woven tape in half and sew each piece to one corner of the tent. Thread tapes through rings to tie back opening edges.
☐Sew the remaining eight curtain rings to the edge of the roof as shown in the photograph.
☐To make the center pole, drill a hole in one end of the long piece of dowel. Apply glue to one end of the short piece and insert it into the hole. Stick the pole into the ground and slip the tent over it.
☐Cut the rope into 8 59in lengths and tie each one through one of the rings. Secure the other end to a skewer or tent peg inserted in the ground at the correct distance to pull the tent out to its full width.
☐Decorate the top of the tent with streamers or balloons, or make a flag from bright-colored fabric.

Toys for learning

Mastering facts and skills can be fun with the aid of colorful, sturdy toys like the ones in this section. Tying a shoe, for example, is easier for little hands if they can start with a big shoe such as the one on page 136. Coping with zippers, snaps and other fastenings becomes a game with a "Learner's laundry bag." A "Numbers game" provides an opportunity to develop motor skills. Telling the time is much more entertaining when the toy clock has two frisky mice to run up its sides. A splendid Noah's ark will serve not only to illustrate the Bible story but also to introduce different types of animals and to help small hands learn dexterity as they place the animals inside it.

Numbers game

Size
53 × 35in

Materials
3yd of 36in-wide unbleached muslin
½yd of bright-colored printed
  fabric, any width, for binding
Scraps of assorted other printed
  fabrics

Making the patterns — cutting out
For the binding cut enough 2¼in-wide bias strips from the main printed fabric (cut at a 45° angle to the selvage) to make up a length of 5½yd.
☐Draw and cut paper patterns for the shapes and numbers — 1 to 10. The numbers should be about 5in tall; the shapes should be in roughly decreasing order of size — the largest being the square for one point and the smallest the O for the ten points. Draw only the outer edges of the shapes — not the inner ones. Cut each number and shape from printed fabric.
☐Also from printed fabrics cut 6 strips on the straight grain measuring 2¼ × 17in.

To make the game
Fold the unbleached muslin in half widthwise and baste the edges together. Stitch the bias strips together on the straight grain to make up the length. Press under ⅜in on both long edges of the strip, then fold the strip in half lengthwise and press again. Place the strip over the edge of the muslin and baste, mitering the corners. Topstitch all around.
☐Tack the various shapes on to the calico as shown in the photograph, remembering to leave space for the numbers. Stitch around the edge of each shape, using a close zigzag stitch. Stitch again, about 1¼in in from the first stitching. Cut out the printed fabric and muslin close to the inner line of stitching. Baste and stitch the numbers next to the corresponding shapes.
☐Press under ⅜in on all four edges of each tie strip. Fold the strips in half lengthwise and press again. Topstitch close to all edges. Stitch the strips in pairs to the top edge of the game.

Weather story clock

Making the pattern — cutting out
Enlarge the pattern pieces as indicated on the graph and cut them from the appropriate fabrics, adding ¼in seam allowance to the pieces of the summer section. Trace the arrow pattern and cut it twice from red felt.

Making the clock
Using a pencil and yardstick, divide the piece of interfacing into 6 sections. Mark a ¾in border around the edges.
☐Stitch and glue the fabric pieces and ribbons to the background. For the sun section, first stitch the terry cloth piece to the background, using straight stitch, then apply the ribbons, using straight stitch, zigzag or slipstitch as desired. Cut a circle of batting and glue it to the position for the sun. Cover it with circles of orange and yellow felt (with the edges pinked if desired), baste them in place and straight stitch as shown in the photograph.
☐For the cloud section, fit the individual pieces together, baste them in place and work around the edges with close zigzag stitch.

Each square = 2in

Size
18in square

Materials
For sun section
Piece of gold-colored terry cloth
  8in square
Scraps of felt in bright orange and
  yellow
Assorted gold and orange ribbons
Scrap of thin polyester batting
For cloud section
Scraps of pale blue, gray and white
  fabric
For storm section
Scraps of dark gray, medium-gray
  and white fabric
Silver embroidery thread
Gray buttonhole twist
For summer section
Scraps of pale blue, pale green and
  tan fabric
For winter section
Piece of white felt 8in square
Scraps of red and brown felt
Scrap of thin polyester batting
Small amount of brown yarn
For autumn section
Piece of dark green fabric 8in
  square
Scraps of felt in brown, three
  shades of green and two shades
  of orange
For the board
Piece of heavy non-woven
  interfacing 18in square
Piece of stiff cardboard 18in
  square
2¼yd of ¾in -wide rainbow-striped
  ribbon
2¼yd of ¾in -wide braid for edges
Scrap of red felt
⅝in of nylon tape

☐For the storm section, apply main pieces as for the cloud section. Using gray buttonhole twist, work lines of straight stitch over lower part. In between, work large running stitches with silver thread. Glue lightning flash in place.

☐For the summer section, first turn under ⅛in around the edge of the tree foliage, left side of trunk, hill and all edges of fence, and baste edges in place. Position the pieces within the section with edges overlapping as shown in the photograph, and slipstitch them together, catching in the interfacing occasionally.

☐For the winter section, stitch the felt triangle to the interfacing, then stitch the snowman in place with an open zigzag stitch, first inserting a piece of batting underneath. Glue on features and accessories. Bind a few strands of yarn to form the broom and sew them in place.

☐For the autumn section, first stitch dark green fabric to the background. Glue the tree in place, then apply leaves with short lines of straight stitch down the centers.

☐Slipstitch the rainbow-striped ribbon over the dividing lines. Glue the panel firmly to the cardboard. Glue braid around the edges, mitering the corners. Topstitch the two arrow pieces together. Sew half of the nylon tape to the arrow and the other half to the center of the clock.

Hickory dickory

Size
30in tall × 10in wide × 4¾in deep

Materials
For the clock
Piece of foam rubber the same size
   as clock
1⅜yd of 36in-wide light blue felt
¼yd of 36in-wide wide royal blue
   felt
Piece of yellow felt 12in square
Piece of red felt 4 × 2in
2 safety eyes 1¼in in diameter, or
   eyes made from scraps of black
   and white felt
1 skein of black stranded
   embroidery floss
Piece of balsa wood 8 × ⅝ × ¼in
Emery board
1 black double screw-in upholstery
   button
⅜yd of ⅝in-wide yellow velvet
   ribbon
3½yd of gold braid ⅝in-wide
3in of dark blue or black nylon
   fastening tape (Velcro)
Piece of thick cardboard
15¾in square
2¼yd navy Russian braid
Small can of non-toxic black enamel
   paint
For three mice
Piece of orange-brown felt 9in
   square
Piece of brown felt 9 × 3in
Small amount of stuffing
9 small beads for eyes and noses
A few strands of horsehair or paint-
   brush bristles for whiskers
5in of nylon tape

Making the pattern — cutting out
Enlarge the pattern pieces for the clock face and door and cut them from the appropriate fabrics. Use the measurement diagram to cut the pieces for the sides, base and top. Use the trace patterns to cut the other pieces. Cut the balsa wood hands with a sharp craft knife. Trim the pointed end of one hand to make the hour hand. Smooth the edges with the emery board. Transfer all pattern markings. A seam allowance of ½in is included on the clock pieces where necessary; ¼in seam allowance is included on the mouse pieces.
☐ If the foam has not already been cut to shape, make a template by trimming off seam allowances from the clock case pattern. Draw around the template onto the foam, then cut out shape, using a sharp knife or hacksaw.

To make the clock
Join the sides, top and base of the clock along the short edges, forming a ring. Join the case back to the sides, RS facing, matching corners to seams.
☐ For the door, cut a piece of cardboard slightly smaller than the door pattern and insert this between the two pieces of royal blue felt. Stitch all around with a zigzag stitch. Trim the edges of the door with gold braid, stitching it on either by hand or by machine, using straight stitch.
☐ On the clock face, draw the numerals, using fabric marking pen. Outline them with a double row of backstitch, using 3 strands of embroidery floss. Stitch the mouth in place with a zigzag stitch, and slipstitch the eyes in place if using felt ones.
☐ Cut a circle of cardboard slightly smaller than the clock face and place this under the felt face. If using safety eyes, make holes through felt and cardboard, and press the eyes through, snapping washers on the underside. Make a hole in the center of the circle for the upholstery button and screw. Zigzag stitch the clock face to the clock front.
☐ Apply at least three coats of paint to each hand. When hands are dry, bore a hole at each pivot point. Insert the upholstery button through the hands, with the minute hand on top, then through the clock face. Screw it firmly in place.
☐ Straight stitch the yellow braid to the clock front, ⅜in in from edge and straight across the top. Miter the corners as you go. Straight stitch 2 lines of Russian braid to the outline of the pendulum case.

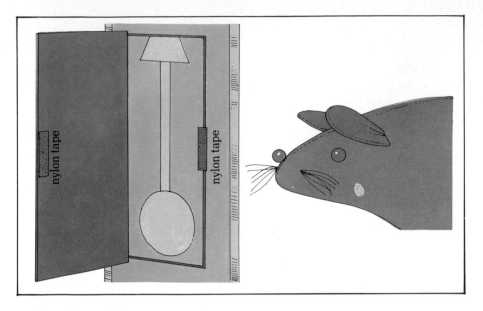

☐For the pendulum, first stitch the velvet ribbon to the vertical line and trim off the excess. Cover the raw ends with the two yellow felt pendulum pieces and zigzag stitch them in place.

☐Place the door over the Russian braid, and stitch down the left-hand side, inside the gold braid, using a fairly wide, closely-spaced zigzag stitch. To close the door, stitch one half of the nylon fastening tape (Velcro) under the right-hand side of the door, and its matching piece over the Russian braid on the pendulum case.

☐Place the foam inside the clock case. Pin the seam allowance on all sides to the top of the foam. On the top piece turn the seam allowance under the braid and pin it in place. Slipstitch the top to the sides of the case, removing pins as you go.

To make the mice

Placing RS together, stitch two body sections together from A to B, around the nose and back, leaving the base open and inserting the tail just above it. Turn body RS out. Hand-sew the base to the lower edges, leaving a gap for stuffing. Fill the body with stuffing and slipstitch the opening edges together.

☐Pleat each ear slightly and hand-sew it to the head, so that it turns forward. Stitch 3 beads onto each mouse — 2 for the eyes and one for the nose. Thread a needle with horsehair and push through behind the nose to make whiskers. Secure the whiskers carefully.

☐Separate the nylon tape and stitch a 1½in piece of the stiff side to the base. This should cling easily to the felt.

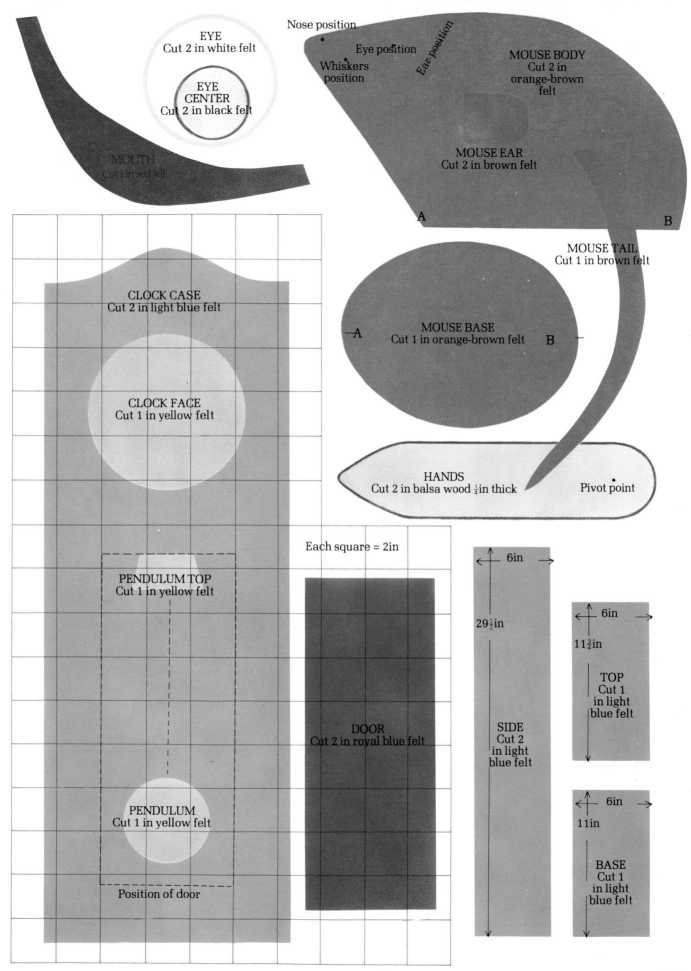

EYE
Cut 2 in white felt

EYE
CENTER
Cut 2 in black felt

Nose position

Eye position

Whiskers
position

Ear position

MOUSE BODY
Cut 2 in orange-brown
felt

MOUSE EAR
Cut 2 in brown felt

MOUTH
Cut 1 in red felt

A

B

MOUSE TAIL
Cut 1 in brown felt

MOUSE BASE
Cut 1 in orange-brown felt

A

B

CLOCK CASE
Cut 2 in light blue felt

CLOCK FACE
Cut 1 in yellow felt

HANDS
Cut 2 in balsa wood $\frac{1}{4}$in thick

Pivot point

Each square = 2in

6in

PENDULUM TOP
Cut 1 in yellow felt

$29\frac{1}{2}$in

6in

$11\frac{3}{4}$in

TOP
Cut 1
in light
blue felt

DOOR
Cut 2 in royal blue felt

SIDE
Cut 2
in light
blue felt

PENDULUM
Cut 1 in yellow felt

Position of door

6in

11in

BASE
Cut 1
in light
blue felt

133

Rug dice

Size
Approximately 13 x 13 x 13in

Materials
Rug canvas with 12 threads,
approximately, to 4in: a
rectangle 49 threads wide and
168 threads long and 2 squares,
each 49 threads wide and 48
threads deep
Packs of cut rug yarn pieces (240
2¾in lengths): 34 packs in main
color and 3 packs in each of 3
contrasting colors
Latch hook
Linen tent thread
Curved upholstery needle
Polyurethane foam cube
12½ x 12½ x 12½in
Masking tape
Graph paper (small scale)

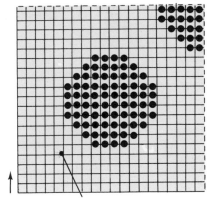

Diagram A   Starting knot

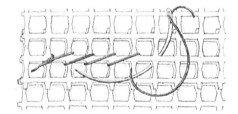

Making the pattern
On the sheet of graph paper draw the pattern for the entire cube
following the arrangement given in Diagram C and using the detailed
representations of the work in diagrams A and B as a guide in
placing the dots. These diagrams each show one corner of a square
after the cube is completed: four rows on each edge of the long strip
and the two side pieces are worked after the edges are stitched
together. Diagram A is the basis for the "1" square (with the edge
dots omitted), for the "4" (with the central dot omitted) and for the
"2," "3" and "5"; Diagram B is used for the "6."

To make the cube
Bind the canvas edges with masking tape to prevent fraying and
catching on clothes. Begin with the long strip. Count 8 threads up
from the lower edge and 8 spaces in from the left-hand edge, and
work the first knot, in main color, on the 9th horizontal thread and
the 9th vertical space. This first knot is marked on Diagram A. Work
31 more knots across the canvas, thus leaving the last 8 spaces
unworked. (For the method of working a knot see the illustrations
below right.)

☐Work 10 more rows in main color. On the 11th row from the
starting point begin the central dot, following your diagram. After
completing the dot, work 15 rows in the main color to complete the
first face of the cube.

☐Mark the canvas on each side of the work to denote the edge, then
continue working the other squares. On the last square (the "3"),
leave the last 4 threads of the diagram (the last 8 of the canvas)
unworked, to correspond with the starting edge. You should have
152 rows completed (40 on each inner square and 36 each on the
outer squares).

☐Now work the two sides, leaving 8 horizontal threads and 8
vertical spaces unworked all around and starting with the knots
marked on diagrams A and B.

☐Join the squares to the rectangle along the sides marked x-x and
y-y, using linen tent thread and a curved needle, as shown, and
overlapping the canvas edges so that each side gains 4 knots. There
will be grooves of 8 unworked strands between each of the sides.
Remove the masking tape and trim the edges slightly if necessary so
that they lie smooth. Work the knots over the double canvas threads,
still working in the same direction, so that the pile slants correctly.

☐Join the seams marked a-x and b-y, as before. (In some cases,
minor variation in vertical and horizontal spacing of canvas threads
may make it necessary to work an extra row in order to match the
sides accurately for a perfect square.) When working the knots,
make sure to work in the same direction as the rest of the knots on
that side.

☐Join the sides c-x and d-y, and complete the knotting on these sides
through the double canvas.

☐Slip the foam cube into the open edges. You may find this easier if
you first insert the cube into a thin plastic bag, as the foam tends to
catch on the canvas. When the cube is inserted, pull out the bag.

☐Join the remaining three edges and work knots as before to
complete the cube.

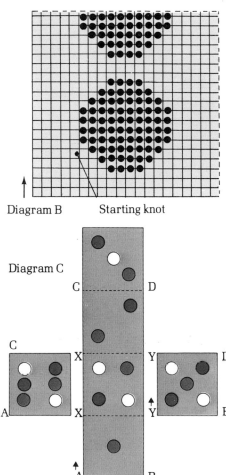

Diagram B Starting knot

Diagram C

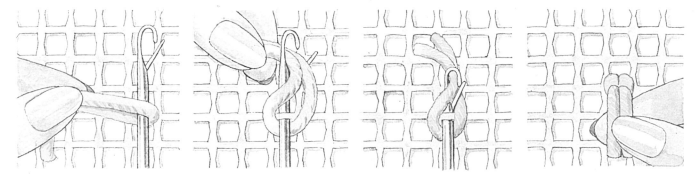

1 Fold the piece of rug yarn in half and slip it over the hook as shown. Holding the two ends firmly between index finger and thumb, slip the hook under one horizontal canvas thread.
2 Bring the two yarn ends into the hook as shown.
3 Pull the hook back toward you, under the canvas thread. As you do so, the latch will close over the yarn ends, pulling them through the loop.
4 Pull the two ends firmly to ensure a tight knot.

Super sneaker

Size
15in long

Materials
$\frac{3}{8}$yd of 36in-wide green canvas
$\frac{3}{8}$yd of 36in-wide white canvas
Piece of white stretch terry cloth
 8in square
$\frac{1}{4}$in-diameter eyelet pliers and 8
 eyelets
$1\frac{1}{8}$in of $1\frac{1}{2}$in-wide striped grosgrain
 ribbon
$1\frac{1}{8}$yd of 1in-wide red bias binding
Small amount of fusible webbing
Piece of stiff cardboard 6×16in
7oz of stuffing
Large decorative shoelace

Making the pattern — cutting out

Enlarge the pattern pieces as indicated on the graph and cut them from the appropriate fabrics. Also cut the sole from cardboard, preferably using a craft knife. Transfer pattern markings.

To make the shoe

Working on RS, baste the toe cap to tongue, ovelapping the tongue by $\frac{1}{4}$in. Sew cap in place using red thread and a closely-spaced zigzag stitch. Bind end of tongue with bias binding.

☐Join heel seam on side pieces, with RS facing, taking $\frac{1}{4}$in seam allowance. Bond heel pieces and side flashes to sides with fusible webbing, following the manufacturer's instructions. Cover the raw edges with closely-spaced red zigzag stitching. Work 2 more lines of zigzag down center of heel piece, spacing them $\frac{3}{8}$in apart.

☐Bind curved edges of sides with red bias binding. Following manufacturer's instructions, insert 4 eyelets along each side, as shown in the photograph. Position sides over tongue and toe section and baste them in place. Using red thread, zigzag stitch along marked line on each side.

☐Using matching thread, and starting at the heel, topstitch grosgrain ribbon around lower edge, overlapping the ends by $\frac{1}{4}$in. Sew the sole to the ribbon, RS facing, taking $\frac{3}{8}$in seam allowance.

☐Insert cardboard sole. Fill shoe firmly with stuffing. Insert and tie shoelace. Cut a 7in-diameter circle from stretch terry cloth. Tuck the edges inside top of shoe and sew them over stuffing.

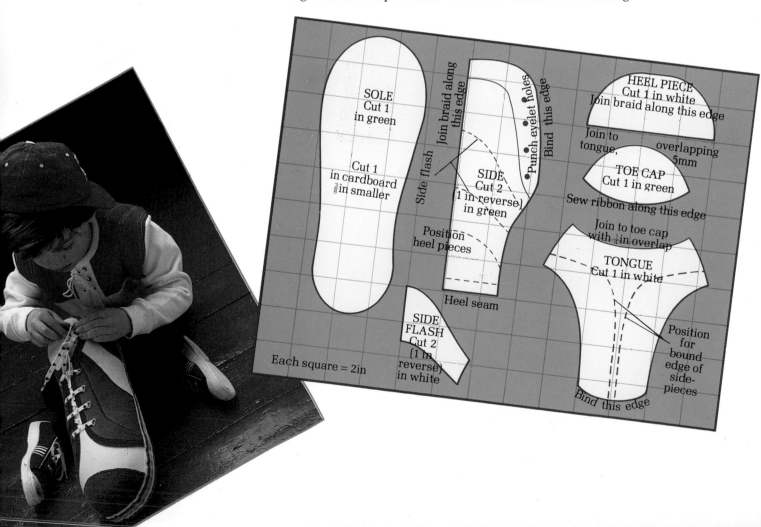

Furry friend glove puppet

Size
Approximately 10in long

Materials
Piece of fur fabric 10 × 14in
Piece of beige felt 8 × 10in
Scraps of white, black and brown
    felt
Small amount of stuffing

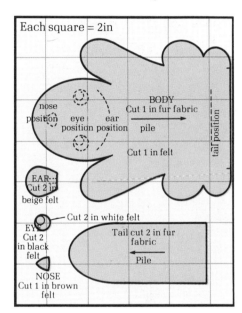

Each square = 2in

nose
position
eye
position
ear
position

BODY
Cut 1 in fur fabric
pile

tail position

Cut 1 in felt

EAR
Cut 2 in
beige felt

Cut 2 in white felt

EYE
Cut 2
in black
felt

Tail cut 2 in fur
fabric
Pile

NOSE
Cut 1 in brown
felt

Making the pattern — cutting out
Enlarge the pattern as indicated on the graph and cut it from the appropriate fabrics, making sure to align the pieces correctly with the fur pile, as marked. A seam allowance of $\frac{3}{8}$in is included.

To make the puppet
Make a small pleat at the base of each ear and sew ears to fur fabric at the positions marked. Sew eyes and nose in place. Sew body pieces together, pile side inward, leaving an opening between A and B. Clip the curved edges. Hem remaining fur fabric edge. Turn puppet RS out. Sew tail pieces together, with pile side inward. Clip curves and turn tail RS out. Fill the tail with stuffing, turn in the opening edges and slipstitch them together. Sew the tail to the body.

Mobile

Size
Most of the characters are about 5½in tall.

Materials
¼yd of 36in-wide printed fabric
10 pieces of felt, 9in square, in assorted colors (see patterns)
Scraps of blue and white felt
Gold-colored sequin waste for cheese
Bits of pink velvet and satin ribbon and narrow lace edging
Black embroidery floss
Tiny gold beads for dog's collar, sequins for eyes, a jingle bell, 2 small buttons
Bit of red yarn
4 pipe cleaners
Lurex ® yarn for embroidery on owl's wings
Nylon whiskers
Small amount of stuffing
Wire ring 6in in diameter
7 small metal rings
Transparent nylon thread
¼yd of 36in-wide thick polyester batting
1yd of cord
2 medium-sized buttons

Making the pattern — cutting out
Enlarge the pattern pieces as indicated and cut them from felt in the colors shown, noting that all main shapes are to be cut twice. For each character cut one shape the full size (e.g. in red for the man, green for the woman), to which other pieces can be glued or stitched.

To make the mobile characters
Man Glue the face and other pieces to the main shapes; sew on buttons. Stitch the front and back together, WS facing, close to the edges, using small running stitches. Leave an opening in the seam. Insert stuffing and stitch the opening edges together. Cut a ⅜ × 5½in strip of felt and sew it around neck to form a scarf.

Woman Make the shape as for man. Trim the apron and dress neckline with lace. Tie 6in of satin ribbon around the waist.

Dog Glue ears and eyes to face. Using black embroidery floss, embroider features and paws with satin and stem stitch. Make the shape as for man. Decorate a ¼in × 5½in strip of felt with gold beads and sew it around neck to form collar. Cut a 4in piece of pipe cleaner, fold a strip of black felt around it and stitch the side edges together. Curl tail around a pencil and sew it in place.

Owl Using Lurex ® yarn and fly stitch (individual chain stitches left open at the top), embroider wings and one tail piece. Glue beak in place and sew on sequins for eyes. Make the shape as for man. Fold a 4¼in piece of pipe cleaner into a "V" shape. Join tail pieces with pipe cleaner sandwiched in between; sew tail in place.

Cat Sew paws and ears to front shape, glue eyes (using sequins for pupils) and nose to front and embroider mouth. Make the shape as for man. Sew bell to 6in of velvet ribbon and sew it around neck to form collar. Make and attach tail as for dog. Attach whiskers as shown.

Mouse Sew sequins in place for eyes. Make the shape as for man. Make and attach tail as for dog. Make a pompon (see page 98) and attach to tip of nose.

Cheese Tack sequin waste on to one side; make up shape as for man.

Each square = 1in

138

To assemble the mobile

Bind the wire ring with strips of batting. Press under a ⅜in hem on both long edges. Fold the fabric in half lengthwise and press again. Work a line of gathering stitches close to both long sides — the single fold and the turned-in edges. Place the fabric strip around the padded ring, with the single folded edge on the bottom. Pull up the gathers to fit and fasten thread securely. Repeat with the other edge. Stitch the fabric ends together.

☐ Sew cord to top of ring at each side. Sew on two buttons to cover the cord ends.

☐ Attach a metal loop to the top of each shape and suspend them from the ring with varying lengths of nylon thread.

(Note: these characters make excellent individual finger puppets.)

Learner's laundry bag

Size
Approximately 26 × 24in

Materials
1½yd of 36in-wide denim
1½yd of 36in-wide cotton fabric for
   lining
Piece of white cotton fabric
   16 × 24in
Scraps of assorted fabrics as shown
   in photograph
¼yd of medium-weight polyester
   batting
1½yd of heavyweight sew-in
   interfacing
Piece of fusible webbing about
   8 × 24in
¾yd of filler cord
¼yd of narrow beige ribbon for
   "clothespins"
Nylon tape (Velcro)
2 small slide stocking fasteners
4in zipper
Shoelace
6 small eyelets
Small button
Small snap
Bits of lace edging and narrow
   ribbon

Making the pattern — cutting out
From denim cut 2 pieces, each 25 × 32in. Also cut 2 straps, 2¾ × 8in. Cut 4in off the long edge of the piece of lining fabric to make a piece 32in wide.

☐Enlarge the pattern as indicated on the graph. The clothes on the line, the girl's clothes and the washing in the basket can be sketched in roughly, as they are not cutting patterns.

☐Using the graph pattern as a guide, draw separate patterns for the clothes, adding ⅜in to all edges for turning under. (The clothes need have only one side; though you can, of course, make real miniature clothes if you prefer.) Cut all appliqué pieces and clothes from appropriate fabrics, cutting the cloud (in one piece) twice from white cotton. Cut the cloud pattern once from batting; trim the edges slightly.

To make the bag
Press under ⅜in on one short edge of each denim piece and topstitch hem in place.

☐Using fusible webbing, following the manufacturer's instructions, bond all the shaded appliqué pieces, except the basket, to one piece of denim in the correct positions. Slip a bit of lace edging under the edge of the girl's skirt before bonding. Do not bond upper ends of poles. Set the machine to a close zigzag stitch and stitch around all the bonded appliqué pieces. Leave a gap unstitched above and below pole crossbars. Work zigzag stitch over the basket to form a pattern, then stitch it to the background along the side and bottom edges. Baste the batting and cotton cloud pieces together, with batting in the middle. Baste clouds to denim in the position shown, then zigzag stitch close to the edges all around. Trim away any excess fabric, being careful not to cut the stitches.

☐Make the separate clothes as shown in the photograph, adding trimmings and fastenings as appropriate.

☐Cut the beige ribbon and the nylon tape into 8 pieces, each ⅞in long. Overcast the two sides of each piece of the tape at one short end to form a "hinge." Place the fuzzy side of the fastening under the shoulder of a garment and place a strip of ribbon on top. Backstitch through all three layers as shown in the photograph.

☐Wrap each end of the filler cord around the poles as shown and sew it firmly in place.

☐Cut heavyweight interfacing the same size as bag pieces. Baste the interfacing around the raw edges and slipstitch it to the hem across the top. Place the two bag pieces togther, RS facing, and stitch them together, taking ⅜in seam allowance. Trim the interfacing close to the stitching and turn the bag RS out.

☐Turn under and press ⅜in on long edges of straps. Fold straps in half lengthwise, WS facing, and topstitch along both edges. Baste them to the WS of bag as shown in the photograph, about 2in in from each side.

☐Fold the lining piece in half widthwise, RS facing, and stitch along both long sides, taking ⅜in seam allowance. Turn ⅜in to the WS along the upper edge; press. Slip the lining into the bag and slipstitch bag and lining together firmly along the upper edge.

☐Fold scraps of fabric and slip them into the finished basket to suggest laundry.

Each square = 2in

Noah's ark

Size
The ark is 27in long and 18in tall.

Materials
For the ark
1½ yd of 36in-wide double-sided
  quilted fabric
1½yd of 36in-wide lining fabric
1¼yd of ¼in -diameter filler cord
For the lions
¼yd of 36in-wide golden velour
  fabric
Scraps of brown yarn for tails and
  male lion's mane
Black stranded embroidery floss
Small amount of stuffing
For the camels
¼yd of 36in-wide golden brown
  velour
Small amount of stuffing
Black stranded embroidery floss
Small amount of brown yarn
For the giraffes
¼in of 36in-wide orange or yellow
  patterned fabric
Small amount of stuffing
Pale brown embroidery floss
For the zebras
¼yd of 36in-wide black and white
  striped fabric
Small amount of stuffing
Black stranded embroidery floss
For the elephants
¼yd of 36in-wide gray velveteen
Small amount of stuffing
Black stranded embroidery floss
Scraps of white felt
For the dove
Scrap of white felt 3 × 2½in
Cream embroidery floss
Blue felt-tip pen
For Noah and his wife
¼yd of 36in-wide cotton stockinet
Pale and dark blue, red, gray and
  green stranded embroidery
  floss
Small amount of stuffing
Scraps of fabric for clothes
Light and dark brown yarn for hair

Making the pattern — cutting out
Enlarge the pattern pieces as indicated on the graph and cut them from the appropriate fabrics. Transfer all pattern markings. A seam allowance of ¼in is included where necessary. (Numbers on pattern pieces are for one animal.)

To make the ark
Placing RS together, stitch the side seams of the quilted side pieces. Repeat with the lining pieces. Stitch the quilted base piece to the quilted side pieces. Place the lining over the quilted boat, RS facing, and stitch them together along the top edges. Tuck the lining inside the boat.

☐Join quilted and lining roof pieces along the two long edges. Turn the roof RS out. Fold the roof in half widthwise, with quilted side on top, and topstitch ⅜in from the fold. Pin the roof to the ark in the position shown on the pattern.

Join the short ends of the quilted pocket strip, RS facing. Repeat with the lining strip. Join the two pocket pieces along their top edges, RS facing, then turn pocket RS out. Slip the pocket strip inside the boat quilted side inside, as shown. Matching the lower edges and working from the top to the bottom of the strip, topstitch the pocket of the ark to each end. Topstitch the mid-section of the pocket to the boat as shown, catching the lower edges of the roof in place at the same time. Finally, stitch the lower edge of the pocket to the lower edge of the boat side pieces.

☐Turn under and press ⅜in all around the edges of the base lining and slipstitch it neatly in place, above the line of the topstitching.

☐Catch-stitch opposite sides of the pocket strip together, 2in from the front end of the boat to give a pointed shape.

☐Leaving loops as shown, catchstitch filler cord at intervals around the top edge, and then secure the two ends at the front of the boat.

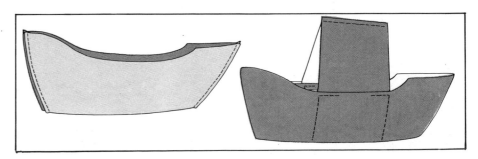

To make the lions
Fold the tail piece in half lengthwise, with RS facing, and stitch the long edges together. Turn the tail RS out and turn in and slipstitch one end. Pin the tail to the RS of one body piece with raw edges matching, in the position marked on the pattern.

☐Place the two body sections together, RS facing, with the tail sandwiched between them, and stitch along the top edges from points A to B. Join the underbody to the main body, RS facing and leaving a gap for stuffing. Turn the body RS out, stuff it firmly and slipstitch the opening edges together.

☐Fold each ear in half, RS facing, and stitch around the curved edge. Turn each ear RS out, turn in the lower edge, gather it slightly and slipstitch it to the lion's head as indicated on the pattern.

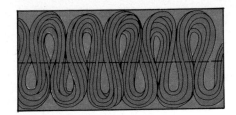

Following the illustration on the pattern and using 2 strands of embroidery floss, work the facial features of each lion. Cut a piece of brown yarn, fold it into several ⅜in loops and bind it securely to the end of each lion's tail. For the male lion's mane, cut several 24in lengths of brown yarn. Fold yarn accordion fashion as shown and backstitch it through the center to the lion's head, as indicated on the pattern.

To make the camels
Make the tail, body and ears as for the lions.
Following the pattern and using 2 strands of embroidery floss, work the eyes of each camel.
Cut several ⅜in loops of brown yarn and sew them to the top of each camel's head. Brush back the loops to stand upright. Cut several ⅜in pieces of yarn and bind them to the tail to form a tuft.

To make the giraffes
Make the tail, body and ears as for the lions.
Following the illustration on the pattern and using 2 strands of embroidery floss, embroider each eye.
Using 2 strands of embroidery floss, knot ¼in tufts down the back neck seam of each giraffe to make a mane. Knot a ⅝in tuft of black embroidery floss at the end of each giraffe's tail.

To make the zebras
Make the tail, body and ears as for the lions.
Following the pattern, using 2 strands of black embroidery floss, work the eyes of each zebra.
Knot ⅝in tufts down the back neck seam of each zebra to form a mane. Knot a ⅝in tuft of black embroidery floss at the end of each zebra's tail.

To make the elephants
Make the tails as for the lions. Placing RS together and catching the tail between them, join the main body pieces around the top edge from point A to B and from the trunk to the chest, C to D. Join the underbody to the main body pieces, RS facing and leaving a gap for stuffing. Turn each body RS out, stuff it firmly and slipstitch the opening edges together.

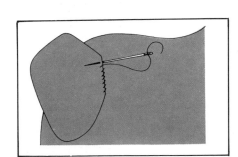

Join each pair of ear pieces, RS facing, leaving seam open between points E and F. Turn the ears RS out. Turn in the raw edges and slipstitch them together. Working from the back of each ear to help it stand out, overcast ears to the elephant's head in the positions indicated on the pattern.
Following the pattern, and using 2 strands of black embroidery floss, embroider each elephant's eye. Using white thread and working as invisibly as possible, slipstitch the tusks in place. Using gray thread, topstitch along the center of each elephant's tail and trim the end of each tail with a ⅝in tuft of black floss.

To make the doves
Following the markings on the pattern, using cream embroidery floss, work the lines of the tail in backstitch.
Fold the body of the dove in half and, following the stitching lines marked on the pattern, slipstitch the two sides together, as invisibly as possible, from the beak to the tail. Fold back wings and press them open.
Following the pattern, mark the eyes of the dove with felt-tip pen.

To make Noah and his wife

Join each pair of body pieces with RS facing, leaving a gap for stuffing. Turn the bodies RS out, stuff them firmly and slipstitch the opening edges together.

☐Following the pattern and using 2 strands of embroidery floss in colors shown, work the facial features of each character.

☐For Noah's hair, cut 4in pieces of dark brown yarn and backstitch them through the center from the top of his head to the nape of his neck. For his beard, work ¼in loops of brown yarn around the chin. For his mustache, sew 3 strands of yarn under his nose as shown.

☐For Mrs Noah's hair, cut 6in pieces of yarn and backstitch them through the center from the top of her head to the nape of her neck. Braid Mrs Noah's hair at each side of her face and bind the ends of the braids with short lengths of thread.

☐For the clothes, place each pair of tunic pieces together, with RS facing, and stitch the side and shoulder seams. Turn in the seam allowances around the neck, armhole and hem edges and slipstitch them in place. Put the tunics on the figures. For belts, twist together a few strands of embroidery floss in different colors and knot them around the waist of each doll, as shown in the photograph.

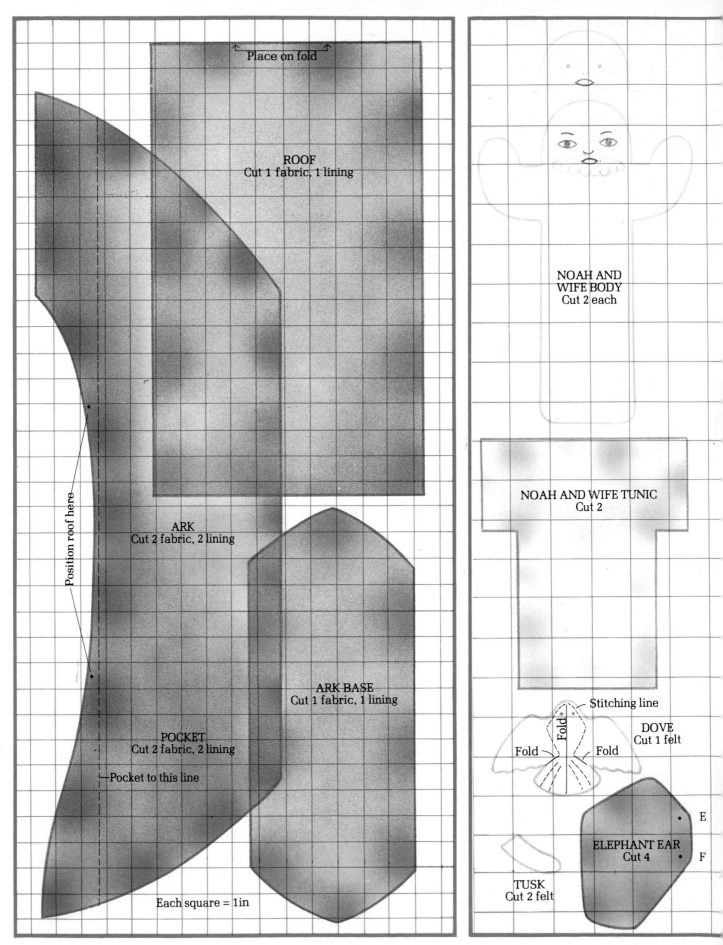

↑ Place on fold ↑

ROOF
Cut 1 fabric, 1 lining

Position roof here

ARK
Cut 2 fabric, 2 lining

ARK BASE
Cut 1 fabric, 1 lining

POCKET
Cut 2 fabric, 2 lining

Pocket to this line

Each square = 1in

NOAH AND
WIFE BODY
Cut 2 each

NOAH AND WIFE TUNIC
Cut 2

Stitching line

Fold

Fold   Fold

DOVE
Cut 1 felt

E

ELEPHANT EAR
Cut 4

F

TUSK
Cut 2 felt

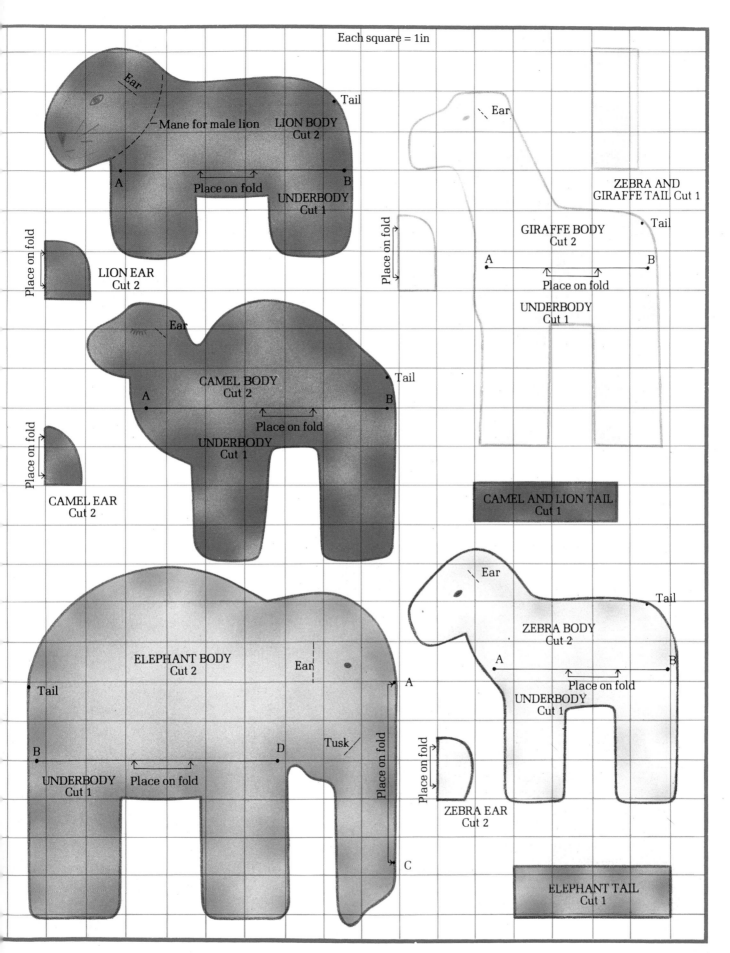

Each square = 1in

LION BODY
Cut 2

Ear

Mane for male lion

Tail

A   B

Place on fold

UNDERBODY
Cut 1

Place on fold

LION EAR
Cut 2

Ear

CAMEL BODY
Cut 2

Tail

A   B

Place on fold

UNDERBODY
Cut 1

Place on fold

CAMEL EAR
Cut 2

Place on fold

ZEBRA AND
GIRAFFE TAIL Cut 1

Ear

GIRAFFE BODY
Cut 2

Tail

A   B

Place on fold

UNDERBODY
Cut 1

CAMEL AND LION TAIL
Cut 1

ELEPHANT BODY
Cut 2

Ear

Tail

A

B   D

Tusk

UNDERBODY
Cut 1   Place on fold

Place on fold

C

Ear

ZEBRA BODY
Cut 2

Tail

A   B

Place on fold

UNDERBODY
Cut 1

Place on fold

ZEBRA EAR
Cut 2

ELEPHANT TAIL
Cut 1

Toys for tots

Soft, colorful toys are best for babies and toddlers. A string of bright pompons will divert an infant for long stretches, and a soft knitted clown doll will survive a lot of hugging and being hurled to the floor. All small children should have a teddy bear; make one yourself from soft fur fabric.

A word of warning: when making toys for small children, do not include trimmings, such as beads, that could easily be pulled off, swallowed and possibly choked on. For eyes use safety eyes (available from toymaking and notions departments) or felt eyes, sewn on securely.

A "growler" or "squeaker" adds a lifelike dimension to toy animals. To insert one, first make a small bag of unbleached muslin; insert the growler in the bag and sew the opening edges together. Sew the bag to the center back of the toy, then fill it with stuffing as usual.

Play blocks

Size
4 × 4 × 4in

Materials
2oz of a knitting worsted yarn in each of 3 colors: red, blue and yellow
3 pieces of foam, each 4 × 4 × 4in
Pair of size 3 knitting needles

Gauge
10 sts and 14 rows to 2in in st st on size 3 needles

To make a play block
For each block make 6 pieces of knitting as foll: Using size 3 needles and red, cast on 24 sts. Starting with a K row, work 28 rows in st st (1 row K, 1 row P).
Bind off.
K another square of red, then 2 each of blue and yellow. Foll charts and using Swiss darning (see page 191) work letters on 3 squares.
K and Swiss darn squares for 2 more blocks, varying the color combinations on each as shown in the photograph.

To finish
Place 6 pieces of knitting tog as shown in diagram. Join the sides around the center square and join top square. Place a piece of foam on WS of center square and stitch remaining pieces together. Use an invisible seam to join the pieces of the square.

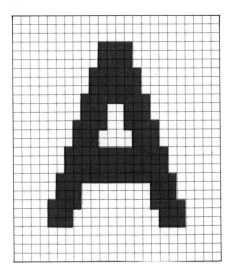
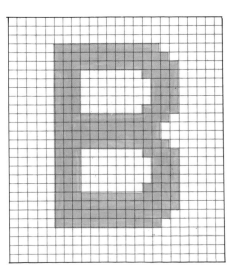
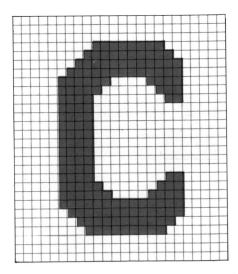

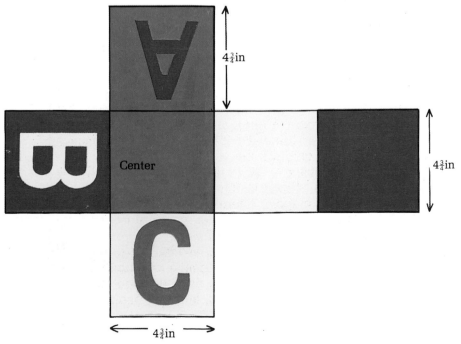

$4\frac{3}{4}$in

$4\frac{3}{4}$in

Center

$4\frac{3}{4}$in

Pompon busy bar

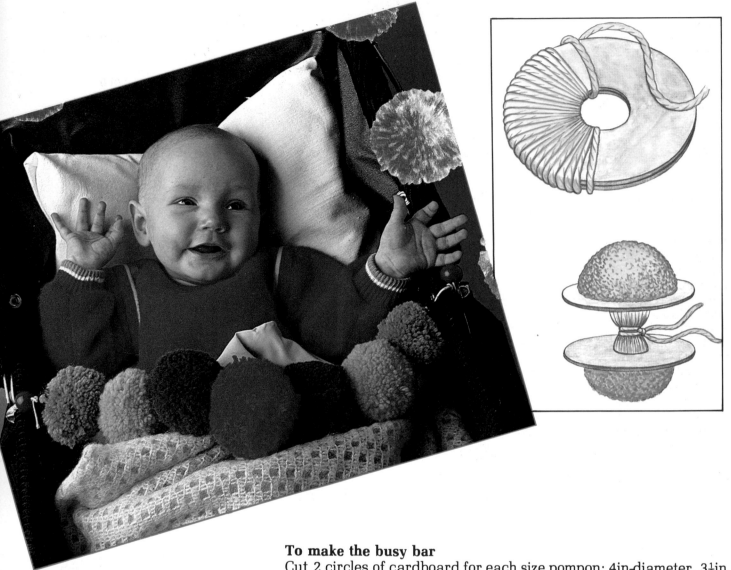

Size
28in long, or to fit across crib

Materials
Small amounts of yarn in red, navy, gold and medium blue
10 wooden beads
1yd of cord elastic
Piece of cardboard about 8 × 14in
Large tapestry needle

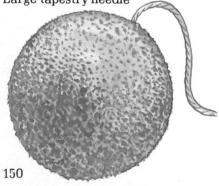

To make the busy bar

Cut 2 circles of cardboard for each size pompon: 4in-diameter, 3½in, 3in and 2¾in. Cut a hole about ¾in in diameter in the center of each disk.

☐Place two equal-sized cardboard disks together. Wind yarn closely and evenly around the disks until the hole is well filled. Use a tapestry needle for inserting yarn when hole becomes tight.

☐Cut through the yarn at the edge of the disks. Pull the disks apart slightly and tie a length of yarn tightly around the center of the strands. Gently pull off the disks. Trim the ends if necessary.

☐Use this technique to make one red, 2 navy, 2 gold and 2 medium blue pompons measuring 4, 3½, 3 and 2¾in respectively. Make the pompons in the order shown in the photograph. Before cutting the strands on the first pompon, thread a tapestry needle with elastic and insert the needle through the center of the strands. Pull the elastic through, leaving about 4in at the end. Pull both disks upward, off the pompon and elastic. Thread a wooden bead onto the elastic, then make more pompons, threading them onto elastic as before and placing beads between them. Place a bead at each end of the cord, knot it, then form the ends into loops, knotting each loop twice and threading a bead between the knots.

150

Baby's ball

Gauge
22 sc and 14 rows to 4in worked on size E hook

To make one section
Using size E hook and one of the 6 colors, make 2ch.
1st row 1sc into 2nd ch from hook, turn.
2nd row (RS) Ch 1, 2sc into next st, turn. 3 sts.
3rd row Ch 1, 2sc into next st, 1sc into last st, turn.
4th and 5th rows Ch 1, 1sc into next st, 2sc into next st, 1sc into each st to end, turn.
6th and 8th rows Ch 1, (1sc into next st) twice, 2sc into next st, 1sc into each st to end, turn.
7th and every alt row Ch 1, 1sc into each st to end, turn.
10th and 12th rows Ch 1, (1dc into next st) 3 times, 2sc into next st, 1sc into each st to end, turn.
14th and 16th rows Ch 1, (1sc into next st) 4 times, 2sc into next st, 1sc into each st to end, turn.
18th row Ch 1, (1sc into next st) 5 times, 2sc into next st, 1sc into each st to end, turn.
20th row As 18th row. 14 sts.
22nd and 24th rows Ch 1, (1sc into next st) 5 times, work 2sc tog, 1sc into each st to end, turn.
26th and 28th rows Ch 1, (1sc into next st) 4 times, work 2sc tog, 1sc into each st to end, turn.
30th and 32nd rows Ch 1, (1sc into next st) 3 times, work 2sc tog, 1sc into each st to end, turn.
34th and 35th rows Ch 1, (1sc into next st) twice, work 2sc tog, 1sc into each st to end, turn.
36th and 37th rows Ch 1, 1sc into next st, work 2sc tog, 1sc into each st to end, turn.
38th row Ch 1, work 2sc tog, 1sc into last st, turn.
39th row Ch 1, work 2sc tog, turn.
40th and 41st rows Ch 1, 1sc into next st, turn.
Fasten off. Make 5 more sections.

To finish
Place WS of two sections together and, using cream yarn, sl st into point through both sections. Work 1 row of sc through both edges to other point. Join other sections in the same way. Leave half of last seam open. Fill ball with stuffing. Close the opening. Fasten off.

Size
Approximately 5in in diameter

Materials
1oz of baby yarn in each of 6 colors
1oz of sport-weight yarn in cream
Size E crochet hook
Small amount of washable stuffing

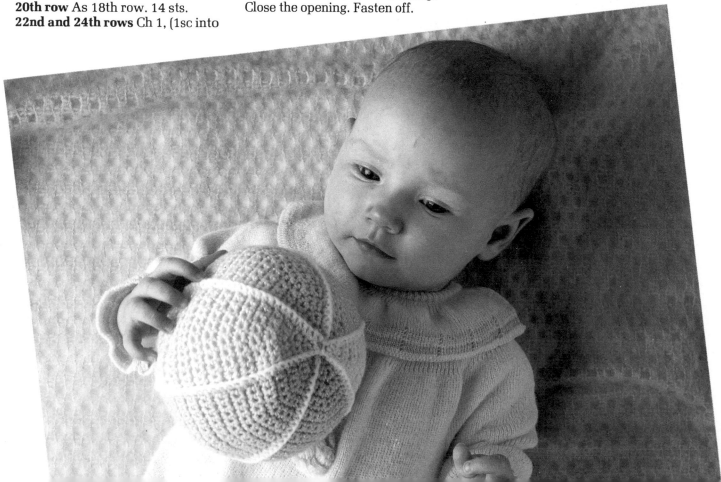

Teddy bear

Size
16in tall

Materials
½yd of 36in-wide brown fur fabric
2 safety eyes
Small amount of black yarn
9oz of washable stuffing
Darning needle
Knitting needle

Making the pattern — cutting out
Enlarge the pattern pieces as indicated on the graph and cut them from fur fabric, placing them on the WS and aligning them as shown on the cutting diagram so that the pile runs correctly. Cut through the backing fabric and not the pile. Transfer pattern markings to the WS of the fabric with tailor's chalk. A seam allowance of ⅜in is included.

To make the teddy bear
Place the left arm and left-side body pieces together RS facing, with angled arm edge toward back, matching seamlines A-B on both pieces. Pin and stitch the seam. Clip the curved edges of the seam and press them open. Fold the arm along the fold line indicated, RS facing. Matching both points E, pin and stitch along the seamline E-F.
☐Join the right arm and right-side body piece in the same way.
☐Place the body pieces together with RS facing, and pin and stitch the center front seam G-H. Clip curves and press seams open. Join the center back seam from H to P and from J to O.

☐With the body still WS out, pin and stitch the inside leg seams and press them open. Pin and baste a foot pad to the bottom of each leg, with the pile running toward the back. Stitch pads in place.

☐On each side head piece, carefully slit the fabric in the positions marked, and insert the plastic eyes.

☐Pin and stitch the right and left side head pieces together along seamline C-G (from the crown past the nose, to the chin). Then pin the front side pieces and back piece together along seamlines E-C and C-E, going around the edge of the ears. Stitch the seam. Clip the curves, and press seams open.

☐With both pieces still WS out, pin the head to the body around the neck edges. The shoulders form a "V" shape up toward the ears a little.

☐Match up points A, B, E, G and J on both pieces. Stitch the seam, clip the seam allowances and press the seam open.

☐Turn the teddy RS out. Stitch across the ear as indicated.

☐Fill the body and head firmly with stuffing, beginning with the legs. After filling each leg, stitch diagonally across the top of the leg from the base of center front at point H, to the side of the body at point M. This enables the legs to bend freely. Stuff the head next, making sure that it is firmly packed. Then stuff the arms and the body. Slipstitch the opening edges together.

☐To work the features, first clip the fur in a triangular shape below the tip of the nose. Thread a darning needle with black yarn and knot the end. Stitch through the tip of the nose (the knot will be covered by stitches). Make long stitches fanning out over the tip of the snout, passing the needle right through the nose each time, to form a round shape of close stitching.

☐Take a long stitch down from the base of the nose to the center of the mouth. Stitch out to the right, and slightly upward, then back again to the center to form a smiling mouth. Make another stitch upward to the left and back. Bring the needle back through to the tip of the nose and fasten off with two or three tiny stitches.

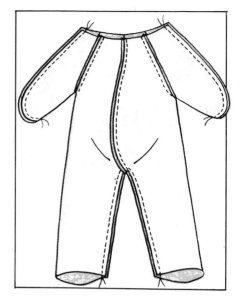

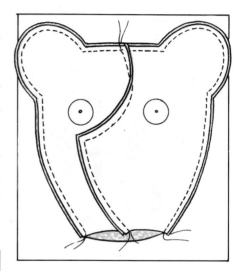

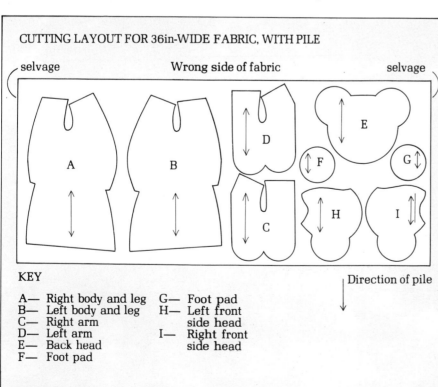

CUTTING LAYOUT FOR 36in-WIDE FABRIC, WITH PILE

selvage   Wrong side of fabric   selvage

A   B   D   E   F   G   C   H   I

KEY

A—	Right body and leg	G—	Foot pad
B—	Left body and leg	H—	Left front
C—	Right arm		side head
D—	Left arm	I—	Right front
E—	Back head		side head
F—	Foot pad		

Direction of pile

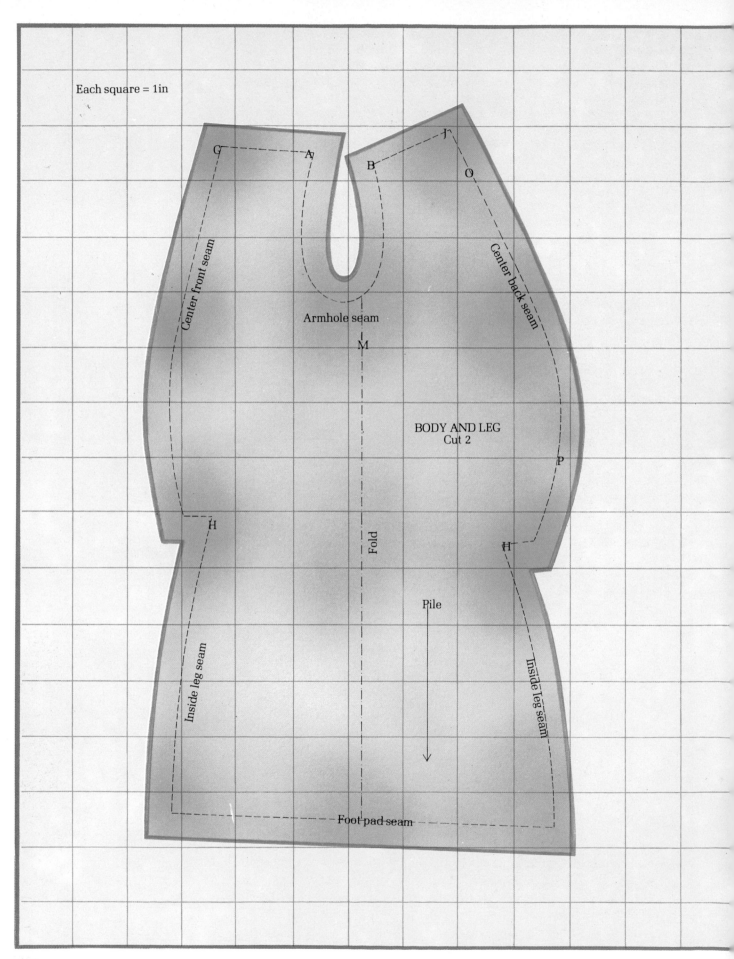

Each square = 1in

G   A

B   T

O

Center front seam

Armhole seam

Center back seam

M

BODY AND LEG
Cut 2

P

H   H

Fold

Pile

Inside leg seam

Inside leg seam

Foot pad seam

154

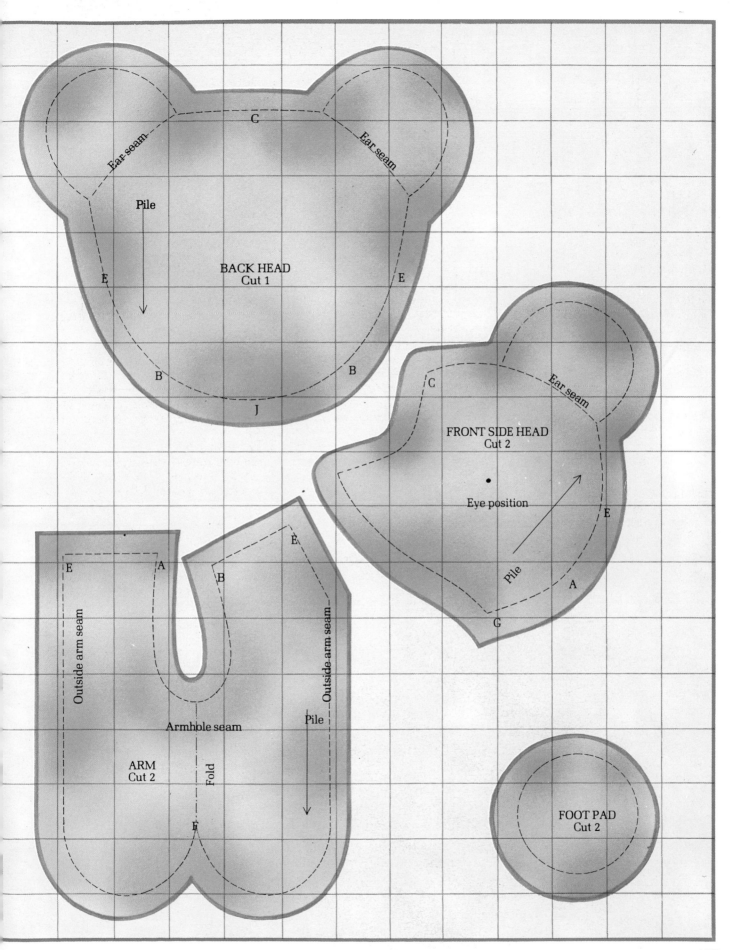

BACK HEAD
Cut 1

Ear seam

Ear seam

C

Pile

E

E

B

B

J

FRONT SIDE HEAD
Cut 2

Ear seam

C

Eye position

E

Pile

A

G

ARM
Cut 2

E

A

Outside arm seam

B

E

Outside arm seam

Pile

Armhole seam

Fold

F

FOOT PAD
Cut 2

Clarence the clown

Size
Approximately 14in tall

Materials
Small amounts of knitting worsted
in 5 colors: A (red), B (blue), C
(green), D (yellow) and E (cream)
3yd of bouclé or mohair yarn in
golden brown
Pair of size 5 knitting needles
Size E crochet hook
7oz of stuffing
2 safety eyes ½in in diameter
Strip of cardboard 2¼in wide

Gauge
24 sts and 32 rows to 4in in st st on
size 5 needles

Front and back (alike)
*Using knitting needles and B, cast
on 12 sts for first leg. Work in seed
st as foll:
1st row (K1, P1) to end.
2nd row (P1, K1) to end.
Rep rows 1 and 2 once.
Starting with a K row, work in st st
stripes as foll: 2 rows each in C, D,
A and B. Carry yarn loosely up side
of work. Work 6 more rows, ending
with A stripe.* Break off yarns.
Rep from * to * for second leg, but
do not break off yarns.
Working across both legs (24 sts),
cont striped patt for 24 rows, beg
with B and ending with A. Break off
C and D.
In B work 4 rows g st (every row K).
In A work 16 rows st st (1 row K, 1
row P), beg with K row. Break off A.
Join in E and work 18 rows g st.
Cont in g st for 6 more rows, dec 1
st at each end of every row. 12 sts.
Bind off.

Arms (both alike)
Using A, cast on 20 sts. Work 14
rows st st, beg with K row.
Change to E. Work 8 rows g st. Bind
off.

Nose
Using crochet hook and A, make 4
ch and join into a ring with a sl st.
1st round ch 1, 9sc into ring, join
with sl st to beg ch.
2nd–5th rounds ch 1, 1sc into each
st of previous round, sl st to beg ch.
Fasten off.

Hat
Using crochet hook and C, work as
for nose for 5 rounds. Change to D.
6th round ch 1, 1sc in first st, 2sc in
each st to end, sl st to beg ch.
7th and 8th rounds ch 1, 1sc into
each st, sl st to beg ch. Change to B.
9th round Rep round 8. Fasten off.
Brim will curl up automatically.

Bow tie
Using crochet hook and C, make
30ch. Break off C. Using D, 1sc into
each ch. Fasten off. Tie in a bow.

To finish
Sew front and back main sections
tog, leaving an opening at top of
head. Sew toy eyes to face. Fill body
and head with stuffing and sew up
opening. Using red, work a row of
gathering stitches around body on
last row of red st st; pull up to make
neck and fasten securely. With red,
embroider mouth in chain stitch.
Stuff nose and sew it to face. Fold
arms lengthwise, RS tog, and sew
long edges, leaving cast-on ends
open. Stuff arms and sew up
openings. Gather up wrists as for
neck. Sew arms to body.
Sew bow tie to neck. For hair, cut
length of brown yarn in half. Wind
each piece around the strip of
cardboard. Tie the loops tog at one
edge and cut them at the other. Sew
the tied point of each hair piece to
each side of head.

Prancing ponies

Making the pattern — cutting out

Trace the pattern pieces, which are actual size, and cut them from fabric. (The pieces are shown in different colors only for the sake of clarity.) Transfer the pattern markings. A seam allowance of ¼in is included.

To make the pony

Place the body pieces together with RS facing. Baste and stitch from point A to B along the top edge of the body.

□Place the gusset and body pieces together and baste. Stitch the gusset in place, leaving seam open along one edge between legs. Turn pony RS out and fill it firmly with stuffing. Slipstitch the opening edges together.

Size
7in tall

For each pony
⅝yd of 36in-wide lightweight fabric
4oz of stuffing
½yd of ¼in-wide ribbon
Scraps of blue and white felt for eyes
Small amount of yarn for mane and tail
2 jingle bells
Large chenille needle for mane

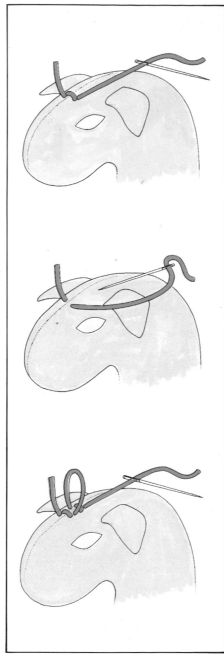

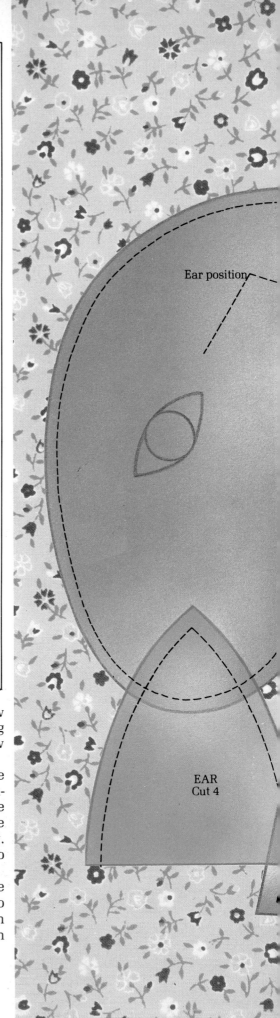

Ear position

EAR
Cut 4

☐Sew each pair of ear pieces together, RS facing. Turn in the raw edges and slipstitch them together. Sew the ears to the head, making a small pleat at the base of each ear. Cut eyes from felt and sew them to the head.

☐Using a chenille needle and a double strand of yarn, work the mane as shown. Start just above the eyes and work loops and back-stitches alternately along the seam. Do not stitch too close to the seam, as the extra thickness of the seam allowances will make stitching more difficult. For the tail, cut 20 strands of yarn 14in long. Double them and tie a knot in the looped end. Sew the knot firmly to the pony's back. Trim tail ends with scissors.

☐Stitch ribbon around the nose. Stitch a 16in piece of ribbon to the nose to make the reins. Tie remaining ribbon in a bow and sew it to the tail. Sew the bells to reins on each side of the head. Sew ribbon or braid around the body to decorate a solid color fabric, as shown on the red pony.

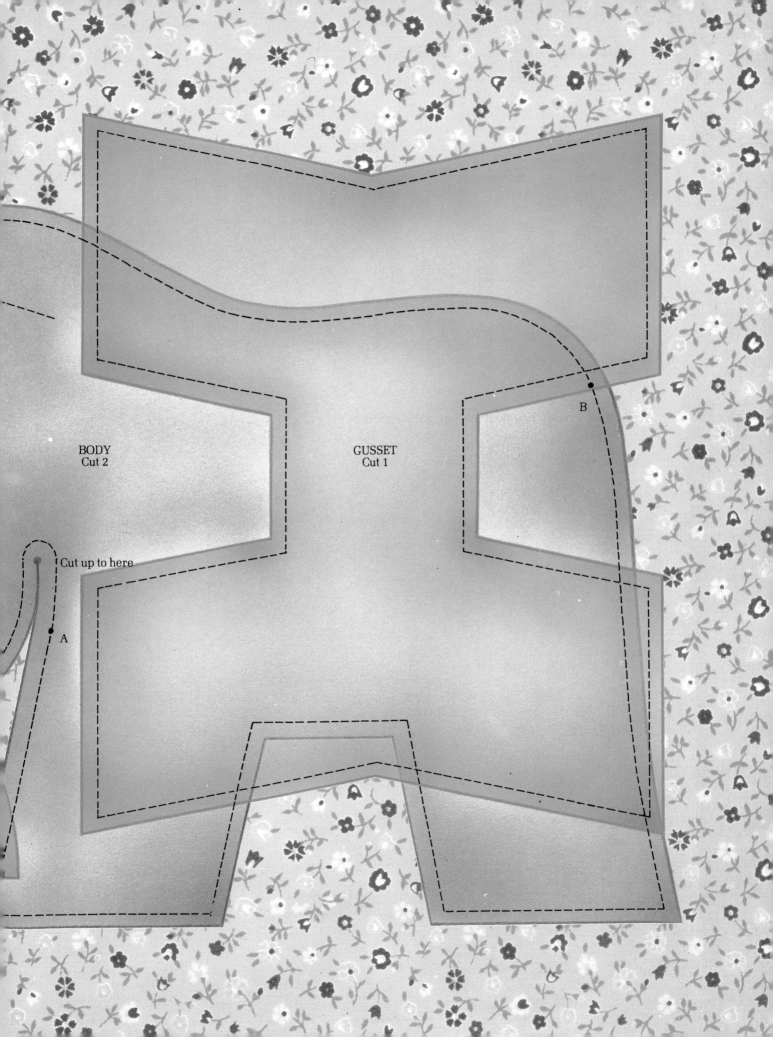

BODY
Cut 2

GUSSET
Cut 1

Cut up to here

A

B

Cushions and pillows

Here is a selection of practical toys — objects that will add a splash of color and whimsy to the playroom or bedroom and at the same time serve a useful purpose. Among them are an endearing cat and mouse pajama case, giant orange and grapefruit sag bags and a spectacular caterpillar sleeping bag. These witty toys will appeal to adults as well as children.

Tommy tortoise

Size
16in long

Materials
5oz of a knitting worsted yarn in main color A (green)
1oz each in contrasting colors B (red), C (yellow) and D (orange)
Size E crochet hook
Scraps of black and white felt for features
7oz of washable stuffing

Gauge
19 dc and 11 rows to 4in on size E hook

Lower body
With size E hook and A make 21ch. 1hdc into 3rd ch from hook, 1hdc into each ch to end, turn. 20hdc.
Next row Ch 2 to count as first hdc, 2hdc into hdc at base of 2ch, 1hdc into each of next 18hdc, 3hdc into last hdc, turn. 24hdc.
Next row Ch 3, 2hdc into hdc at base of 3ch, 1hdc into each st to last st, 3hdc into last st, turn.
Rep this row once more. 32hdc.
Next row Ch 3, 1hdc into hdc at base of 3ch, 1hdc into each st to last st, 2hdc into last st, turn.
Rep this row until there are 40hdc.
Work 23 rows straight in hdc, turn.
Dec 1hdc at each end of next and every foll row until there are 32hdc.
* Dec 2hdc at each end of next and foll 2 rows, turn. Do not break yarn.

Head
Sl st over 6hdc, ch 2, 1hdc into each of next 7 sts, turn.
Work 2 rows of hdc.
Inc 1hdc each end of every row until there are 16 sts.
Work even for 4 rows.

Dec 1hdc at each end of every row until 6 sts rem, fasten off. *

Upper body
Work first 4 rows as for lower body.
5th row Ch 2, 1hdc into st at base of 2ch, 1hdc into each of next 5 sts, 2hdc into next st, 1hdc into each of next 18 sts, 2hdc into next st, 1hdc into each of next 5 sts, 2hdc into last st, turn.
6th row Ch 2, 1hdc into st at base of 2ch, 1hdc into each of next 5 sts, 2hdc into next st, 1hdc into each of next 22 sts, 2hdc into next st, 1 hdc into each of next 5 sts, 2hdc into last st, turn.
7th row As 6th row, working 26hdc between inc instead of 22, turn.
8th row As 7th row, working 30hdc instead of 26, turn.
9th row Ch 2, 1hdc into each of next 36 sts, 1sc into each of next 2 sts, sl st into next st, turn (leaving 8 sts unworked).
10th row Sl st into each of next 2sc, 1sc into each of next 2 sts, 1hdc into each of next 24 sts, 1sc into each of next 2 sts, sl st into next st, turn.
11th row Sl st into each of next 2sc, 1sc into each of next 2 sts, 1hdc into each of next 34 sts, 1hdc into turning ch, turn.
12th row Ch 2 to count as first st, 1hdc into each st to end. 48 hdc.
13th to 21st rows Work straight in hdc.
22nd to 25th rows As 9th-12th rows.
26th to 33rd rows Work straight in hdc.
34th to 36th rows As 9th-12th rows.

37th row Ch 2, dec 1 hdc over next 2 sts, 1hdc into each of next 5 sts, dec 1hdc over next 2 sts, 1hdc into each of next 29 sts, dec 1hdc over next 2 sts, 1hdc over next 5 sts, dec 1hdc over last 2 sts.

38th row As 37th row, working 25hdc instead of 29.

39th row As 38th row, working 21hdc instead of 25.

40th row As 39th row, working 17hdc instead of 21.

Now work from * to * as on lower body, inc to 12hdc and working 10 rows of hdc instead of 4, then dec 1hdc each end of every alt row until 6hdc rem. Fasten off.

Head gusset (make 2)

Make 24ch. 1hdc into 3rd ch from hook, 1hdc into each ch to end. 23hdc.

Next row Ch 2, 1hdc into each of next 19 sts, turn.

Next row Sl st over first 3 sts, ch 2, 1hdc into each of next 15 sts, turn.

Next row Ch 2, 1hdc into each of next 13 sts, turn.

Next row Sl st over first 2 sts, ch 2, 1hdc into each of next 10 sts, turn.

Next row Ch 2, 1hdc into each of next 8 sts, turn.

Next row Sl st over first 2 sts, ch 2, 1hdc into each of next 5 sts, fasten off.

Feet (make 4)

Make 20ch. 1hdc into 3rd ch from hook, 1hdc into each ch to end, turn. 19hdc.

Next row Ch 2 to count as first hdc, 1hdc into each st to end, turn. Rep this row 3 more times.

Next row Ch 2, 1hdc into each of next 8 sts, 3hdc into next st, 1hdc into each of last 9 sts, turn.

Next row Ch 2, dec 1hdc over next 2 sts, 1hdc into each of next 7 sts, 3hdc into next st, 1hdc into each of next 8 sts, dec 1hdc over last 2 sts, turn. 21 sts. Rep this last row twice.

Next row Ch 2, dec 1hdc over next 2 sts, 1hdc into each of next 5 sts, dec 1hdc over next 2 sts, 1hdc into next st, dec 1hdc over next 2 sts, 1hdc into each of next 6 sts, dec 1hdc over last 2 sts, turn.

Next row Ch 2, dec 1hdc over next 2 sts, 1hdc into each of next 3 sts, dec 1hdc over next 2 sts, 1hdc into next st, dec 1hdc over next 2 sts, 1hdc into each of next 4 sts, dec 1hdc over last 2 sts, fasten off.

Tail

Make 4ch. Sl st to first ch to form ring.

1st round Ch 2, * 2hdc into next st, 1hdc into each of next 2 sts, rep from * to end, finishing with sl st in top of 2ch.

2nd round Ch 2, * 2hdc into next st, 1hdc into each of next 2 sts, rep from * to end. Finish with sl st in top of 2ch.

3rd round As 2nd.

4th round Ch 2, 1hdc into each sl st to end, finishing with sl st in top of 2ch. Fasten off.

Shell motif (make 19)

With D make 4ch. Sl st to first ch to form ring.

1st round Ch 3, 11dc into ring, sl st to top of 3ch, break yarn.

2nd round Change to B, ch 3, (3dc into next dc, 1dc into next dc) 5 times, 3dc into next dc, sl st to top of 3ch, break yarn.

3rd round Change to C, ch 3, 1dc into next dc, (3dc into next dc, 1dc into each of next 3dc) 5 times, 3dc into next dc, 1dc into next dc, sl st to top of 3ch, fasten off.

Make 6 more motifs as first, then 6 using C, D and B in that order, then 6 using B, C and D in that order.

To finish

Stitch head gussets in place from A to B on upper and lower body. Stitch around body, from C to B, across nose, then from B to D on other side. Fill head and body with stuffing, then stitch from C to D. Fold legs in half, stuff and stitch. Stuff tail lightly and stitch. Cut features from felt and sew them in place. Assemble shell with one motif in center, 6 motifs joined around it, and 12 motifs in a circle around the 6. Join by placing WS tog and working a row of sc in A through both edges along one side of motif. Join the next motif by working sc along adjacent edges, and finally working a row of sc around shell edge. Lay shell over body and stitch it in place.

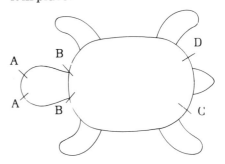

Caterpillar sleeping bag

Size
71in long

Materials
4yd of 36in-wide green fabric
4yd of 36in-wide yellow lining
    fabric
4yd of 36in-wide batting
1⅞yd of 36in-wide red fabric for
    appliqué
1⅞yd of 36in-wide yellow fabric for
    appliqué
⅜yd of 36in-wide white fabric for
    appliqué
⅜in of 36in-wide black fabric for
    appliqué
43in zipper
White shirring elastic

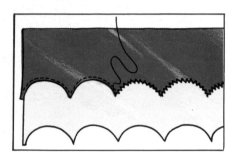

Making the pattern — cutting out
Enlarge the pattern pieces as indicated on the graph and cut them from the appropriate fabrics. Using dressmaker's carbon paper and tracing wheel, transfer the quilting lines from pattern piece 1 to the right side of the green fabric piece and to one yellow lining piece. Then transfer the ruching lines on pattern piece 2 to the green fabric piece. Transfer the notches. A seam allowance is included.

To make the sleeping bag
Place one red scalloped strip on one yellow strip, matching straight edges, RS upward. Baste and stitch around the scalloped edges, first with a straight stitch and then with a close zigzag. Repeat with the remaining strips.
☐Lay the green fabric piece 2, RS up, on a flat surface and place the red and yellow strips, RS up, along the edges, making sure that the base of each scallop overlaps the edges of the green fabric by at least 1½in. Match the points of the scallops and the ruching lines. Baste and stitch around the scallops, then zigzag stitch as before. Trim away the surplus green fabric on the WS.
☐Wind a machine bobbin by hand with shirring elastic. Using green sewing thread, stitch along each ruching line, extending the stitching at both sides through the points of the scallops. Also stitch along the top and bottom, ¾in from the edges.
☐Position pieces 4 to 8 on the RS of head piece 3; baste and straight stitch close to the edge on each shape; zigzag over first stitching.
☐Pin the head to the shirred body section with RS facing, matching center marks and with points X and Y at the edges. Baste and stitch pieces together.
☐Lay the ruched top on the green back piece, RS together, matching ruching and quilting lines and with the head farthest from you. Baste and stitch the right-hand edges together up to the head section.
☐Place the lining piece with the quilting lines RS up, on a flat surface with head end farthest from you. Place the other piece, RS down, on top. Baste and stitch the right-hand edges together up to the head section

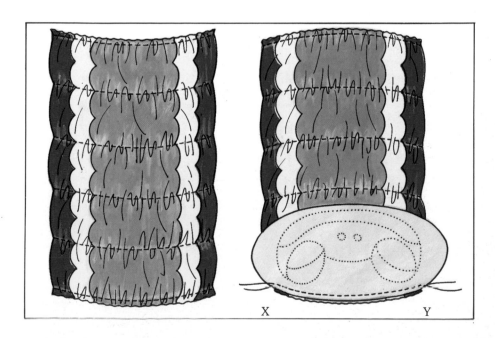

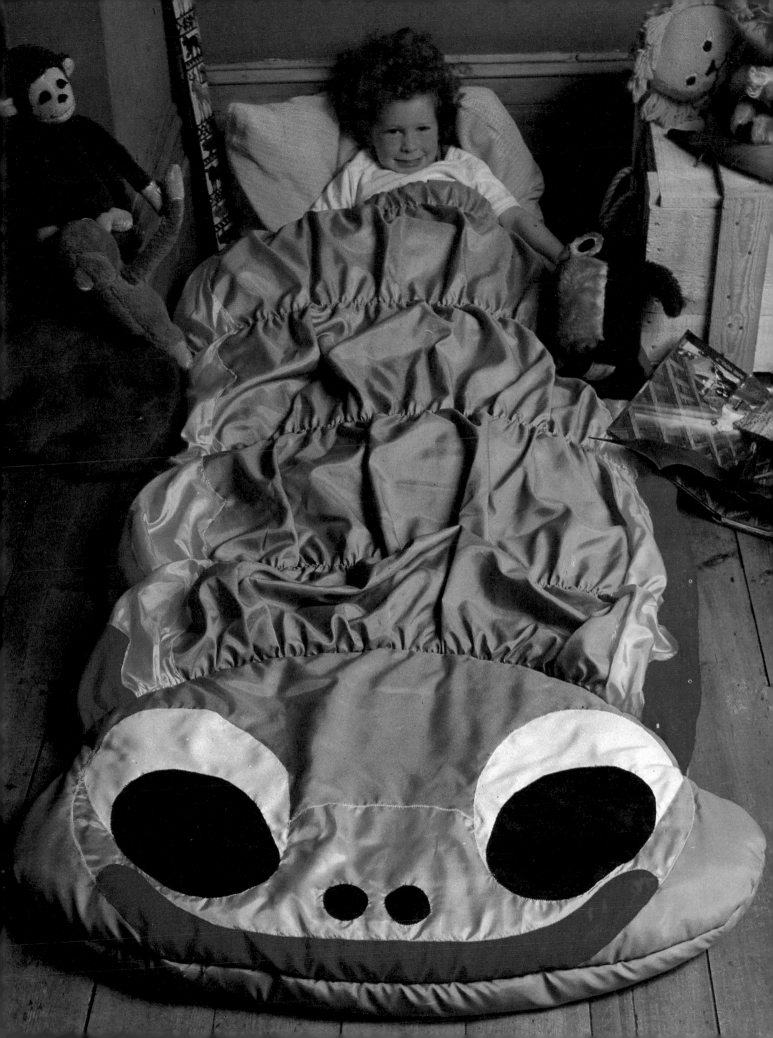

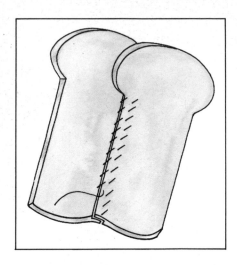

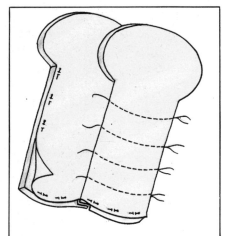

□To avoid lumps, joinings in batting must always be graded. On one piece of batting measure and mark a line 4in from the edge from A to B. Slip your hand into the cut edge, and separate it into two equal layers. Cut the upper layer along the marked line. Repeat the process on the reverse side of the other piece of batting.

□Butt the two pieces together as shown to form a flat piece of equal thickness. (The head sections will overlap.) Using a long needle and strong white thread, stitch diagonally through both layers of batting along both sides of the overlap.

□Lay the lining fabric, RS up, on top of the batting, with outer edges matching. Pin around edges and along the quilting lines on one section of the lining. Using matching thread, and starting from the center, stitch along the quilting lines, omitting the line marking off head section.

□Place the quilted lining RS upward and place the main fabric RS down, on top. Pin layers together along the side edges and the curved ends opposite the head. Baste and stitch, making sure that the batting is caught in the seam; turn bag RS out.

□Lay the bag flat, and pin along the line where the head meets the body (X-Y) on the front section. Using green upper thread and yellow bobbin thread, stitch along this line through all layers. On the back section pin along the curved quilting lines and, using matching thread, quilt through all layers from the center outward, allowing the green fabric to roll under slightly at the edges.

□Fold back the lining from the head sections and pin it to the body to keep it out of the way. Fold the bag lengthwise RS together, and pin around the head section through the green fabric and batting. Stitch ¾in from the edge from Y around the head to X. Push the head section into the body section. Unpin the lining, lay it flat and pin the edges together as for green fabric. Stitch as before, and finish raw edges with a small zigzag stitch. Turn the bag RS out and push the lining into the head.

□Pin the zipper to the open side of the bag, beginning a couple of inches from the open end, with the pull tab at that end. Starting from the head section, baste and stitch zipper in place. Tuck in the end of the zipper and finish neatly by hand. If you like, make a 5in-long tie, and thread it through the zipper pull tab.

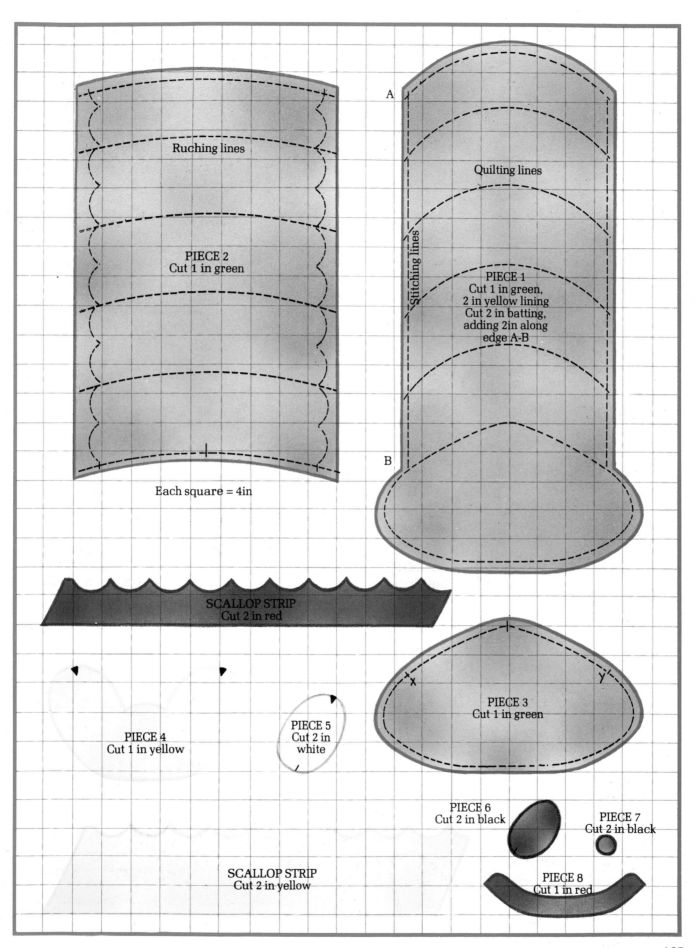

Ruching lines

PIECE 2
Cut 1 in green

Each square = 4in

A

Quilting lines

Stitching lines

PIECE 1
Cut 1 in green,
2 in yellow lining
Cut 2 in batting,
adding 2in along
edge A-B

B

SCALLOP STRIP
Cut 2 in red

PIECE 4
Cut 1 in yellow

PIECE 5
Cut 2 in
white

x

PIECE 3
Cut 1 in green

y

PIECE 6
Cut 2 in black

PIECE 7
Cut 2 in black

SCALLOP STRIP
Cut 2 in yellow

PIECE 8
Cut 1 in red

Citrus sag bags

Size
Grapefruit is approximately 105in in circumference.
Orange is approximately 84in in circumference.

Materials

For the grapefruit
3¼yd of 60in-wide wide yellow cotton drill

3¼yd of 60in-wide unbleached muslin

½yd of 60in-wide white cotton drill

Scrap of dull green cotton fabric

13yd of ⅛in-diameter filler cord

Approximately 9 cubic ft of polystyrene granules

¼yd of bright green cotton fabric for the leaf (optional)

¼yd of lightweight batting for padding leaf

Snap for attaching leaf

For the orange
3⅞yd of 36in-wide orange cotton drill

2⅝yd of 60in-wide unbleached muslin

⅜yd of 60in-wide white cotton drill

Scrap of dull green cotton fabric

13yd of ⅛in-diameter filler cord

Approximately 7 cubic ft of polystyrene granules

¼yd of bright green cotton fabric for the leaf (optional)

¼yd of lightweight batting for padding leaf

Snap for attaching leaf

Making the pattern — cutting out

Enlarge the pattern pieces as indicated on the graph and cut them from the appropriate fabrics. Use the smaller leaf, if desired, for the orange and the larger for the grapefruit. Cut the leaf shape once from batting as well as from green fabric. Transfer leaf markings to RS of fabric. Cut top piece from dull green fabric and bottom piece from orange or yellow fabric. Cut all pieces except leaf from unbleached muslin for lining. A ⅜in seam allowance is included.

☐ For the cording cut enough 1in-wide bias strips from white fabric to make a length of 13yd. Join the strips on the straight grain and fold the strip, RS outside, around the cord. Baste close to cord.

☐ Cut a length of cording to fit one side edge of one segment and baste it to RS with raw edges matching. Baste another segment on top, RS facing. Using the zipper foot, machine stitch all layers together as close to the cord as possible.

☐ Continue adding segments with cording until all nine are joined together, inserting cording into each joining. Cord one of the two remaining free edges, then join these edges for 3in from each end, leaving the rest of the seam open.

☐ Clip the edges of the top and bottom circles, to a depth of just under ⅜in, and turn ⅜in to the WS; pin and baste. Trim away excess cording from the top opening. Lay the top piece over the hole, RS upward, pin and baste edges together. Stitch by machine ¼in from the edge of the circle, then stitch again with a wide, close zigzag over the edge. Attach bottom piece in the same way.

☐ Make the muslin bag by joining the nine segments, leaving a small opening for turning. Turn bag RS out and close the opening. Hem the top piece as described above; pin, baste and stitch it in place with a straight stitch . Fill the bag with granules until it is about two-thirds full. Hem bottom piece and stitch it in place.

☐ Insert the filled muslin bag into the orange or grapefruit cover. Slipstitch the opening edges together.

☐ To make the leaf, lay the fabric leaf and batting on the green fabric with RS outward; pin and baste. With a medium zigag, stitch around the edge; trim away excess fabric and zigzag stitch around the edge again to finish it.

☐ Stitch one half of a snap to one segment, ⅜in from the top piece. Stitch the other half to the WS of the leaf, ⅜in from the top. Attach the leaf to the bag.

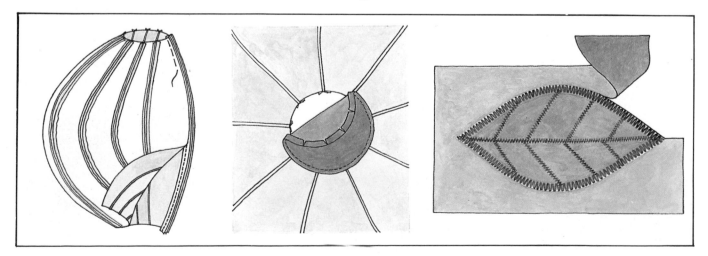

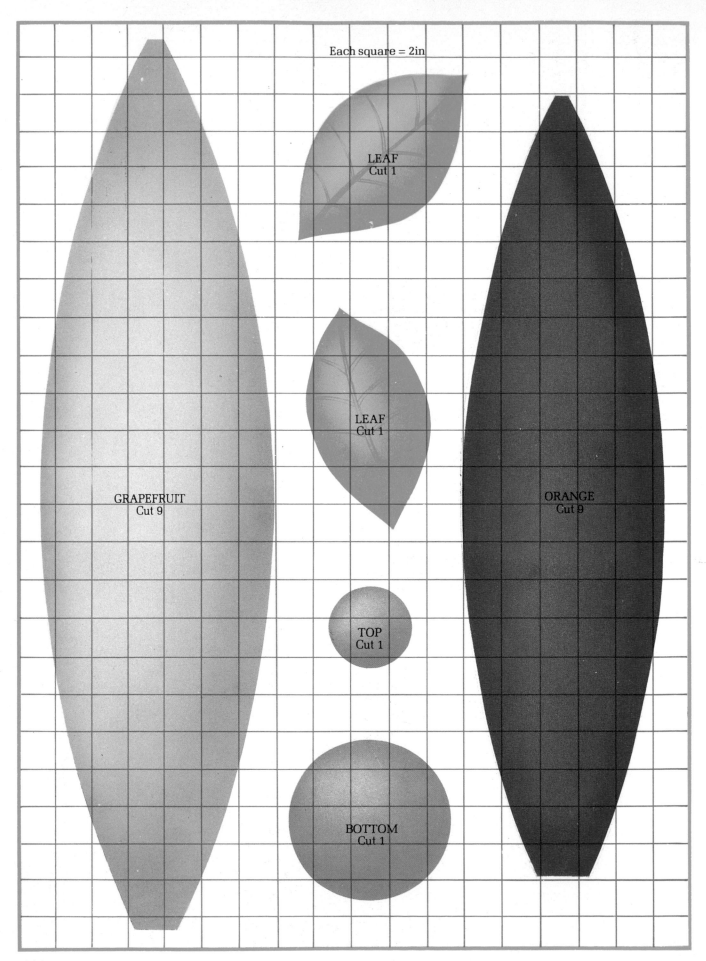

Each square = 2in

LEAF
Cut 1

LEAF
Cut 1

GRAPEFRUIT
Cut 9

ORANGE
Cut 9

TOP
Cut 1

BOTTOM
Cut 1

Banana cushion

Making the pattern — cutting out

Enlarge the pattern pieces as indicated on the graph and cut them from the appropriate fabrics. From the brown fabric cut enough 1in-wide strips on the true bias (at a 45° angle to the selvage) to make a strip about 4½yd long. Also cut 2 circles 2in in diameter.

To make the cushion

Fold and stitch the darts at each end of each muslin piece. Stitch the two pieces together. RS facing, taking ⅝in seam allowance and leaving gap in one end as shown on pattern. Turn inner cushion RS out, fill with foam chips. Slipstitch edges together.

☐ Pin yellow segments around cushion. Mark seamlines, including those on ends extending beyond inner cushion. Remove segments, trim to marked lines.

☐ Cut a 3in piece of the bias strip, and stitch it to the bottom end of the zipper. Cut a 29½in piece and stitch it to the top of the zipper. Place the zipper and binding strip face down on to one of the "2" segments with edges matching. Baste and stitch, taking a scant ⅜in seam allowance. Repeat to join the other "2" segments to the other side of the zipper. Join lengths of bias strip to other edges of these segments in same way; join a "3" segment to each bias strip. Turn cover RS up, topstitch ¼in to both sides of bias strips. Join remaining bias strip to free edges, first opening zipper. Topstitch again, working through zipper opening.

☐ Turn under edges of fabric and stalk and stem end binding, insert circle of brown fabric to close ends. Baste and sew in place. Put cover on the cushion, smoothing it to fit.

Size
Approximately 43in long

Materials
2¼yd of 36in-wide yellow terry cloth
1⅛yd of 36in-wide unbleached muslin
½yd of 36in-wide brown fabric for contrasting trim
16in brown heavyweight zipper
3½lb of foam chips

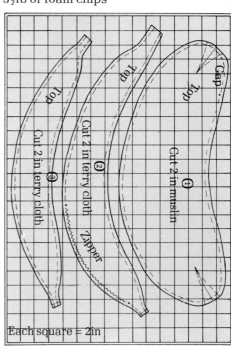

Each square = 2in

169

Pajama pillow

Size
Cat measures 16 × 10in.
Mouse measures $4\frac{3}{4} \times 1\frac{1}{2}$in.

Materials
For the cat
$\frac{5}{8}$yd of 60in-wide gray fur fabric
$\frac{3}{8}$yd of 36in-wide thick batting
$\frac{1}{8}$yd of 36in-wide white fur fabric
$\frac{5}{8}$yd of 36in-wide lining fabric
8in gray nylon zipper
2 toy safety eyes $\frac{1}{2}$in in diameter
Black and red stranded embroidery
  floss
Plastic thread for whiskers
  (optional)
Small amount of stuffing for tail
1yd of $\frac{3}{8}$in-wide pink ribbon for neck
For the mouse
Scraps of white fur fabric
Scraps of pink and gray felt
Black embroidery thread
6in of pink cord for tail
Black plastic thread for whiskers
Small amount of stuffing

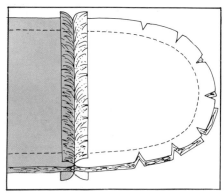

Making the pattern — cutting out
Enlarge the pattern places as indicated on the graph and cut them from the appropriate fabrics. Cut fur fabric pieces from a single layer, placing them on the WS and reversing them where necessary. Make sure that pile runs as indicated. Cut through backing only. Transfer all pattern markings. A seam allowance of $\frac{3}{8}$in is included, except where otherwise stated.

To make the cat
Pin together the main body pieces with RS facing. Stitch from point A to B around the curved edge, leaving an opening for the tail. Pin the base pieces together, RS facing, and baste the straight edges together. Baste and stitch the zipper into this seam by hand or machine. Pin, baste and stitch the base to the main body around the curved edges. Clip the seam allowances at $\frac{3}{4}$in intervals.

☐Stitch a white tip to the end of each tail piece. Place the tail pieces together with RS facing and, leaving the straight end open, stitch all around. Clip the seams and turn the tail RS out. Fill the tail firmly with stuffing and insert it into the body opening. Working from the WS, pin, baste and stitch the remainder of the curved body seam, catching the tail in place.

☐Position the white mask on one gray fur head piece as shown on the pattern and secure it in place with the safety eyes. Using 2 strands of black embroidery floss, work the eyebrows in straight stitches and work a small triangular nose in satin stitch. Cut 6in pieces of plastic thread for whiskers, if desired, and catch them in place. Work the mouth in red embroidery floss, using satin stitch.

☐Turn under the raw edges of each white ear piece and stitch them to the center of two of the four gray ear pieces. Place each pair of ear pieces together with RS facing; stitch around curved edges only. Turn the ears RS out.

☐Place the two head pieces together with RS facing. Insert the ears between the head pieces in the positions marked, with raw edges matching. Leaving a gap for turning and stuffing, stitch all around. Fill the head lightly with stuffing and stitch the opening edges together. Stitch head to the body in the position shown on the pattern. Tie the ribbon around the cat's neck as shown.

☐Place each pair of paw pieces together with RS facing and stitch around the curved edges. Turn paws RS out and fill them firmly with stuffing. Turn in the straight edges, and slipstitch them together neatly. Stitch paws to the base seam of the cat's body in the positions shown on pattern.

To make the lining
Stitch the two pieces of batting together around the curved edge, taking $\frac{3}{4}$in seam allowance. Trim the seam allowance to $\frac{1}{4}$in, and cut $\frac{3}{8}$in from the lower straight edges of batting.

☐Place the batting inside the cat's body and smooth it to fit. Catch-stitch the batting neatly to the inside of the body along the seams.

☐Place the body lining pieces together with RS facing, and stitch the curved seam. Clip the seam allowance. Baste the base lining pieces along the straight edge, and press this seam open.

☐Stitch the base to the body lining, RS facing. Remove basting.

☐Slip the lining inside the body of the cat and, working from the inside, catch-stitch it neatly in place along the seams. Hand-sew the turned edges of the lining to each side of the zipper inside the base opening. Check that zipper opens and closes easily.

To make the mouse
Place the body pieces together with RS facing and with the tail sandwiched between them in the position shown. Stitch around the edges, leaving a gap for turning. Turn the body RS out and fill it firmly with stuffing. Slipstitch the opening edges together.
☐Using 2 strands of black embroidery floss, work the mouse's eyes, eyebrows, and nose. Cut and attach 4in-long whiskers as for cat. Place the pink ear pieces on top of the gray ear pieces, fold each pair in half and sew them securely to the top of the head.
☐Sew mouse to back of cat.

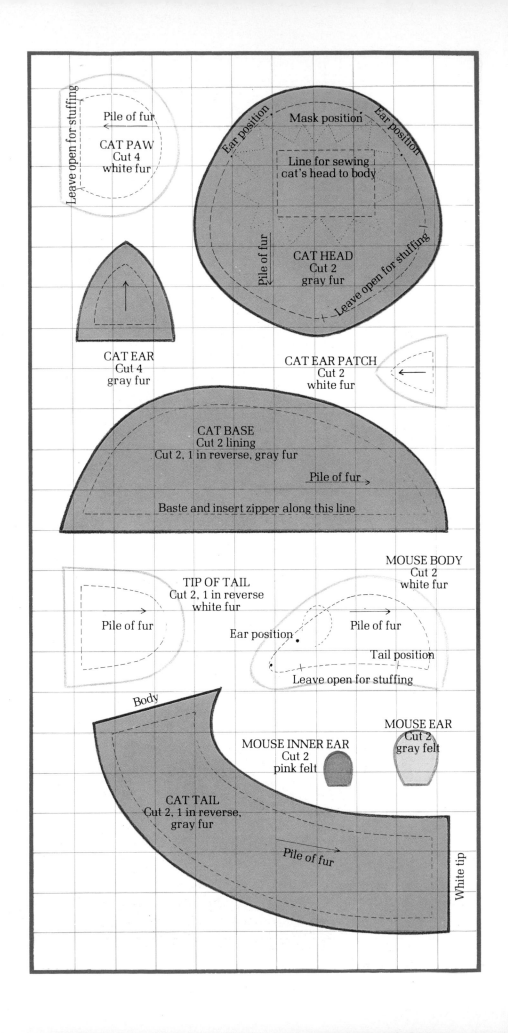

Pile of fur

Leave open for stuffing

CAT PAW
Cut 4
white fur

Mask position

Ear position   Ear position

Line for sewing
cat's head to body

Pile of fur

CAT HEAD
Cut 2
gray fur

Leave open for stuffing

CAT EAR
Cut 4
gray fur

CAT EAR PATCH
Cut 2
white fur

CAT BASE
Cut 2 lining
Cut 2, 1 in reverse, gray fur

Pile of fur

Baste and insert zipper along this line

MOUSE BODY
Cut 2
white fur

TIP OF TAIL
Cut 2, 1 in reverse
white fur

Pile of fur

Ear position

Pile of fur

Tail position

Leave open for stuffing

Body

MOUSE EAR
Cut 2
gray felt

MOUSE INNER EAR
Cut 2
pink felt

CAT TAIL
Cut 2, 1 in reverse,
gray fur

Pile of fur

White tip

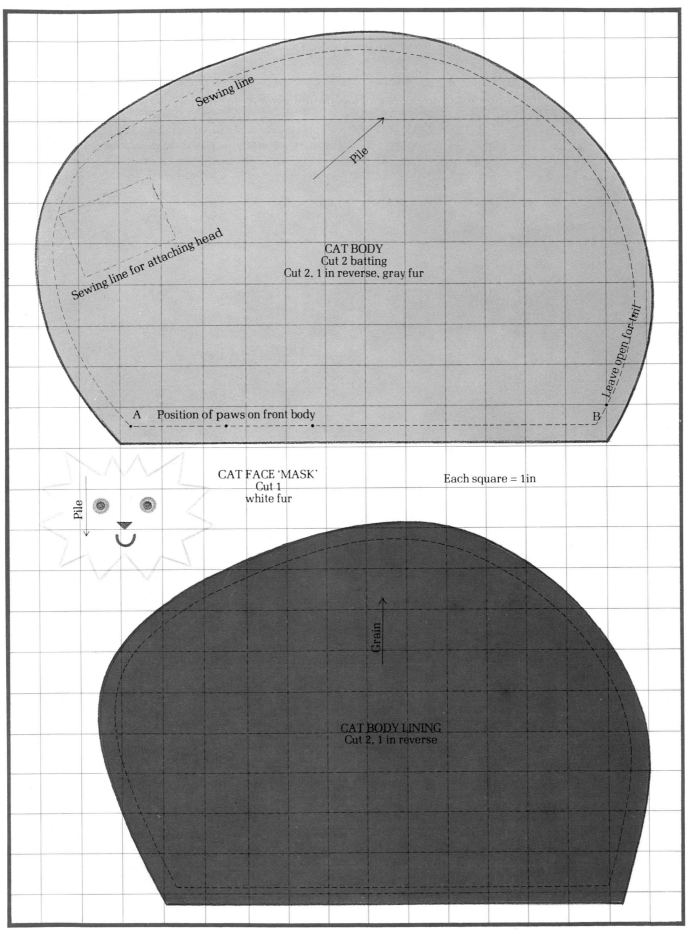

Sewing line

Pile

Sewing line for attaching head

CAT BODY
Cut 2 batting
Cut 2, 1 in reverse, gray fur

Leave open for tail

A Position of paws on front body B

CAT FACE 'MASK'
Cut 1
white fur

Each square = 1in

Pile

Grain

CAT BODY LINING
Cut 2, 1 in reverse

Novelties

Putting away those tiny toys that get underfoot and drive Mom crazy can almost be fun if you can store them in a super balloon basket, or a jolly little train that doubles as a wall hanging or a cunning container disguised as a toadstool, topped with a grinning elf. These and other imaginative — and useful — toys, including a set of amusing duck toys for the bathtub and a happy-face handbag for a little girl, are shown in these pages. They're fun to make, and they may also give you ideas for designing your own original toys.

Happy face handbag

Size
Approximately 8in in diameter

Materials
½yd of 36in-wide firmly-woven
    pink fabric
Scraps of white and blue fabric
6in red zipper
8in pink zipper
2 D-rings
Compass

Making the pattern — cutting out
Using the compasses, draw 3 circles, each 8¾in in diameter, on the pink fabric; cut them out. For the gussets, cut 2 rectangles, each 1½ × 10in, and one 2¼ × 16½in. Cut a strap measuring 3¼ × 36in. From white fabric cut 2 circles 1½in in diameter; from blue, 2 circles ⅝in in diameter. A seam allowance of ⅜in is included.

To make the bag
Glue or baste each blue circle to a white circle to make eyes, and glue or baste these to one pink circle as shown in the photograph. Stitch them in place with a close zigzag stitch, using blue and brown thread as shown. Work eyelashes and nose in zigzag stitch.
☐For the mouth draw a curved line 6¼in long. Cut along the line, then clip diagonally outward about ¼in at the end of each line in a "V" shape. Turn under and press ⅛in along both edges and the short ends, clipping the curves as necessary. Baste the 6in zipper to the opening edges and topstitch it in place close to the teeth, using the zipper foot.
☐Stitch the face circle, RS upward, to one of the other pink circles just inside the seam allowance.
☐Fold the strap in half lengthwise and stitch along the long edges. Turn strap RS out and topstitch ¼in from each edge. Cut off 2 4in strips. Thread each of these through a D-ring and stitch the ends together.
☐On each 10in gusset strip press under ⅜in on one long edge. Baste these edges to the 8in zipper, and stitch. Stitch the ends of the zipper gusset to the ends of the 16½in gusset, RS facing, with a D-ring tab inserted in each seam.
☐Place the gusset on the edge of the face circle with RS together, edges matching and the center of the zipper at the top of the face. Stitch all around.
☐Open the gusset zipper and join the other edge of the gusset to the remaining pink circle, RS facing. Turn the bag RS out.
☐Thread the ends of the strap through the rings and topstitch them in place.

Wall storage basket

Size
Approximately 36in tall

Materials
$\frac{5}{8}$yd of 36in-wide poplin in each of
red, yellow, green and blue
Piece of polyester batting 20in
square
$1\frac{1}{8}$yd of heavyweight non-woven
sew-in interfacing
$2\frac{1}{4}$yd of thin cord in each of red, blue
and green
Child's bicycle basket
Wire coathanger

Making the pattern — cutting out
Enlarge the balloon pattern as indicated and cut one pattern for the whole shape and a pattern for each section, adding $\frac{5}{8}$in seam allowance to all edges. Cut the sections from the fabrics as shown. Cut the whole shape once from blue fabric, twice from interfacing.

To make the balloon
Pin, baste and stitch the seven sections together, RS facing. Place this over the batting and baste the two layers together vertically and horizontally at 3in intervals. Stitch along the seamlines. Trim away excess batting, including seam allowance. Baste fabric edges to WS of batting. Slipstitch a length of cord over each seam.

☐ Trim the seam allowances from the interfacing balloon shapes. Place one on top of the other and place them on the WS of the blue shape. Turn the fabric seam allowances over the interfacing and baste them in place. Lay the quilted shape on the interfaced shape, WS facing, and slipstitch them together, leaving lower edges open.

☐ Bend the coathanger into a diamond shape and hand-sew it to the back of the balloon using strong thread.

☐ Cut the remaining lengths of cord in half and tie a knot at one end of each piece. Thread the cords through the basket so that the knots are on the inside. Knot the other ends and slip them between the lower edges of the balloon. Baste them in place, then slipstitch the lower edges together. Hang the balloon from a hook on the wall.

Each square = 2in

Pencil case

Cutting out
Cut 2 pieces of gray fabric, lining and batting, each 11 × ¾in. A seam allowance of ⅜in is included.

To make the pencil case
Cut 10 strips of fabric, each 10 × ½in, for pencils. Pink one short end of each. From light brown fabric cut 120 triangular pencil points.
□Arrange the pencils side by side on RS of one piece of gray fabric, starting ⅜in from the top. Trim some pencils to give a variety of lengths, and align the ends with the edges of main fabric at right-hand side. Use fabric glue stick to apply the pencils to the background fabric, leaving about ⅛in unglued on the pinked ends. Glue each pencil point to the fabric, with the wide end slightly under the pinked end of the pencil.
□Place appliquéd piece RS up over lining with batting in between. Baste the layers together. Stitch around pencil points and along the edge of each pencil with small zigzag stitch in matching thread. Zigzag stitch pencil points. Straight stitch 2 lines on each pencil.
□Baste the other piece of gray cotton to batting and lining to make back of case. Zigzag stitch one long edge on front and back pieces. Turn ⅜in to WS on stitched edges and baste. Baste folded edge to each side of zipper and machine stitch using zipper foot.
□Fold pieces with RS together and, starting at end of zipper, machine stitch around remaining edges. Finish seam allowances.

Size
10¼ × 5in

Materials
¼yd of 36in-wide firmly-woven gray fabric
¼yd of 36in-wide lining fabric
¼yd of 36in-wide lightweight batting
Scraps of firmly-woven fabric in 11 colors, including light brown for pencil points
10in zipper
Fabric glue stick
Pinking shears

Duck bath toys

Size
As shown in photograph

Materials
⅝yd of 36in-wide yellow terry cloth
¾yd of 36in-wide orange
    terry cloth
¼yd of 36in-wide orange shower
    curtain plastic
Scraps of turquoise and black
    cotton fabric
⅜yd of ⅝in-wide elastic
Piece of 2in-thick foam rubber
    6in square
Piece of ¼in-thick foam rubber
    20in square
Scraps of 1in-thick foam rubber
2¾in-thick oval bath sponge
    measuring 8 × 6in

Making the pattern — cutting out
Enlarge the pattern pieces as indicated on the graph and cut them from the appropriate fabrics and foam (taking care to use the correct thickness). Note that for visor front band the fabric must be folded in both directions. A seam allowance of ⅜in is included, except where otherwise stated.

To make the mitt
Join the two orange top beak pieces to yellow top pieces along the straight edges. Press seams open. Baste foam mitt lining to WS of each piece. Stitch orange inside beak piece to top beak pieces, matching dots. Join side seams of yellow top pieces. Turn mitt RS out.
☐Placing RS together, sew yellow inside back to terry cloth linings, matching dots. Join side seams. Place lining inside mitt. Bind wrist with yellow bias strip, taking ¼in seam allowance.
☐To make the eyes, zigzag stitch pupils to center of irises, then stitch irises to center of terry cloth eyes. Trim foam eyeballs into domes. Gather eyes ¼in in from edge and place them over foam. Draw up gathering thread and secure across back of eyes with a few stitches. Sew eyes in place on top of the mitt.

To make the visor
Stitch the two visor beak pieces together along the outer edge. Trim seam to ¼in and turn beak RS out. Place foam beak piece inside beak.
☐Fold back head band in half lengthwise. Stitch long seam edges together. Turn band RS out and position seam in center of band; press. Topstitch close to both long and bottom edges.
☐Thread elastic through band and secure it at both ends.
☐Fold front band in half lengthwise. Baste elasticized band to each end as shown and stitch across each one and around curved edge to dots. Stitch one curved edge to top edge of beak. Turn headband RS out and pad it with ¼in-thick foam. Turn under and slipstitch other curved edge to stitching line. Make eyes as for mitt and sew them in place.

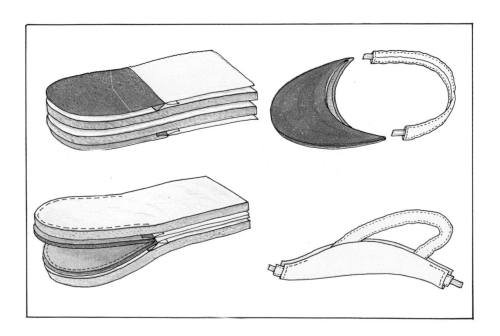

To make the duck sponge
Place the two tail pieces together and stitch along outer, pointed edge. Turn tail RS out. Join short ends of side strip to form band. Sew band to top piece, inserting tail between dots. Stitch other edge of side band to bottom piece, leaving an opening. Turn sponge cover RS out and insert bath sponge. Slipstitch opening edges together.
☐Trim away corners of foam head with scissors. Stitch beak pieces together along curved edges. Turn beak RS out. Stitch head gusset and under neck gusset to head pieces. Place beak inside head, with RS facing, matching dots; stitch it in place. Turn RS out and fit it over sponge head. Turn under $\frac{3}{8}$in at base of head and hand-sew it to body. Make eyes as for the mitts and sew them in place on duck's head.

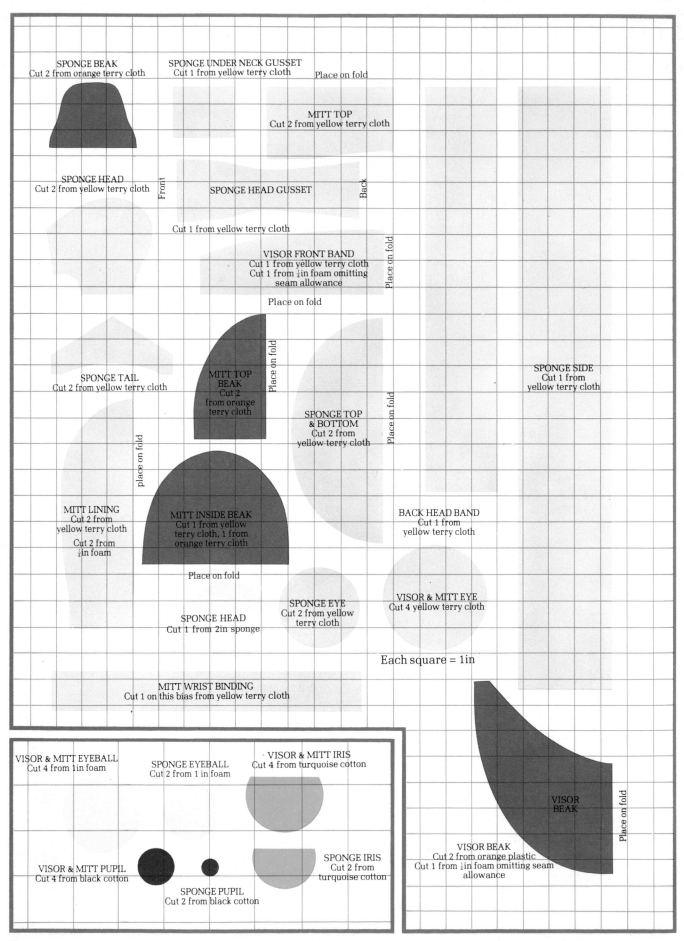

SPONGE BEAK
Cut 2 from orange terry cloth

SPONGE UNDER NECK GUSSET
Cut 1 from yellow terry cloth

Place on fold

MITT TOP
Cut 2 from yellow terry cloth

SPONGE HEAD
Cut 2 from yellow terry cloth

Front

SPONGE HEAD GUSSET

Back

Cut 1 from yellow terry cloth

VISOR FRONT BAND
Cut 1 from yellow terry cloth
Cut 1 from ¼in foam omitting
seam allowance

Place on fold

Place on fold

SPONGE TAIL
Cut 2 from yellow terry cloth

MITT TOP
BEAK
Cut 2
from orange
terry cloth

Place on fold

SPONGE SIDE
Cut 1 from
yellow terry cloth

SPONGE TOP
& BOTTOM
Cut 2 from
yellow terry cloth

Place on fold

place on fold

MITT LINING
Cut 2 from
yellow terry cloth
Cut 2 from
¼in foam

MITT INSIDE BEAK
Cut 1 from yellow
terry cloth, 1 from
orange terry cloth

BACK HEAD BAND
Cut 1 from
yellow terry cloth

Place on fold

SPONGE HEAD
Cut 1 from 2in sponge

SPONGE EYE
Cut 2 from yellow
terry cloth

VISOR & MITT EYE
Cut 4 yellow terry cloth

Each square = 1in

MITT WRIST BINDING
Cut 1 on this bias from yellow terry cloth

VISOR & MITT EYEBALL
Cut 4 from 1in foam

SPONGE EYEBALL
Cut 2 from 1 in foam

VISOR & MITT IRIS
Cut 4 from turquoise cotton

VISOR BEAK

SPONGE IRIS
Cut 2 from
turquoise cotton

VISOR & MITT PUPIL
Cut 4 from black cotton

SPONGE PUPIL
Cut 2 from black cotton

VISOR BEAK
Cut 2 from orange plastic
Cut 1 from ¼in foam omitting seam
allowance

Place on fold

180

Train toy bag

Making the pattern — cutting out

Enlarge pattern pieces as indicated on graph and cut from different colors of felt, using pattern as a guide to color and number.

☐ From red felt also cut the following pieces: one piece $44\frac{1}{2} \times 65\frac{1}{2}$in for the backing and 6 pieces for the pockets — 3 measuring $6\frac{3}{4} \times 9$in and 3 measuring $6\frac{3}{4} \times 12\frac{1}{4}$in.

☐ From white felt cut a rectangle $42\frac{1}{2} \times 9$in for the sky and 3 pieces $8\frac{1}{2} \times 2\frac{1}{2}$in for the coach windows.

☐ From black felt cut 6 strips $8\frac{1}{2} \times \frac{3}{8}$in and 21 strips $1\frac{3}{4} \times \frac{1}{4}$in for coach window frames; 2 strips $\frac{1}{4} \times 3\frac{1}{4}$in and 2 strips $\frac{1}{4} \times 1$in for engine window frames; and 2 strips $\frac{1}{4} \times 7\frac{1}{2}$in and 2 strips $\frac{1}{4} \times 4\frac{3}{4}$in for engine decoration.

☐ From bright and dull green felt cut hill shapes, using the photograph as a guide. The bright green shape should be $42\frac{1}{2}$in wide and about 16in deep at the left-hand edge; the dull green shape should — when added to the other piece — measure about 18in deep at the right-hand edge.

☐ Label all the smaller pieces for easy reference when assembling.

Size

$44\frac{1}{2} \times 23\frac{1}{2}$in

Materials

$1\frac{3}{8}$yd of 36in-wide red felt
$1\frac{1}{4}$yd of 36in-wide white felt
$1\frac{1}{4}$yd of 36in-wide bright green felt
$\frac{3}{4}$yd of 36in-wide dull green felt
Piece of dark green felt 12in square
Piece of gray felt 12in square
Piece of black felt $12 \times 23\frac{1}{2}$in
Scraps of blue, yellow, brown and light gray felt
Fabric glue stick
2 lengths of $\frac{3}{8}$in-diameter dowel 44in long
4 eyelet screws
4 hooks

To make the toy bag

☐Lay the green hills on the red backing, 2½in from bottom edges, and baste them firmly in place along straight edges. Slip sky piece under edges of hills, with its top edge 2½in from edge of red felt; trace along edges of hills, remove sky and cut along traced line.

☐Replace sky and baste around all its edges and around curved edges of hills. Cut about 15 strips of dark green felt, ⅜in wide, to fit diagonally across the bright green hill shape, spaced about 2¼in apart. Use the fabric glue stick to fix them in place, then stitch them to the background using a medium-width zigzag stitch.

☐Cut enough ⅜in-wide black felt strips to make a length of 42½in. Glue them to the green felt, 1½in up from the lower edge, to form the track. Zigzag stitch the track in place.

☐Use fabric glue to apply the sun, birds and trees to the hills and sky, and zigzag stitch around the edges.

☐Glue the gray wheel circles to the black circles. Using gray thread, zigzag stitch around the edges of the gray circles, and, using black thread and a straight stitch, add the spokes. Place two wheels on the track 1½in from left edge of green hill and with a 3½in gap between them. Glue and then zigzag stitch them in place.

☐Baste the engine in place directly above the wheels, with the front 1¼in from the side edge of the hill. Glue the window, its frame, the two chimneys and smoke, the bell and the black edging to the engine. Using matching threads, zigzag stitch pieces in place.

☐Baste the white felt windows to the 6¾ × 9in red felt coach pieces. Glue the black felt window frames to the windows as shown, and zigzag stitch them in place.

☐Place the right-hand edge of the end coach 1¼in from the edge of green felt, with lower edge of coach 2in above the track. Baste and zigzag stitch the side edge in place. Position the left-hand edge 9in from the right-hand edge; baste and zigzag stitch. Fold the edges into pleats as shown, and zigzag stitch the lower edge of the coach to hold it in place.

☐Attach the center pocket in the same way, starting 1¼in from the left edge of the end coach. Repeat to attach the front coach.

☐Apply the remaining six wheels as for the engine wheels, placing them 1in from each end of each coach. Glue and stitch foot plates between engine and coaches.

☐Turn under top and bottom edges of red felt to make two 1in channels for the dowel. Straight stitch edges in place, just outside picture area. Trim side edges with pinking shears. Thread the dowel through channels and insert eyelet screws into both ends of each rod.

☐Insert 4 hooks in the wall for hanging up the toy bag.

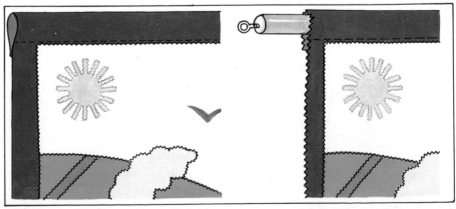

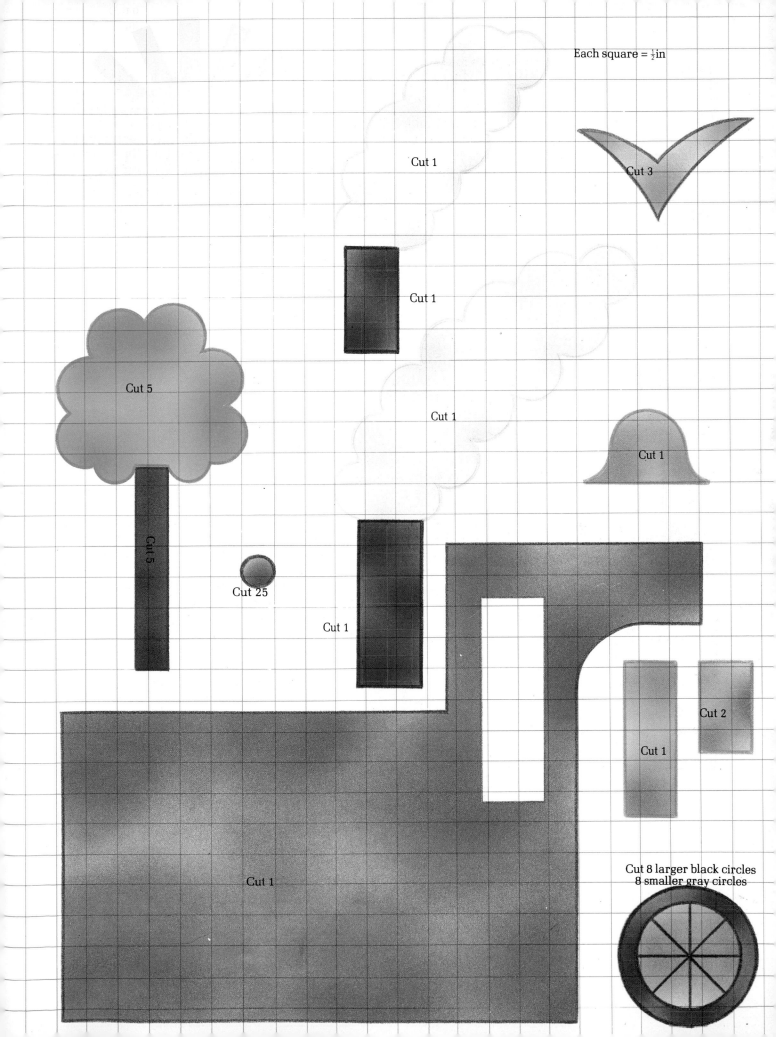

Each square = $\frac{1}{2}$in

Cut 1

Cut 3

Cut 1

Cut 5

Cut 1

Cut 1

Cut 5

Cut 25

Cut 1

Cut 1

Cut 2

Cut 1

Cut 1

Cut 8 larger black circles
8 smaller gray circles

Toadstool toybox with elf

Size
Toadstool is approximately 14in tall.
Elf is approximately 11in tall (seated).

Materials
For the toadstool
One wicker waste basket, 11in tall and 10in in diameter*
$\frac{7}{8}$yd of 60in-wide cream fabric
$\frac{3}{4}$yd of 36in-wide red and white dotted fabric
$\frac{3}{4}$yd of 36in-wide beige twill fabric
$\frac{3}{8}$yd of 36in-wide synthetic batting
1lb of stuffing
Piece of stiff cardboard, at least 18in square
$1\frac{1}{8}$yd of $1\frac{1}{2}$in-wide cream cotton webbing
$1\frac{5}{8}$yd of $\frac{5}{8}$in-wide woven tape
Piece of $\frac{3}{4}$in-thick foam, 10in square

For the elf
$\frac{1}{2}$yd of 36in-wide green felt
$\frac{3}{8}$yd of 36in-wide felt in yellow, red and cream
$\frac{1}{4}$yd of 36in-wide brown felt or imitation suede
4oz of stuffing
Scrap of peach felt for nose
$\frac{3}{4}$in-diameter domed button
$2 \times \frac{3}{8}$in-diameter black beads
Peach stranded embroidery floss
Red pencil

*If you are unable to find a wastebasket with these dimensions, add or subtract the difference to the stalk and lid plug pieces.

Making the pattern — cutting out
Enlarge the pattern pieces for the elf as indicated on the graph, and cut them from the appropriate fabrics. Cut the toadstool pieces from the specified fabrics and from cardboard and foam, following the measurements on the diagram and making patterns first where it is necessary. Transfer all pattern markings. A seam allowance of $\frac{3}{8}$in is included, except where otherwise stated.

To make the toadstool
Cut each stalk ruffle piece from A to B. Join the two pieces along their short ends with French seams. Zigzag stitch close to the outside edge of ruffle; trim away any loose threads. Join stalk top along short ends, C-D, and stalk bottom along ends E-F. Join stalk top to bottom, RS facing, inserting the ruffle in the seam.

☐Glue the piece of batting to the side of basket. Place stalk over basket and glue its top edge to inside of basket, and bottom edge to the base, pleating the fabric to fit. Cover raw edges inside basket with webbing, gluing it in place. Cover cardboard stalk base with fabric, gluing edges of fabric to underside. Glue base to bottom of basket.

☐Work a line of gathering stitches around the edge of the toolstool cap and draw up edge to measure $56\frac{1}{2}$in. Adjust the gathers evenly. Trim woven tape to 57in and sew it to wrong side of fabric, $\frac{3}{8}$in in from edge, overlapping the ends of the tape by $\frac{1}{2}$in.

☐Join the three gill pieces to form a ring. Placing RS together, stitch gill section to edge of cap top. Run a gathering thread through base of gills, but do not pull up gathers.

☐Place cap and gills over cardboard lid and fill cap loosely with stuffing. Glue the tape to edge of cardboard. Draw up the gill gathering thread so that gills lie flat over the lid and glue edges in place. Gather edge of plug fabric, place it over foam circle and draw up gathers. Position plug in center of lid and glue it in place.

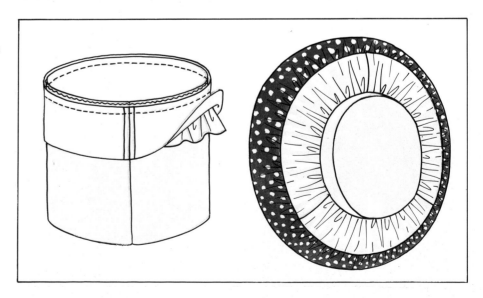

To make the elf
Stitch each pair of ear pieces together, WS facing, close to the edge, leaving straight sides open. Fill ears lightly with stuffing, then stitch along the quilting lines.

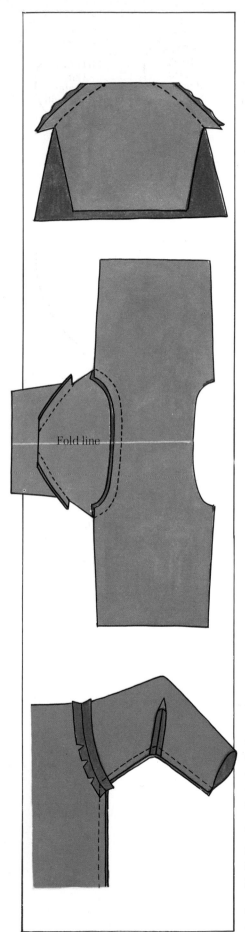

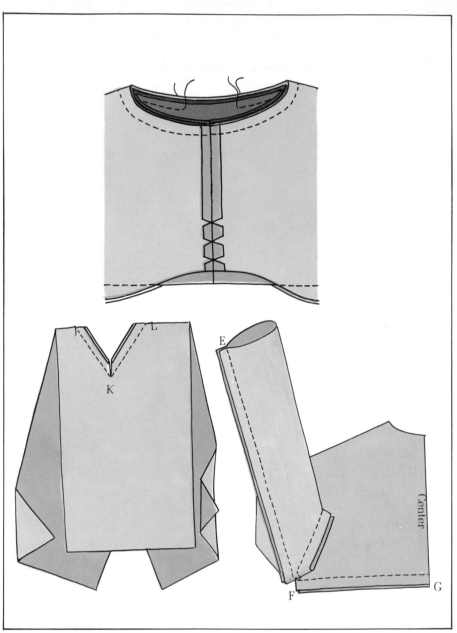

☐Stitch each pair of head pieces together at the side seams, inserting ears in the spaces indicated. Sew the right and left halves together, leaving a space open in back seam. Turn head RS out, stuff it firmly and slipstitch the opening edges together.

☐Fold each arm widthwise at the elbow darts and baste the dart edges together, easing in the longer edge to fit. Stitch darts from edges to dots. Open arms out and open darts. Pin the longer straight edge of arm to curved armhole edge of body, easing the arm around curve to fit. Stitch it in place. Clip seam curve and open seam. Stitch other arm into opposite body armhole in the same way.

☐Fold body and arms in half, RS facing. Stitch along side edges of body and underarm seams. Turn section RS out. Pin inner curved edge of peplum around lower straight edge of body with raw edges even and ends of peplum butted together at the front. Stitch peplum in place.

☐Fold each leg widthwise to bring points K together; stitch from J through K to L. Unfold each leg and refold lengthwise, matching points G, F and E. Pin, then stitch the long edges together from center

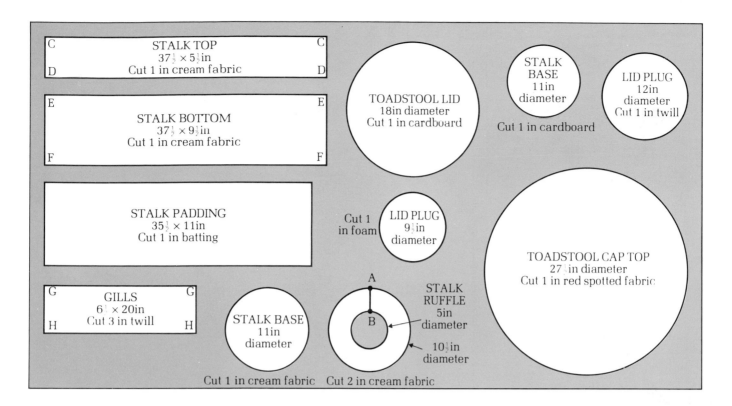

STALK TOP
37½ × 5½in
Cut 1 in cream fabric

STALK BOTTOM
37½ × 9½in
Cut 1 in cream fabric

STALK PADDING
35½ × 11in
Cut 1 in batting

GILLS
6½ × 20in
Cut 3 in twill

TOADSTOOL LID
18in diameter
Cut 1 in cardboard

STALK BASE
11in diameter
Cut 1 in cardboard

LID PLUG
12in diameter
Cut 1 in twill

Cut 1 in foam

LID PLUG
9½in diameter

TOADSTOOL CAP TOP
27½in diameter
Cut 1 in red spotted fabric

STALK BASE
11in diameter
Cut 1 in cream fabric

STALK RUFFLE
5in diameter
10½in diameter
Cut 2 in cream fabric

edge toward darts, then continuing past darts to the lower edge. Open seams and darts and press lightly to hold them open and so reduce bulk.

☐Stitch the two legs together along the center. Place body and arms, turned RS out, inside leg section, so that waist edge of body (with peplum) is level with curved waist edge of legs and peplum ends are aligned with center front seam of legs. Stitch waist seam, leaving a gap at the back for turning. Turn body RS out.

☐Stitch each pair of hand pieces together in the same way, leaving straight edges open. Fill hands lightly, then stitch along the quilting lines. Fill palms of hands firmly, then push each hand into end of arms, with arm edges overlapping by ⅜in. Stitch hands in place.

☐On each boot piece, bring the two edges M-N together, WS facing, and stitch close to the edge of the fabric. Join edges O-P in the same way. Bring the two points Q together, WS facing, and sew seam Q-R close to edge of fabric. Fill boot firmly with stuffing and push each boot into end of leg, matching points Q and overlapping by ⅜in. Stitch boots in place.

☐Fill the legs and arms firmly with stuffing, molding elbows and knees as you work. Stuff body firmly, then slipstitch opening edges in back waist seam.

☐Glue cuffs to wrists and ankles, with ends of cuffs meeting edge to edge. Sew center point of collar to neck of body.

☐To make the nose, cover the button with a 1½in-diameter circle of peach felt, gluing the edges to the underside. Glue nose to face. Sew on two black beads for eyes. Embroider mouth in stem stitch, using 3 strands of peach floss. Color cheeks with red pencil.

☐Stitch hat pieces together from S through T to U. Clip curves and trim away fabric at point. Turn hat RS out and glue it to head. Fold down point of hat and catch it to head with a few stitches. Pin head to body and stitch securely through collar and body fabrics. Cross legs of elf and secure them with a few stitches where legs touch. Sew palms of hands to knees with a few stitches.

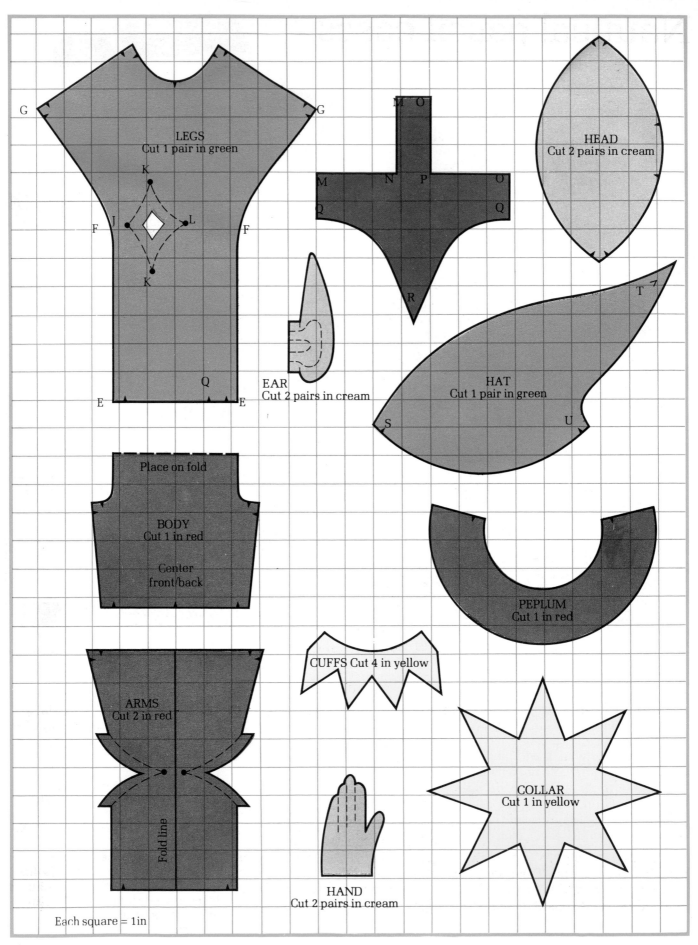

LEGS
Cut 1 pair in green

G

G

K

F J L F

K

Q

E E

HEAD
Cut 2 pairs in cream

M O

M N P O

Q Q

R

EAR
Cut 2 pairs in cream

HAT
Cut 1 pair in green

T 7

S U

Place on fold

BODY
Cut 1 in red

Center
front/back

PEPLUM
Cut 1 in red

CUFFS Cut 4 in yellow

ARMS
Cut 2 in red

Fold line

COLLAR
Cut 1 in yellow

HAND
Cut 2 pairs in cream

Each square = 1in

Nautical pencil cases

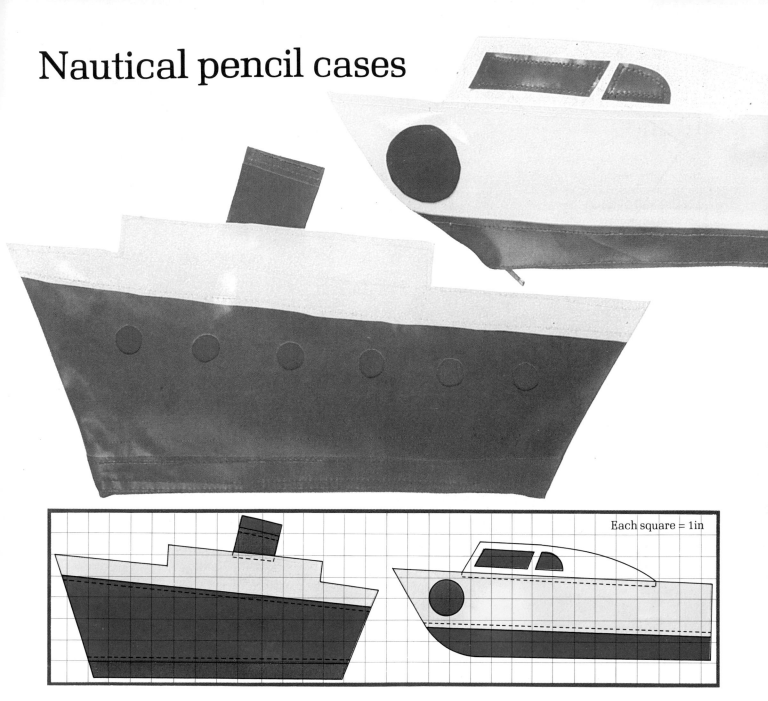

Each square = 1in

Making the pattern — cutting out

Enlarge the pattern pieces as indicated on the graph, drawing each piece up to the broken line, where given, to allow for an overlap. Use thin cardboard or stiff paper for patterns and draw around pieces on fabric. Cut each piece twice from the appropriate color of vinyl.

To make either pencil case

Assemble the pieces for each side of the case and tape them together on the WS, overlapping them as shown on the pattern. Working on the RS, topstitch the pieces together to form each side of the boat. ☐Topstitch the zipper to the lower edges of the boat, leaving equal margins at each end. Turn boat WS out and stitch the remainder of the lower seam and the side seams, taking ¼in seam allowance. Turn boat RS out and topstitch the upper edges together.

Size

Liner is approximately 11½in long.
Cabin cruiser is approximately 11in long.

Materials

For liner pencil case

Piece of blue vinyl about 11 × 6½in
Piece of yellow vinyl about 12 × 3in
Piece of red vinyl about 10½in × 1½in
8in zipper

For cabin cruiser pencil case

Piece of yellow vinyl about 12 × 4in
Piece of blue vinyl about 13½ × 3in
Piece of white vinyl about 7 × 5½in
Scrap of red vinyl
7in zipper

Functional stitches

The following stitches are used mainly – in toymaking – to join sections, to attach fastenings and trimmings and to finish fabric edges.

Running stitch

This is the simplest of all stitches. It is worked by weaving the needle in and out of the fabric evenly, taking several stitches on the needle before pulling it through. It is a weak stitch, so is not recommended for seams.

Large running stitches are used for basting.

Stab stitch

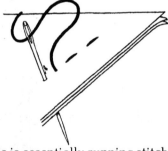

This is essentially running stitch, but it is worked in an up-and-down movement. It is especially useful when joining layers of fabric including batting or other filling – for example, to suggest fingers on a doll's hand.

Backstitch

This can be used for joining seams by hand (and also for embroidering lines). To work backstitch, bring the needle up a short distance (about $\frac{1}{16}$ in) beyond the beginning of the stitching line. Insert it at the

Stitches

starting point and bring it up the same distance ahead of the point at which it emerged. Then take it back to meet the first stitch and bring it up as before. Keep the stitches the same length.

A couple of backstitches, worked on the same spot, are used to secure thread at the end (and sometimes at the beginning) of a line of stitching.

Overcasting

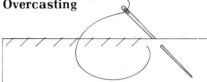

This is used to finish seam allowances and sometimes to join edges. Bring the needle up about $\frac{1}{8}$ in below the fabric edge, take it over the edge and about $\frac{1}{4}$ in to the right (or to the left if left-handed) and insert it as before. Continue working over the edge to the end.

Slipstitch

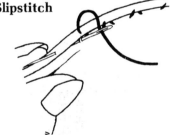

This stitch is used to join two folded edges – for example, when closing a gap left for stuffing. It is easiest to work if the edges are first basted together. Hold the fabric with the edges upward. Fasten the thread in the farther edge, bring the needle straight across into the near edge and, in one movement, take it through the fold for about $\frac{1}{8}$ in then into the farther fold for about $\frac{1}{8}$ in. Pull the thread through. Repeat. The stitches should be almost invisible.

Hemming stitch

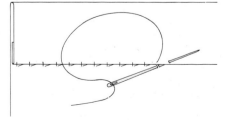

There are several stitches used for hemming, but this is one of the most useful. Work with the folded edge away from you (it may be basted in place first). Secure the thread in the fold. Take a tiny stitch in the main fabric, then, without pulling the thread through, take another stitch in the hem edge; pull the thread through. Repeat.

Ladder stitch

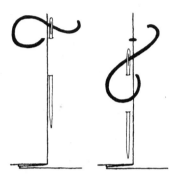

This stitch is used in toymaking to join two sections where one or both have been filled with stuffing. Turn under one raw edge and place it over the other edge. Baste the edges together. Secure the thread in the folded edge, then take the needle just over the edge and into the other fabric, bringing it out about $\frac{1}{4}$ in farther on. Take it directly across into the folded edge, through the fold for about $\frac{1}{4}$ in, then out. Repeat.

Faggot stitch

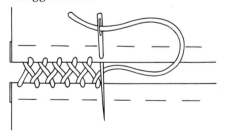

Faggot stich is especially useful for joining sections of a puppet so that they remain flexible. Fasten the thread in the lower edge, then bring it up to the front and into the other edge from front to back, leaving about $\frac{1}{8}$–$\frac{1}{4}$ in between the sections. Bring the needle over the thread then take it down into the lower section again from front to back.

Decorative stitches

These include some of the most often-used embroidery stitches, used in toymaking for facial features and for decoration of various kinds.

Stem stitch

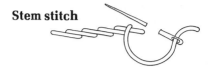

This is used for working thin, smooth lines, as for eyebrows. Bring the needle up at the starting point, then take it down along the stitching line, about $\frac{1}{8}$–$\frac{1}{4}$in farther on, bringing it up halfway between the two points. Re-insert it the same distance along the line as before, and bring it up at the end of the first stitch. Repeat, always bringing the needle up on the same side of the thread, producing a rope-like effect.

Satin stitch

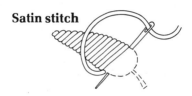

Bring the needle up on one edge of the space to be filled, then take it across to the opposite edge and insert it. Bring it out next to where it first emerged and take it down on the other edge as before.
No fabric should show between the two threads. Repeat to fill the space, keeping the stitches close together and exactly parallel.

Long and short stitch

This is used either to fill a space too large for satin stitch or to produce shaded effects. In toymaking it is often used for the irises of eyes. A little practice is required to produce a smooth, natural effect.
First work a row of satin stitches along the outer edge of the shape, alternating long and short ones as

shown. On following rows work stitches of the same length, either meeting the ends of the first ones, as shown, or inserting the needle into the very end of each stitch. To fill a curved shape, you will need to adjust the number and length of stitches as the space narrows. For shading, change color on subsequent rows.

French knots

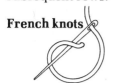

These are used wherever a small dot is required. Bring the needle up and pull the thread through. Wind the thread once or twice around the needle, close to the point where it emerges. Holding the thread taut, re-insert the needle close to the starting point. Pull the needle quickly and smoothly to the wrong side.

Feather stitch

Work this stitch vertically. Bring the needle up at the beginning of the stitching line, then re-insert it a short distance to the left, leaving a shallow loop. Bring it up just above the center of the loop, forming a wide "V" shape. Take it down to the right, forming another loop, and bring it out in the center of the loop as before. Repeat.

Chain stitch

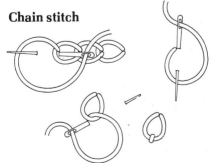

This may be worked in a line or individually (known as "lazy daisy stitch"). Bring the needle out at the beginning of the stitching line and take it down just beside this point, leaving a loop. Bring the needle up $\frac{1}{8}$–$\frac{1}{4}$in along the line, inside the loop,

and pull the thread through, not too tightly. Take it down inside the loop, leaving a new loop. Repeat. To work a detached chain stitch, make a loop as described above, bring the needle up inside the loop, then take it down just outside, to hold the loop in place.

Swiss darning

Also called "duplicate stitch," this is a method of embroidering a stockinette stitch fabric by covering the stitches with embroidered stitches that appear to have been knitted. It is usually worked from a chart, in which each square represents one stitch. Use a tapestry needle and yarn the same thickness as that used for the knitting.

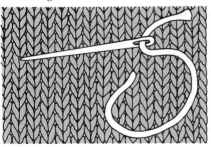

1 Secure the yarn at the back of the work, and bring the needle up at the bottom of the first stitch to be covered.

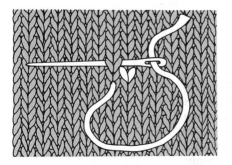

2 Insert the needle from right to left at the upper right-hand corner of the stitch, and bring it out at the upper left-hand corner. Take it down at the starting point. This completes the first stitch.

3 Bring the needle up at the base of the next stitch and take it under the top, as shown. Continue in this way, following the chart and changing colors as necessary. Do not pull the yarn tightly; it should be at the same tension as the knitted background.

191

Enlarging a grid pattern

Most of the projects in this book are made from patterns which are given in reduced size and must therefore be enlarged to the original size before cutting out. This is not difficult to do. All you need by way of materials are: graph paper ruled in inches, a ruler and a pencil. You may also want a flexible curve – a length of pliable plastic that serves as a guide in drawing curved lines.

On the pattern you will find the scale to which it has been reduced. This is expressed in the form: "Each square = 1in" (or 2in for example). Graph paper is ruled in 1in squares, (smaller squares ruled within the inch marks), with so if the scale is one square to 1in you have a ready-made grid. If the squares on the pattern correspond to 2in, you should darken these lines on the grid, using a different color, so that you will not be confused by the intermediate lines. If the scale of a design does not correspond to inch markings, you will need to draw a grid to the correct scale on plain paper. Once the grid is marked out, you can enlarge the design. The example given here is a corner of a sag bag pattern (see page 168).

1 Select a starting point on the pattern piece (here marked "A"). Note the location of this point in relation to the lines of the grid and mark this point on your full-size grid, the same distance, proportionately, from the corresponding grid lines. (There is no need to label the points, which we have done simply to make the procedure clear.)

2 Similarly, locate the next point ("B") on the pattern and locate the equivalent point on the large grid. In the case of straight lines, the "next" point is simply the next corner – moving either clockwise or counter-clockwise.

3 Using the ruler, draw a line between these two points. To transfer curved lines, mark the points on the enlarged grid lines corresponding to the points where the pattern line crosses the lines of the small grid. In the example, C is a little over halfway along the next horizontal line, and D is just past the intersection with a vertical line. You should also mark the points where the pattern crosses vertical lines; this is essential for patterns with more intricate curves. After marking several points on the grid, join the points, using the flexible curve, if desired, as a guide.

Continue marking and joining coresponding points on the full-size grid to complete the pattern.

Knitting and crochet abbreviations used in this book

alt	alternate
approx	approximately
beg	begin(ning)
ch	chain(s)
cont	continu(e) (ing)
dc	double crochet
dec	decrease(e) (ing)
foll	follow(s) (ing)
g st	garter stitch
hdc	half double crochet
inc	increas(e) (ing)
K	knit
P	purl
patt	pattern
psso	pass slipped stitch over
rem	remain(s) (ing)
rep	repeat
RS	right side
sc	single crochet
sl	slip
sl st	slip(ped) stitch
st(s)	stitch(es)
st st	stockinette stitch
tbl	through back of loop(s)
tog	together
tr	triple
WS	wrong side
yo	yarn over (hook or needle)

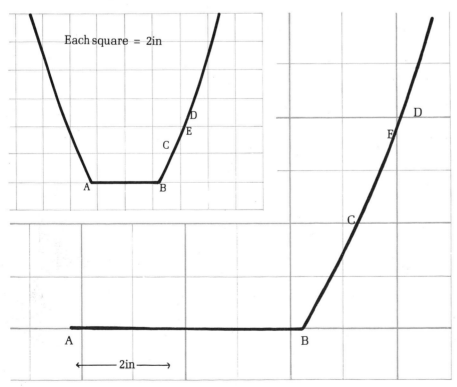

Each square = 2in

2in